T0330071

A Research Agenda for the Gig Economy and Society

Elgar Research Agendas outline the future of research in a given area. Leading scholars are given the space to explore their subject in provocative ways, and map out the potential directions of travel. They are relevant but also visionary.

Forward-looking and innovative, Elgar Research Agendas are an essential resource for PhD students, scholars and anybody who wants to be at the forefront of research.

Titles in the series include:

A Research Agenda for Public–Private Partnerships and the Governance of Infrastructure
Edited by Graeme A. Hodge and Carsten Greve

A Research Agenda for Governance
John Pierre, B. Guy Peters, Jacob Torfing and Eva Sørensen

A Research Agenda for Sport Management
Edited by David Shilbury

A Research Agenda for COVID-19 and Society
Edited by Steve Matthewman

A Research Agenda for Civil Society
Edited by Kees Biekart and Alan Fowler

A Research Agenda for Tax Law
Edited by Leopoldo Parada

A Research Agenda for Food Systems
Edited by Colin L. Sage

A Research Agenda for International Political Economy New Directions and Promising Paths
Edited by David A. Deese

A Research Agenda for Social Networks and Social Resilience
Edited by Emmanuel Lazega, Tom A.B. Snijders and Rafael P.M. Wittek

A Research Agenda for the Gig Economy and Society
Edited by Valerio De Stefano, Ilda Durri, Charalampos Stylogiannis and Mathias Wouters

A Research Agenda for the Gig Economy and Society

Edited by

VALERIO DE STEFANO, PHD

PhD, Canada Research Chair in Innovation, Law and Society, Osgoode Hall Law School, Toronto, Canada

ILDA DURRI

PhD Candidate, Institute for Labour Law, KU Leuven, Belgium

CHARALAMPOS STYLOGIANNIS

PhD Candidate, Institute for Labour Law, KU Leuven, Belgium

MATHIAS WOUTERS, PHD

PhD, Legal Adviser, Swiss Institute for Comparative Law, Lausanne, Switzerland

Elgar Research Agendas

Cheltenham, UK • Northampton, MA, USA

© Valerio De Stefano, Ilda Durri, Charalampos Stylogiannis and Mathias Wouters 2022

All rights reserved. No part of this publication may be reproduced, stored in a retrieval system or transmitted in any form or by any means, electronic, mechanical or photocopying, recording, or otherwise without the prior permission of the publisher.

Published by
Edward Elgar Publishing Limited
The Lypiatts
15 Lansdown Road
Cheltenham
Glos GL50 2JA
UK

Edward Elgar Publishing, Inc.
William Pratt House
9 Dewey Court
Northampton
Massachusetts 01060
USA

A catalogue record for this book
is available from the British Library

Library of Congress Control Number: 2022944631

This book is available electronically in the **Elgar**online
Sociology, Social Policy and Education subject collection
http://dx.doi.org/10.4337/9781800883512

ISBN 978 1 80088 350 5 (cased)
ISBN 978 1 80088 351 2 (eBook)

Printed and bound by CPI Group (UK) Ltd, Croydon, CR0 4YY

Contents

Figures

Tables

Contributors

Alberto Barrio, Postdoctoral Researcher, Centre for Legal Studies in Welfare and Market, University of Copenhagen, Denmark

Alessio Bertolini, Postdoctoral Researcher, Oxford Internet Institute, University of Oxford, United Kingdom

Alan Bogg, Professor in Law, University of Bristol Law School, University of Bristol, United Kingdom

Ricardo Buendia, PhD Student, University of Bristol Law School and the Centre of Law at Work, University of Bristol, United Kingdom

Iain Campbell, Honorary Senior Fellow, Centre for Employment and Labour Relations Law, Faculty of Law, University of Melbourne, AUSTRALIA

Aude Cefaliello, Researcher, European Trade Union Institute, Belgium

Eleni De Becker, Professor of Social Security Law, Free University of Brussels. and Substitute Lecturer, KU Leuven, Belgium

Valerio De Stefano, Canada Research Chair in Innovation, Law and Society, Osgoode Hall Law School, York University, Toronto, Canada

Ruth Dukes, Professor of Labour Law, School of Law, University of Glasgow, United Kingdom

Ilda Durri, PhD Researcher, Institute for Labour Law, Faculty of Law, KU Leuven, Belgium

Nora Gobel, Junior Research Officer, Research Department, International Labour Office (ILO)

Mark Graham, Professor of Internet Geography, Oxford Internet Institute, University of Oxford

Elena Gramano, Assistant Professor of Labour Law, A. Sraffa Department of Legal Studies, Università commerciale L. Bocconi, Milan

Kelle Howson, Postdoctoral Researcher, Oxford Internet Institute, University of Oxford, United Kingdom

Cristina Inversi, Lecturer in Employment Law at The University of Manchester, Alliance Manchester Business School and Research Fellow at Università degli Studi di Milano, Social and Political Science Department

Srujana Katta, Doctoral Student, Oxford Internet Institute, University of Oxford, United Kingdom

Miriam Kullmann, Associate Professor of Labour Law, Faculty of Law, Department Social Law, Radboud University Nijmegen, the Netherlands

Rishabh Kumar Dhir, Research Officer, Research Department, International Labour Office (ILO)

Nastazja Potocka-Sionek, PhD Researcher, Law Department, European University Institute

Uma Rani, Senior Economist, Research Department, International Labour Office (ILO)

Paul Schoukens, Professor of Social Security Law (comparative, European, international law), Institute for Social Law, Faculty of Law, KU Leuven, Belgium, and Tilburg University, the Netherlands

Natalie Sedacca, Assistant Professor in Employment Law, Durham University, United Kingdom

Charalampos Stylogiannis, PhD Researcher, Institute for Labour Law, Faculty of Law, KU Leuven, Belgium

Funda Ustek-Spilda, Postdoctoral Researcher, Oxford Internet Institute, University of Oxford, United Kingdom

Mathias Wouters, Legal Adviser, Swiss Institute for Comparative Law, Lausanne, Switzerland

Acknowledgments

First and foremost, we are incredibly grateful to all the authors who contributed to this collection for their outstanding, innovative and profound work. They made our job as editors pleasant and instructive and enormously facilitated our tasks. We also owe many thanks to Daniel Mather and the whole editorial team at Edward Elgar Publishing.

We are also greatly thankful to our institutions, the Institute for Labour Law of the KU Leuven, Belgium, and Osgoode Hall Law School, York University, Toronto, for their support throughout this project. Finally, we are very indebted to all the colleagues, the students, and the staff that we met and who worked with us at these institutions.

This book was also possible thanks to the generous funding provided to Professor De Stefano under the Canada Research Chair in Innovation Law and Society and the Odysseus grant "Employment Rights and Labour Protection in the On-Demand Economy" awarded by the FWO Research Foundation, Flanders. This funding immensely helped us carry out the broader research activity that partially fed into this book. The Odysseus grant also allowed, among other things, to fund the positions of Ilda Durri, Charalampos Stylogiannis, and Mathias Wouters.

We are also deeply thankful to the many colleagues with whom we could discuss the results of our multi-year research on platform work. Beyond the authors who contributed to this book, it is possible to name only some of them: Antonio Aloisi, Janine Berg, Jeremias Adams-Prassl, Nicola Countouris, Frank Hendrickx, Miriam Cherry, Martine Humblet, Simon Taes, Filip Dorssemont, Pieter Pecinovsky, Stan Buurs, Silvia Rainone, Ewan McGaughey, Sara Slinn, Cindy Estlund, and Brishen Rogers.

1 Introduction to *A Research Agenda for the Gig Economy and Society*

Valerio De Stefano, Ilda Durri, Charalampos Stylogiannis, Mathias Wouters

This book comes at a moment when some "disruptors", more specifically platform businesses, are, indeed, starting to be "disrupted". Such disruption is driven by crucial court decisions and regulatory developments, which attempt to address the ongoing challenges in the so-called "gig economy". For quite some time now, digital labour platforms have avoided labour regulations by hiding under the cloak of technological innovation. The businesses operating these platforms have long alleged that people can work autonomously, as self-employed persons, and "be their own bosses" away from any supervision or control thanks to their technologies.

By now, nonetheless, there is an abundance of evidence that suggests that a considerable number of platform workers are, in fact, subject to forms of direction and monitoring comparable to the ones that traditional employers exercise. As observed elsewhere, these supposed "liberating business models" are often nothing more than "a rebrand of casualised forms of work" (De Stefano and Aloisi 2019, 361). Casual work arrangements were used long before their platform-based instantiations came to be to reduce labour costs, increase productivity, and escape employment and labour law regulations (Prassl 2018). Such understanding, as noted, seems at least to a certain extent to be incorporated into the recent actions of lawmakers and judges.

Before editing this book, we decided to collect and analyse judicial and legislative developments about platform work worldwide. A good deal of these developments regarded, in particular, the employment status of platform workers or, in any case, their access to labour, employment, and social protection. This part of our research has, among other publications, materialised into a working paper published by the International Labour Organization (ILO) (De Stefano et al. 2021).

What struck us in writing this paper was the constant effort required to keep pace with platform work's changing legal landscape, as our research risked becoming outdated even while we were writing it. National and regional regulatory developments, including case law, follow each other quickly. Platform operators are not sitting idle either. One notable feature of platform work is the ease with which platforms tweak their terms and conditions to avoid or countermine legal challenges. Sometimes the corresponding transformation is also factual, materially altering the working conditions of platform workers; at other times, the changes are merely cosmetic.

Our ILO working paper served as a starting point for our chapter in this book. However, much has happened since then. Most notably, a transnational regulation has been proposed at the EU level in a draft directive on improving working conditions in platform work. Together with other domestic legal developments, this legal instrument could arguably mark the end of platform work's legal exceptionalism (De Stefano and Aloisi 2021). It is about time. Indeed, we are firmly convinced that platform work and the gig economy are a part of broader and long-standing societal and labour issues. Therefore, the book's core theme is to link critical aspects of platform work, like those found in the existing literature, to more extensive discussions regarding the world of work.

The first aim of this book is to provide insights into how platform work fits into this bigger picture; hence, its title mentions the gig economy and society. It has thus been clear to us since the beginning that the book should not solely feature legal research. Instead, it embraces a multidisciplinary approach by including crucial scholarship outside the legal field; authors from different scientific and geographical backgrounds were invited to contribute to this endeavour and assess the impact of platform work in the contemporary world of work. The collective result is a comprehensive analysis of platform work from diverse angles, including sociological, geographical, economic, and, of course, legal perspectives.

Most importantly, the chapters of this book go much beyond the issue of the employment classification of platform workers, a subject that has already been significantly covered in recent literature. Instead, they delve into many of the other manifold issues raised by platform work, such as occupational health and safety, discrimination, social security coverage, restrictions in the enjoyment of collective labour rights, and cross-border coverage of labour standards, among others. Many of the authors in this volume are right to point out that the legal woes do not stop at solving the misclassification of workers under sham self-employment. Many more questions stand between platform workers and decent working conditions.

As part of the effort to move beyond the already well-known challenges, authors were also entrusted with the mission of advancing a "research agenda" for going forward. Much remains to be said about the future development of platform work and the gig economy. Despite the wealth of research that has already been published, many angles of these phenomena have received scant attention so far.

It is undeniable, nonetheless, that the regulatory struggles around the employment status of platform workers are far from over and will continue to occupy the agendas of policymakers, courts and, therefore, scholars for a long while. Thus, this collection begins with *the editors' contribution*, featuring a comparative discussion of **recent trends in case law and legislation** about the inclusion of platform workers in labour, employment, and social protection. This analysis is also done against the background of the ILO Employment Relationship Recommendation 2006 (No. 198), which still constitutes a valuable guide for lawmakers to adopt policies around the scope of the employment relationship and for courts determining its existence in judicial cases.

As the chapter discusses, historically, challenges about employment status have also been faced by other non-standard workers, such as people engaged in casual or triangular work arrangements, homeworkers, and domestic workers. Nonetheless, our analysis shows how platform work exacerbates these challenges, as it incorporates multiple features of these non-standard arrangements.

Notwithstanding the complex nature of platform work, the alleged incompatibility between digital labour platforms' business models and existing labour law concepts has been widely called into question. As we illustrate, many courts and administrative bodies around the world have, indeed, established that platform workers can have access to protections under existing labour standards. After acknowledging the significance of these judicial outcomes, we highlight the importance of various regulatory responses, both at the national and supranational levels. To this end, we cover a broad range of regulatory instruments. We focus on platform-specific measures and general adaptations of labour law, which attempt to solve issues related to the misclassification of workers. Both types of measures can be equally important for platform workers. The chapter ends by paving the way for a future research agenda on this matter, as platform work constitutes "a house of many rooms." While some of these rooms have been explored extensively, others should not be overlooked.

One of the aspects of platform work that certainly warrants more research is **occupational health and safety (OSH)**, the subject matter of the chapter by *Aude Cefaliello and Cristina Inversi*. They show how OSH hazards can be materially worsened within the context of platform work. Not only is the work itself intrinsically dangerous, for instance, due to the ever-present risk of road accidents in the delivery business, but the current legal environment is also not conducive to their protection.

Using the United Kingdom's legal system as an example, the authors highlight that OSH protections materially lie on the distinction between employees and non-employees (e.g., self-employed and limb-b workers). Yet a material part of OSH regulation only covers employees and limb-b workers. This is not only problematic because it can exclude self-employed platform workers from some vital protections, but it is also at odds with the basic principles of OSH.

As the authors discuss, an essential tension between who is protected and who should be protected still endures. Some OSH standards and principles might trickle down into the area of self-employment, requiring platforms to take care of self-employed workers to some extent. However, this is not sufficient. Most notably, the authors argue that consultation processes between workers' representatives and management are a vital aspect of OSH; yet platform workers are largely excluded from representation in such proceedings due to their legal status and fragmented organisational structure. They convincingly show that exclusion from the consultation processes around health and safety is one of the most significant gaps in the OSH legal framework.

In response to these gaps, the authors propose a coherent and comprehensive ethical and legal framework for the digitalisation of work, drawing on two main streams fundamental to OSH: a "decent work agenda" that universalises health and safety protections and a sound "ethical perspective" concerning the proper governance of AI, networks, algorithms, or information more broadly. This framework could feature a robust "prevention through design" approach, which, among other things, spurs information disclosure for OSH purposes. As the authors lucidly detail in their pages, platform work brings about new combinations of risks. The situation demands both general measures, such as universalising OSH protection and more specific actions, like minimising information asymmetries between platform participants.

Minimising information asymmetries is also essential to mitigate the risk of **discrimination**, particularly tech-powered ones. Unfortunately, limited protection against discriminatory practices is a severe issue faced by many platform workers, making it difficult to counter, among other things, gender pay gaps in the sector (see Kullmann 2018; Adams-Prassl 2021). *Elena Gramano and Miriam Kullmann* focus primarily on discrimination deriving from algorithmic decision-making by assessing the suitability of current EU non-discrimination standards to tackle these problems.

One of the crucial components necessary for algorithmic management is an enormous amount of data collected from workers via numerous tracking systems, such as GPS (Global Positioning System) (De Stefano and Taes 2021, 3). According to Gramano and Kullmann, these tools can be used to directly and more often indirectly discriminate against workers, negatively affecting their access to work. Albeit slowly, the possible discriminatory effects of algorithmic management and the importance of tracking systems in the functioning of platforms have also been acknowledged by some national courts in Europe. The authors refer to two recent cases against Deliveroo in Italy and the Netherlands. Both rulings pay significant attention to the role that ranking and tracking algorithmic tools play in monitoring work performance and productivity, directly affecting the workers' ability to access work. However, as both courts recognise, the criteria used by the platform to assess its workers' performance were far from clear. According to the authors, not only can new managerial technologies exacerbate existing discriminatory risks, but they also generate new ones. They argue that some steps forward have been made at the EU level in this respect. For instance, the new proposed directive on improving working conditions in platform work and the AI Act proposal could potentially address some of the risks posed by algorithmic decision-making. However, much more needs to be done at both national and European levels to ensure the effective protection of platform workers, including self-employed ones, against discriminatory practices. To that end, as the authors remark, the involvement of trade unions is vital.

This, however, also raises the fundamental issue of ensuring that platform workers have meaningful access to **collective labour rights**. Several contributions to this book observe that platform workers' resistance and mobilisation gradually increase, with some remarkable achievements occurring so far. Workers' initiatives have varied, including collective bargaining negotiations with the platforms, strike actions, and online campaigns against exploitative practices. In light of these developments, *Alan Bogg and Ricardo Buendia* explore the philosophical foundations and structures of workers' voice in the platform economy.

In their contribution, three ideal-type strategies are identified, namely, the "exit" approach, the "constitutional rights" approach, and the "radical" republican approach. Then, the authors explore the strengths and shortcomings of each of these models. In doing so, they reject the "exit" approach "as risking a form of deregulatory discourse that will be damaging to the interests of workers in the gig economy". Concomitantly, they accept the benefits of the "constitutional rights" approach, which workers often apply through litigation in courts. By adopting this strategy, some platform workers have achieved critical legal victories in securing worker or employment status. Nonetheless, despite its possible benefits, this approach has some structural limitations. For instance, legal proceedings before courts can be lengthy, complex, and very costly, in addition to the risk of a lack of any substantive impact for the majority of workers.

Therefore, according to the authors, the restrictions in current normative structures (e.g., the need for employment or "worker" status as a prerequisite for the application of the vast bulk of labour and employment protections, such as the exercise of the right collective bargaining) show the importance of the "radical" (resistance) approach. Platform workers around the globe have started to reap the benefits of this model, which is often applied in tandem with the "constitutional rights" strategy. As Bogg and Buendia observe, workers' strategies of radical resistance have taken different forms, including, among other things, spontaneous wildcat strikes, walkouts, and protests at different levels of the supply chain. Notably, such initiatives are often taken by platform workers' associations that do not necessarily fit the traditional model of trade unions. The extent to which these developments can effectively challenge existing exploitative business models constitutes an essential subject for a future research agenda.

Platform workers do not only often fall through the cracks of employment and labour legislation, but they also frequently suffer from inadequate **social security protection**. *Paul Schoukens, Alberto Barrio, and Eleni De Becker* focus on the challenges platform work, as part of the broader phenomenon of non-standard work, poses for social security schemes in providing effective, adequate, and transparent coverage.

As commonly happens in the case of labour and employment regulation, work-related social security schemes remain primarily confined to "subordinate" wage employment and are built around the standard open-ended full-time employment relationship (SER). As a result, non-standard workers, including platform workers, face significant restrictions in accessing social security protections. These limitations put these workers at a significantly higher risk of in-work poverty than those in a SER.

They also point out that the very characteristics of platform work, often corresponding to "irregular work patterns, or very marginal work which deviates from the standard employment relationship, but also the role of the algorithm management", are challenging to fit in the usual framework of social security law. The result is a severe lack of transparency and coverage in their social protection.

Acknowledging how these elements can seriously worsen poverty and social exclusion, the EU launched the Council Recommendation on Access to Social Protection in 2019. Schoukens, Barrio, and De Becker, remaining very critical towards some of the instrument's provisions, admit its importance in setting out some standards and principles that should shape the social security systems of the EU member states. It may, furthermore, constitute a valuable tool to reflect on the future of national social security systems and how non-standard work arrangements, like platform work, can fit into national social security frameworks. Still, the authors remark, the recommendation should by no means be seen as a panacea, and other regulatory solutions with a broader scope of application must also be explored. Importantly, as they argue, "if social protection systems will not start to recalibrate their scope of application [...] they may lose out on new evolving realities of work".

Shortfalls in social security protection also materially exacerbate the **precariousness** experienced by platform workers. In his contribution, *Iain Campbell* points out how platform work is significantly associated with a deterioration of "job quality and a redistribution of costs and risks of employment to workers". He reflects on this subject from a sociology of work standpoint and starts by addressing the essential features of platform work, which entail different outcomes in terms of precariousness. Campbell analyses this precariousness along four fundamental dimensions: low levels of regulatory protection, employment insecurity, low earnings, and limited control over work, exploring these particular last two aspects more in depth. He also suggests that the concept of precariousness is not only influenced by the nature of platform work per se but can also be affected by workers' personal experiences. Social relations outside the workplace (e.g., social security benefits, other sources of income) can also significantly impact the level of precariousness. Finally, his contribution touches upon the big picture of precariousness, which can also be observed in other work arrangements, such as casual work. To this extent, he argues some crucial overlaps exist between platform work and casual work, bringing the author to identify platform work as part of a continuum of casual on-call work.

This observation perfectly links Campbell's contribution with the chapter by *Ruth Dukes*. Dukes understands **"on demand work"** or **"work on demand"** broadly as comprising many different forms of contractual and organisational arrangement that are all designed to keep the worker hungry for the next shift, and so – in effect – "on call", ready and willing to work, often on short notice, whenever the employer requires it. She uses the term "employer" broadly, too, meaning an organisation that contracts – directly or via a contractual chain – for work in exchange for a wage or a fee. The author's primary argument is that "on demand work as a legal framework" shines a light on three matters of importance when it comes to understanding platform work. The first one is the weakness of the platforms' claim to novelty when it comes to platform work, the claim that it is quite different to what has gone before. The second is the weakness of the claim to contemporary uniqueness or difference when it comes to platform work, namely the claim that platform work is quite different to other forms of work today and that, therefore, existing laws should not apply. The final matter is the role of contract as both the key legal institution and as an ideological lens implying the ideas of contractual freedom, market justice, and entrepreneurship providing legitimation of platform work, partially obscuring its true nature.

The claims around the novel or unique nature of platform work, conclusively demystified by Dukes' chapter, sound even shallower if one observes how some of the work activities channelled by platforms are among the most traditional forms of labour in our societies. In this respect, **domestic work in the platform economy** is paradigmatic, as demonstrated by the chapter of *Natalie Sedacca*. In examining challenges associated with this form of work, she takes traditional domestic work as a starting point. Historically, domestic workers have struggled to fall within the protection afforded by labour and social protection legal frameworks. Contrary to the notion that platform work would enhance domestic workers' visibility by improving their labour rights, the author contends that an exacerbation of pre-existing challenges can, instead, be observed. The use of apps to "connect" domestic workers and clients, together with a "longstanding distrust" towards these workers, has magnified the surveillance and control over them. Moreover, the use of algorithmic decision-making, for instance, through ranking systems, can supersede the domination of one single employer, thus creating "new means for the domination of workers".

The author also highlights how the devaluation of domestic work, perceived as work predominantly executed by women in the household, constitutes a recurring issue within platform work. Reference is then made to the problematic application of collective labour rights, such as the right to collective bargaining, to domestic workers in the platform economy. Both practical and legal obstacles continue to restrict the enjoyment of these rights. Despite these challenges, some critical collective initiatives are discussed by the author, including a collective agreement concluded between the 3F trade union in Denmark and the cleaning platform Hilfr. Nevertheless, this initiative has faced practical difficulties related to a "lack of mandate from the workers" and legal ones deriving from competition law. In concluding her contribution, Sedacca convincingly emphasises the role that human rights law can play for domestic workers and other platform workers.

Domestic work is not the only age-old work activity channelled by platforms. The transportation of people, as performed, for instance, in the taxi sector, is another obvious example. The chapter of *Uma Rani, Nora Gobel, and Rishabh Kumar Dhir* addresses this form of platform work by focusing specifically on the experiences of traditional and **app-based taxi drivers** in countries such as Chile, Ghana, India, Indonesia, Kenya, Lebanon, Mexico, and Morocco, as they emerge, among other sources, in a survey carried out by the International Labour Office.

In these countries, former traditional taxi drivers are an integral part of the workforce of ride-hailing platforms. Contrary to what is often claimed, these drivers are not afforded any meaningful work flexibility. Instead, they regularly face long working hours on the platforms and diminished levels of autonomy. Even more prominently than in the "Global North", incentive, rewards, and bonus systems are used to exert significant control over workers. These systems affect a material part of the drivers' earnings. Their impact is all the more important as driving is, in fact, the primary source of income for most app-based taxi drivers in these countries. Moreover, the widespread use of rating systems and the tracking and monitoring of the worker's location results in harsh self-disciplining by the drivers to maintain access to work. Notwithstanding the mainstream narrative about autonomy, about half of the surveyed workers in countries like India, Indonesia, and Mexico also faced repercussions for cancelling rides; one-fifth of them also reported the automated deactivation of their account, either on a temporary or permanent basis.

The authors' findings shine a new light on the characteristics of transport-related platform work by highlighting how unsubstantiated the platforms' claims about flexibility and autonomy in this sector are. Recent strike activity also suggests that workers are increasingly ready to challenge existing business practices. Unionising efforts are also ongoing, while policymakers and courts are starting to acknowledge and address the concerns of app-based taxi drivers. Yet, as Rani, Gobel, and Kumar Dhir stress, many legislative and judicial initiatives remain "disjointed and dispersed". The authors conclude by observing that a coordinated and cohesive policy response at the international level may prove essential to better the working conditions of platform workers in the "Global South".

This argument seems all the more valid after reading the chapter of *Kelle Howson, Alessio Bertolini, Srujana Katta, Funda Ustek-Spilda, and Mark Graham* about the "**geographies of platform labour**". They observe that platforms have been designed to function on different scales (locally, regionally, and globally) in a very tactical manner. To this extent, they can allocate and control work via algorithms from a "central point of coordination", which is often many miles away from the workers' local context. Platforms have thus managed to take advantage of existing social and geographical disparities and further exacerbate those inequalities, especially in the "Global South". In doing so, they can also influence "local spatialities", such as transportations systems and patterns of urban inclusion and exclusion. This situation, in many instances, can result in a pronounced commodification of labour, whereby work is exchanged for the lowest price like any other commodity. The authors, moreover, claim that territorial unevenness is not the only form of inequality that platform workers have to deal with. Exploitation across intersecting lines of class and gender issues are severe additional challenges stemming from platform work.

These problems have prompted strong reactions from workers, policymakers, and other stakeholders. The authors observe four "multiscalar" initiatives that have been adopted thus far, and are capable of mitigating the so-far largely unrestricted power of platforms to evade labour regulations. These include workers' mobilisation and resistance through collective actions, such as strikes; the use of online tools by workers to rebalance the information asymmetries between them and the platforms; the enactment of national policies, which regulate the phenomenon of platform work, for instance, by addressing concerns about the employment status of workers; and the active role of supranational organisations, such as the ILO, in promoting and setting global standards for decent work in the platform economy. The authors, thus, conclude that a significant platform countermovement is on the rise that "has the potential to reshape the labour geographies created by digital platforms on local, global, and virtual terrains".

An essential pillar of this countermovement will arguably rest on **transnational regulatory strategies** and instruments. The chapter of *Nastazja Potocka-Sionek* draws a striking parallel between crowdwork, or "digital piecework", a major segment of platform work, and global supply chains (GSCs). The author compares the position of crowdwork platforms with that of lead firms, namely the entities which set parameters for other subjects in GSCs. A crucial common factor lies in their "decisive influence on working conditions in their ecosystems and the evasion of liability".

Starting from this consideration, the author sets out to identify a regulatory strategy to establish and maintain the accountability of crowdwork platforms in terms of labour rights. First, she scrutinises various public and private governance mechanisms, including the UN Guiding Principles, the ILO Home Work Convention, the ILO Fundamental Principles and Rights at Work, and the proposal for an EU Directive on Corporate Sustainability Due Diligence, as well as corporate codes of conduct. She also examines targeted regulatory responses to platform work, such as the recent draft directive of the European Commission on improving working conditions in platform work. Finally, the author advances "a multi-level response" as a pathway towards sustainable platform work concerning these existing normative solutions. Some policy responses in this regard include: promoting private governance mechanisms, establishing the liability of platform companies "for detecting labour law violations by requestors", and setting out an international regulatory framework to govern platform work.

The contribution of Potocka-Sionek is a perfect conclusion for this collection as it addresses some of the most under-researched dimensions of the regulatory challenges posed by platform work to date. The cross-border nature of certain forms of platform work, and the consequent difficulties in governing them, will most likely be an essential preoccupation of policymakers, trade unions, and labour scholars in the future. This issue will not only affect the people who already work online through crowdwork platforms. The normalisation of remote work during the pandemic and technological developments such as the rise of the Metaverse (De Stefano, Aloisi, and Countouris 2022) will likely result in the "platformisation" of growing segments of work activities. The result may well be an additional deregulatory global race to the bottom for labour conditions, underpinned by sham self-employment and inadequate enforcement of labour standards worldwide – issues that have materially shaped both crowdwork and offline-executed platform work.

To avert these risks, it will be essential to address the many complex challenges identified in the different contributions to this collection. The good news, in our opinion, is that these contributions not only pave the way for further research on these matters but also offer some vital insights into how to react to those challenges. As such, we hope this book will not only prove valuable to labour scholars. It will also offer policymakers, social partners, and other stakeholders helpful direction for the road ahead.

Toronto and Leuven, March 2022

V.D.S., I.D., C.S., M.W.

References

Adams-Prassl, Abi. 2021. "The gender wage gap in an online labour market: The Cost of interruptions". Department of Economics Discussion Paper Series. Oxford: University of Oxford.

De Stefano, Valerio and Antonio Aloisi. 2019. "Fundamental labour rights, platform work and human rights protection of non-standard workers". In *Research Handbook on Labour, Business and Human Rights Law*, edited by Janice R. Bellace and Beryl ter Haar, 359–379. Cheltenham, UK and Northampton, MA, USA: Edward Elgar Publishing.

De Stefano, Valerio and Antonio Aloisi. 2021. "The EU Commission takes the lead in regulating platform work". *Social Europe* (blog), 9 December 2021. https:// socialeurope .eu/ european -commission -takes -the -lead -in -regulating -platform -work.

De Stefano, Valerio, Antonio Aloisi, and Nicola Countouris. 2022. "The Metaverse is a labour issue". *Social Europe* (blog), 1 February 2022. https:// socialeurope .eu/ the -metaverse-is-a-labour-issue .

De Stefano, Valerio, Ilda Durri, Charalampos Stylogiannis, and Mathias Wouters. 2021. "Platform work and the employment relationship". ILO Working Paper No. 27. Geneva: International Labour Organization.

De Stefano, Valerio and Simon Taes. 2021. "Algorithmic management and collective bargaining". Foresight Brief. Brussels: ETUI.

Kullmann, Miriam. 2018. "Platform work, algorithmic decision-making, and EU gender equality law". *International Journal of Comparative Labour Law and Industrial Relations* 34 (1): 1–22.

Prassl, Jeremias. 2018. *Humans as a Service: The Promise and Perils of Work in the Gig Economy*. Oxford: Oxford University Press.

2   Exclusion by default: Platform workers' quest for labour protections

Valerio De Stefano, Ilda Durri, Charalampos Stylogiannis, Mathias Wouters

Introduction

Who is entitled to employment and labour protections? Which workers classify as employees? These questions have a long history: "Courts all over the world have been struggling with these issues since the beginning of modern labour law, approximately a century ago, but variations of the same question have been troubling courts for several centuries beforehand" (Davidov, Freedland, and Countouris 2015, 115).

As this contribution discusses, the dawn of the "gig economy" or "platform work" has sparked debates about whether existing labour laws apply to platform workers. Many scholars have argued that existing labour laws can cover these workers. In the meantime, a formidable body of case law has also formed regarding the employment status of platform workers, predominantly focusing on passenger transportation and food delivery. This contribution provides an account of the developments that have taken place in this area of the law. First, it covers case law and highlights some of the steps taken by public authorities to clarify these matters. Subsequently, it points to some of the topics on which additional research is urgently needed.

To do so, this chapter sets the scene by outlining what an employment relationship is, drawing on the International Labour Organization (ILO) Employment Relationship Recommendation, 2006 (No. 198). Next, it contextualises the misclassification of platform workers by shortly recalling how, historically, there have been many other categories of workers whose employment status has also been in doubt. It then turns to recent case law on the employment status of platform workers. The analysis bears out that courts can meaningfully contribute to resolving these issues; however, there are also reasons to believe that, at least in some countries, legislative or governmental interventions are needed to achieve consistent results. Next, we examine some of the many possible "solutions" undertaken by governments and social partners to grant platform workers the legal certainty and protection they need. Finally, the chapter concludes by sketching which questions may warrant further research in light of current developments.

The employment relationship through the lens of ILO Recommendation No. 198

The Employment Relationship Recommendation, 2006 (No. 198) resulted from many years of hard work and negotiations at the ILO (De Stefano et al. 2021, 5–6). To some extent, it can even be considered remarkable for such a recommendation to have been adopted at all. After all, the concept of an employment relationship is strongly connected to that of an employment contract, and these contracts only became a structural feature of European labour law at the beginning of the twentieth century (Veneziani 2010, 31). It is thus remarkable how, within a century, a certain degree of consensus has emerged at the international level regarding the hallmarks of an employment relationship (see, however, De Stefano 2021).

Paragraph 12 of Recommendation No. 198 calls on the Member States to clearly define the conditions applied for determining the existence of an employment relationship. It explicitly refers to "subordination" and "dependence" between the worker and employer as two examples of such conditions. Paragraph 13, then, describes indicators relating to subordination and dependence, pointing to the existence of an employment relationship. These indicators include the fact that the work: (i) involves the integration of the worker in the organisation of the enterprise; (ii) is performed solely or mainly for the benefit of another person; (iii) must be carried out personally by the worker; (iv) is carried out within specific working hours or at a workplace specified or agreed by the party requesting the work; and (v) is of a particular duration and has a certain continuity. These and other indicators describe the features of a stereotypical standard employee in industry or commerce. That itself should not be surprising. One can hardly expect ILO constituents, at the global level, to come up with a radically new approach to identifying employment relationships. It is arguably already a significant achievement for them to form a shared understanding of this legal concept in the first place.

However, things have traditionally become more dubious regarding the legal classification of workers other than standard employees in industry or commerce. At the national level, homeworkers, domestic workers, temporary agency workers, and highly mobile and casual workers have all struggled before courts and labour administrations to be classified as employees. These workers have also historically been more successful in gaining access to labour and social protections in some countries than in others. To some degree, platform workers can be perceived as part of the current generation of workers who face difficulties gaining access to the protective framework of an employment relationship. Some of the specific features of their work may render the determination of the existence of an employment relationship difficult when examining their work arrangements through the lenses of traditional legal doctrines and judicial criteria. Similar to the groups of workers mentioned above, they, too, often have to struggle significantly to gain access to labour and employment rights.

We have (kind of) been here before: Compound non-standard work

Persons involved in multiple-party work relationships are a prominent example of workers whose protection under existing labour and employment standards has long been challenging to secure. Since the late 1960s, governments and courts worldwide have been trying to figure out how temporary agency work and other forms of labour dispatching could be best covered under existing labour and employment regulations. Some of the questions they examined were: Is there an employment relationship between the worker and user enterprise? Or between the worker and agency? Or between the worker and both agency and user? Or between none of them? After decades of uncertainty, both the ILO and the European Union, as well as many national lawmakers, agreed to "forge" an employment relationship between the worker and temporary work agency, sometimes with the understanding that agency workers should have equal treatment with workers engaged through a direct employment contract with the user enterprise. The fact that in some countries, such as Canada, the employment relationship in triangular arrangements can arise between the worker and user enterprise, instead of the agency (Doorey 2009), shows how the ILO's and EU's solution is only one of the possible ways to construct temporary agency work legally. Indeed, the user enterprise usually directs and controls the worker's performance. Therefore, often, this enterprise more factually resembles an actual employer. Nevertheless, temporary work agencies were made the employer of record in many jurisdictions.

Although there may have been good reasons for this decision, such an approach may also lead to employment misclassification once intermediaries and agencies, like platforms, no longer accept their role as the formal employer (Wouters 2021). For instance, Thörnquist describes how many employers in the construction industry in Sweden rely on intermediaries to provide self-employed "subcontractors", mainly from Eastern Europe. The employers in question prefer this option to recourse to temporary agency work covered by EU Directive 2008/104/EC (Thörnquist 2015, 420–21). One response to this issue would be to amend such regulations, introducing a legal mechanism to identify intermediaries that, arguably, evade the regulation on temporary agency work. However, identifying these intermediaries has proven quite challenging. As the ILO recalls, frequently, "specific measures are needed to mitigate the risks for workers in a contractual relationship involving multiple parties, including the risk that they will not know who should be considered as the 'employer' for some specific purposes" (ILO 2016, 275). Unfortunately, the adoption of such measures has historically lagged, something which also impacts workers in the platform economy.

Furthermore, similarly to the need for particular measures for workers in multi-party employment, specific protections for workers who do not perform their work at the workplace of an entrepreneurial employer may also be necessary. Two prominent examples are homeworkers and domestic workers. The ILO's Home Work Convention, 1996 (No. 177) and Domestic Workers Convention, 2011 (No. 189) both aim at ensuring that ratifying Member States develop specific policies to effectively deliver decent work to home and domestic workers by providing at least equal treatment between these workers and workers generally.

Road transport workers are another category of working people who are routinely deprived of labour and employment rights. Many businesses in this sector heavily rely on sham and dependent self-employed workers to undercut the competition (Eichhorst et al. 2013, 93). This tendency might be even more pronounced in some subsectors than in others. Self-employment in the highly competitive parcel delivery market, for instance, is arguably "integral to cost-cutting, the speed-up of delivery and, crucially, the removal of non-delivery costs" (Moore and Newsome 2018, 489). Consequently, targeted measures could be needed for labour protections to be effective in this environment. Nonetheless, as with multi-party, home and domestic work, public authorities often deal with these challenging regulatory issues very timidly.

Platform work is primarily concentrated in a relatively limited number of industries. "App-based" platform work often has to do with passenger transport or food and parcel delivery. Domestic work is also another prominent activity in app-based platform work; platform workers are called upon to perform a range of household tasks (Sedacca 2022). Additionally, online crowdworkers, who perform various digital tasks like transcribing audio, writing or translating short texts, and tagging pictures, often perform the job from their home (De Stefano and Aloisi 2018, 7–13) in a way that resembles some homework arrangements. In other words, many digital labour platforms – and especially the bigger ones – have taken root in parts of the economy that have always been remarkably resistant to effective labour regulation.

In addition, many platform operators establish a sort of multi-party work relationship whereby the platform's user is a business or household, and both the platform and user instruct, monitor and evaluate the worker. Add to this how platform operators assert their ability to offer working time flexibility to provide workers with "autonomy". It is not surprising, then, that both regulators and courts have so far struggled to include these workers in the scope of labour and employment protection. Many platform workers are engaged in arrangements characterised by multiple non-standard and atypical features. Therefore, their work arrangements may deviate from the standard employment relationship across many dimensions. Notably, Eurofound calls work arrangements that combine different non-standard work statutes, like a temporary, part-time, multi-party and self-employed dimension, "compound non-standard work" (Eurofound 2020, 16). Platform work is a conspicuous example of compound non-standard employment. In the words of Eurofound, "[s]uch employment has led to an expansion in the number of individuals with no employment contract, casual workers (including zero-hours contract workers) and people working a very limited number of hours or holding temporary contracts for fewer than six months" (2020, 61).

Many platform operators are keen to take advantage of these atypical features. Their terms and conditions are used to structure the working arrangement to their convenience, including labelling workers on the platform as independent contractors. Each separate "gig" often comes with its short-term contract. These terms, furthermore, tend to downplay the operator's role in the entire construction, implying that the platform is merely a "facilitator" and is not responsible for what happens between workers and users (De Stefano et al. 2021, 12–14). In addition, as just mentioned, many operators strategically profess the virtues of working time flexibility, conveniently highlighting how much workers enjoy such flexibility. Platform workers' desire for flexibility is, concomitantly, presented to mean that workers want to remain self-employed (Dubal 2020, 54). The fact that, in many legal systems, no laws would prevent a platform operator from classifying a worker as an employee and still grant them considerable flexibility is expediently overlooked (Prassl 2018, 115–16).

In other words, operators tend to gravitate towards hard-to-regulate sectors, and they pretendedly and strategically distance themselves from the template of traditional employment relationships. Even so, as the ILO Committee of Experts has also highlighted, this does not mean that labour and employment regulation should not apply to them: "the use of casual work on a regular basis, to carry on activities that concern the main business of the enterprise is a form of disguised employment relationship and contributes to the natural precariousness of this type of work" (ILO 2020, 127).

Platform workers' days in court

In a large number of instances, now, platform workers (together with trade unions and other stakeholders) have demanded the reclassification of their working arrangements under an employment relationship. This has resulted in a growing number of court and administrative decisions from which a few trends have already emerged. For one, although it is anything but simple to convince the courts to override the self-employed classification of platform workers, at least some workers have succeeded in almost all countries where this has been tried. Undoubtedly, workers have been more successful in some countries[1] than in others;[2] still, even in countries where platform operators seem to win cases generally, some adjudicators rule in favour of the workers.[3] In most countries where the courts were called to determine platform workers' employment status, some rulings have questioned the classification of these workers as independent contractors (De Stefano et al. 2021, 30–40).

Second, although it remains to be seen what will happen outside of Europe, workers have mostly prevailed in the European countries where this issue reached the Supreme Court platform. The most notable examples are France, Italy, Spain, and the United Kingdom. For instance, in France, the Cour de cassation argued in March 2020 that the Court of Appeal of Paris had correctly construed the bond between a driver and Uber as constitutive of an employment relationship. The Cour de cassation highlighted how the driver joined a transport service created and entirely organised by Uber, leaving no options to find their clientele or set personal rates; has to follow a particular route, or risk suffering financial consequences; is sometimes unaware of the final destination before accepting the transport request, something that limits their agency; and can be temporarily disconnected from the app as a form of discipline. The Court of Appeal was thus correct to deduce from these facts that the driver was performing work under the authority of Uber and, therefore, as its employee.[4] This 2020 ruling followed an earlier judgment from 2018. Then, the Cour de cassation had overruled a decision of a Court of Appeal that had classified delivery bikers for Take Eat Easy as self-employed workers.[5] However, though the French Supreme Court has drawn a clear line up to now, there might still be room for some disagreement in the judiciary. Most notably, a Court of Appeal in Lyon decided in January 2021 that Uber drivers are self-employed,[6] raising the question of whether the Cour de cassation would quash this decision if the case reached it.

In Italy, in time, platform workers have likewise been successful in front of the courts. Since the first couple of rulings in Milan and Turin, case law has taken a turn. These early decisions had suggested that food delivery drivers for Foodora and Glovo were genuinely self-employed with no access to any meaningful employment protection (Aloisi 2018).[7] After these initial rulings, however, courts were more ready to rely on specific provisions adopted in 2015 and amended in 2019 to extend labour and employment protections to those self-employed persons whose work is organised by someone else. These provisions have eventually benefitted platform workers. Most notably, in January 2020, the Corte di Cassazione disagreed with the assessment of the lower courts, who had ruled either that platform workers were not covered by those provisions or, even when these applied, courts could cherry-pick protections to extend to these workers.[8] The Cassazione, instead, held that under the law of 2015, "[a]ll employment and labour legislation applies to workers whose work is organised by the other party (lavoratori etero-organizzati)" (Aloisi and De Stefano, 2020). Later that year, another noteworthy judgment was issued by a Tribunal in Palermo.[9] Contrary to the Supreme Court, which opened the doors to protection by characterising Foodora bikers as *lavoratori etero-organizzati*, the Tribunal in Palermo decided that a delivery driver for Glovo was an employee plain and simple. Therefore, there would be no need to rely on the 2015 legislation. According to Aloisi, "[t]he significance of [this Palermo judgment] lies in its recognition that the relationship between a platform and a rider fits the model of subordinate employment as a round peg fits solidly in its round hole" (2021, 9).

A decision by the Spanish Supreme Court has also boosted the chances of delivery riders being reclassified as employees in court. In Spain too, initially, there were many contradictory decisions on the employment status of platform workers (Barrio 2020). However, that issue should be resolved now due to the unanimous ruling of the Tribunal Supremo on Glovo in September 2020.[10] Todolí Signes draws attention to one passage, in particular:

> explaining that dependence does not imply absolute subordination, but only insertion into the governing, organisational and disciplinary circle of the company. In post-industrial society the note of dependency has become more flexible. Technological innovations have led to the introduction of digitalised control systems for the provision of services. The existence of a new productive reality makes it necessary to adapt the notes of dependency and alienation to the social reality of the time in which the rules must be applied. (Todolí Signes 2020, 4)

He suggests that the Spanish Supreme Court has been expanding the scope of application of labour laws over the years. In his words: "[i]n short, those who only provide labor, whether they are subject to the employer's instructions or not, will always be employees" (Todolí Signes 2020, 4).

Uber challenged the Employment Tribunal's decision, the Employment Appeal Tribunal's judgment, and the Court of Appeal's majority opinion that Uber drivers are "limb (b) workers" before the Supreme Court of the United Kingdom. That designation meant that in the view of these lower courts, Uber drivers work under a contract, other than a contract of employment, whereby the driver undertakes to perform personally any work or services for Uber, whose status is not by virtue of the contract that of a client or customer of the driver's business.[11] In other words, drivers cannot be considered to be operating a proper business with their clientele. Instead, they personally perform work for Uber, which is the entity with real market access to customers. This is a point of view that the Supreme Court also seemed to share. In his opinion, Lord Leggatt notes that, under Uber's current system, the drivers cannot be "properly regarded as carrying on businesses which are independent of the platform and as performing their services for the customers who purchase those services and not for the platform."[12] Instead, they are "limb (b) workers" and entitled to the corresponding protections.

Some commentators have argued that, in the future, the Supreme Court's purposive approach in Uber "ought to make it more likely for casual and other atypical workers to succeed in claiming statutory employment rights" (Atkinson and Dhorajiwala 2021). Indeed, that would seem to be the case. Nonetheless, since a ruling in June 2021 concluded that Deliveroo bikers are not in an employment relationship for the purposes of their collective rights, caution is still warranted.[13] In the view of the Central Arbitration Committee and Court of Appeal, Deliveroo bikers have a genuine right to substitute themselves, implying that their work is not necessarily performed "personally".

Based on these four countries' examples, it is possible to reach some conclusions. First, at least in Western Europe, platform workers in transportation and delivery services seem to stand a good chance of obtaining labour and social protections by taking their cases to the highest courts. Nevertheless, as the examples of France and the UK show, even at this stage, lower courts may still rule in favour of the platform operator for some reason. Therefore, the lasting effect of these Supreme courts' rulings remains to be seen. Second, in all four countries, the tests that determine the employment classification of the worker seem to be or have been in motion. The French judgments are keenly aware of how digital tools allow directing, monitoring, and disciplining workers differently from how managers have done in the past. Yet, these new ways of managing the workforce can amount to subordination and warrant finding employment status. In Italy, contrary to the majority of the case law, the Tribunal of Palermo decided that a platform worker could be reclassified as an employee despite these workers' somehow flexible schedules. The Spanish Supreme Court, among other things, minimised the importance of the clauses in food-delivery bikers' contracts that allow them to find a replacement if they are unavailable to work. Lastly, the UK Supreme Court in *Uber* assigned far less importance to the wording of the contracts than what it might have done in the past. Therefore, it seems evident that courts can make a considerable difference in the debate about platform workers' employment status.

At the same time, only relying on developments in case law has its drawbacks. Besides the countries mentioned above, Australia, Belgium, Chile, Canada, Germany, Switzerland, the Netherlands, the United States, and Uruguay are also countries where some courts or administrative bodies have accepted the possibility that platform workers be employees (for a detailed discussion, see De Stefano et al. 2021, 30–40). However, it is still uncertain whether platform workers will systematically be entitled to employment protection in these countries. There is arguably still a clear need for more impactful enforcement mechanisms. This could come in various fashions. For example, a class action is a possibility in some countries. A platform may also be barred from the market as long as it resists complying with a ruling, or it might incur criminal or administrative sanctions for deliberately violating existing laws. Instead, what is not possible is for regulators to expect courts to strike the necessary balance and, at the same time, allow these courts' rulings to only have effect between the parties in the dispute. If there is no legislative or administrative follow up to those decisions, platforms can easily alter the terms and conditions and some of their practices cosmetically and keep on treating all the other workers as self-employed ones.

Indeed, past experiences related to the employment status of temporary agency workers, domestic workers, and homeworkers have shown that for this "carnival of litigation" to stop, the courts must be enabled to bring structural change across the industry, or regulators must take it upon themselves to regulate a sector also based on the "inputs" of the court. The second option has been regularly taken in the past. As a result, specific regulations were adopted in many countries for those categories of workers. Lately, some public authorities have also started introducing legislative reforms to help platform workers in their quest for labour protections.

Regulatory approaches to platform work around the world

The national legal tests that govern the classification of employment relationships are often the result of continuous alterations and struggles in business practices and labour relations, changing of policies, overruling of court decisions, and much academic ink. Many national authorities also pay heed to what happens in comparable countries. At the same time, each legal system still has its particularities. Therefore, albeit developments in other countries may inform the domestic response of public authorities, it is impossible for lawmakers to simply transplant a solution from elsewhere and expect it to generate adequate results at home. For this reason, each legal system must develop its multifaceted strategy to embed platform work into existing labour law frameworks satisfactorily. Various approaches are beginning to emerge in this regard.

First, public authorities can take a general stance. This is, for example, what happened in California a few years ago. Following the California Supreme Court ruling in *Dynamex Operations W. v. Superior Court*, Assembly Bill 5 was advanced to incorporate the "ABC-test", advanced by the Court in Dynamex, into statutory law (Cherry 2021).[14] The so-called AB5 reform intended to establish a broad scope of application for labour law in general. Instead of workers having to prove that they are employees of the company, many workers would be presumed to be legally employed unless the hiring entity would show that all three conditions of the ABC-test are fulfilled:

> "(a) the person is free from the control and direction of the hiring entity in connection with the performance of the work, both under the contract for the performance of the work and in fact, (b) the person performs work that is outside the usual course of the hiring entity's business, (c) the person is customarily engaged in an independently established trade, occupation, or business of the same nature as that involved in the work performed".[15]

If the conditions are satisfied, the worker can legitimately perform their activities as an independent contractor. Such a change in methodology, adopting an "employee unless" approach instead of a "self-employed by default" approach, could greatly benefit workers who struggle to prove their employment relationship due to atypical and non-standard features, not least platform workers. Moreover, this kind of approach could be cautiously replicated in other legal systems because it allows for quite a bit of discretion. Policymakers can tweak the content of conditions A, B, and C to strike the correct balance considering the features of their workforces and economies (De Stefano and Wouters 2021). It is thus disappointing that platform workers were artificially "ripped out" of the operation of the AB5 reform by Proposition 22 (De Stefano et al. 2021, 25).

Besides implementing an "employee unless"-approach, there are, of course, other general steps that could significantly benefit some platform workers (De Stefano et al. 2021, 23–29). One example is the Italian case discussed above. The 2015 legislation, as amended in 2019, is unique in the sense that it confers *all* labour and employment protections to workers whose work is organised by a third party (*lavoratori etero-organizzati*), including via platforms, unless a collective agreement says otherwise. As a result, this "particular" category of workers does not lose out on the protections that employees typically receive, even though they are technically not employees but in a type of dependent self-employment (Countouris and De Stefano 2019, 22–28). Moreover, as already said, the judgement of the Italian Supreme Court in 2020 confirmed the applicability of the 2015 legislation to platform workers.

Another general remedy, albeit not necessarily a sufficient one, relates to the possibility to strengthen self-employed workers' collective rights. Around the world, policymakers are exploring options to allow dependent or solo self-employed workers to bargain collectively and enhance their ability to do so (ILO 2020, 113–20). Depending on the legal system, collective agreements could also provide platform workers access to employment status or labour and employment protection. This is the case, for instance, of the collective agreement concluded by the Danish domestic work platform Hilfr and the 3F trade union. Under this agreement, workers are either Freelance Hilfrs (self-employed) or Super Hilfrs (employees). In principle, a worker automatically becomes a Super Hilfr after 100 hours of work, which grants that person employee protection. There are two exceptions to this rule, however. On the one hand, freelancers can individually opt for employee classification even before reaching the 100-hour threshold. On the other hand, domestic workers can also opt-out and continue working as freelancers even though they have reached that threshold (Ilsøe and Jesnes 2020).

Besides general adaptations of employment law, policymakers can also undertake actions that specifically address platform work. Most notably, in Spain, the "Riders' Law"[16] has implemented a targeted presumption. The existence of an employment relationship is rebuttably presumed "for those who provide, in exchange of remuneration, the services of delivering and distributing products for employers who exercise the business powers of organisation, direction and control indirectly or implicitly through a digital platform, or through the algorithmic management of the service or the conditions of work" (Pérez del Prado 2021).

Similarly, the European Commission has proposed a directive on improving working conditions in platform work,[17] which constitutes the most comprehensive response to platform work so far (De Stefano and Aloisi 2021). The scope of this instrument includes all platform workers principally, without being limited to those working in the delivery and transportation sectors.[18] The Directive would also cover platform workers, "who based on an assessment of facts may be deemed to have, an employment contract or employment relationship".[19] To tackle the underlying ambiguity in the employment status of platform workers, the draft Directive specifically emphasises the "primacy of facts" principle, which is also a cornerstone of the ILO Employment Relationship Recommendation, 2006 (No. 198). Furthermore, the proposed instrument also provides a rebuttable presumption of an employment relationship when the platform "controls [...] the performance of work".[20] "Controlling the performance of work", in turn, is understood as fulfilling at least two out of five indicators: (1) remuneration-setting by the platform; (2) a restriction of the workers' freedom to organise their work, including through sanctions; (3) a limitation to the ability to work for another party; (4) the imposition of conduct's standards; and (5) the platform's supervision of the performance of work or the verification of the quality of the results, including by electronic means. Overall, the criteria triggering the presumption reflect key judicial findings from several European courts, ruling in favour of the employment status of platform workers, including the supreme courts of France and Spain (De Stefano and Aloisi 2021). The familiarity of national judges with these criteria may contribute to an easier activation of the legal presumption by workers. Arguably, however, the indicators are still drafted in a very stringent way. This, together with the need to meet at least two indicators to trigger the presumption, can materially hamper its practical application.

Moreover, some of these indicators, such as supervision of work performance or restricting the workers' freedom to organise their work, should already be strong indicia, per se, of the existence of an employment relationship. Proving their existence should be enough to obtain a reclassification – there should be no need to fulfil another indicator to trigger a rebuttable presumption of employment. If these indicators are not significantly revisited, the risk is that some courts will set a very high bar to consider them fulfilled, possibly as high as the one to consider "control" or "subordination" based on traditional domestic criteria. This would be an erroneous interpretation, as supervision and "restricting the freedom, including through sanctions, to organise one's work" are only two indicators of the "control" that activates the presumption of employment. Nonetheless, if the draft directive is not revised, its practical application could paradoxically make it more difficult for platform workers to challenge their employment status.

Public authorities could also issue dedicated laws that confer certain protections to a subset of platform workers. The European Union, for example, has granted certain protections to some self-employed platform workers through EU Regulation 2019/1150 on promoting fairness and transparency for business users of online intermediation services.[21] Limited protection is also provided for self-employed workers under the draft directive on platform work regarding algorithmic management. Likewise, France has issued protections for self-employed platform workers who work on platforms falling under the relevant definitions.[22] Not infrequently, however, the attempt to improve the protection of self-employed platform workers at the national level goes hand in hand with the expectation that they will thereby relinquish their claim to any (quasi-)employment status.

Countries like France and Belgium have also attempted to prevent platform workers from obtaining employment rights, and these efforts have been overruled by the relevant Constitutional Courts (De Stefano et al. 2021, 18–20). However, other countries continue to be attracted to such measures, aiming to foster job creation and "entrepreneurship". In a recent example, Ukrainian lawmakers adopted a law on "stimulating the development of the digital economy in Ukraine".[23] This law creates a virtual free economic zone, referred to as "Diya city". The tech companies residing in this "city" can hire workers under "gig contracts" that exclude them from the Labour Code's standard protections.

As noted, public authorities have an array of options, some of which have not even been mentioned yet (e.g., reliance on external hiring agencies; see Frouin and Barfety 2020). For this reason, the question also becomes how several of these options can be combined, depending on the already existing legal frameworks in place. For example, a country may well succeed in forcing transport and delivery platforms, whether through the courts or broad or targeted legislative amendments, to hire their workers under employment contracts.

Yet, that does not necessarily help people working for cleaning and care services platforms. Nor do they improve the conditions of online crowdworkers. Domestic platform workers and online crowdworkers may have different protection needs from drivers and couriers. Their working conditions are also likely to be governed under another regulatory arrangement (Wouters 2021). Therefore, although platform work has been at the forefront of policy debates for some time now, we are still barely at the outset of any meaningful legal systematisation. Most attention has so far been devoted to ride-hailing and delivery. Still, apart from the draft EU Directive mentioned above, very little is clear about the future regulation of other forms of platform work.

Conclusion: Future topics for research

As discussed in Section 3 above, platform work is in many ways a continuation of ongoing trends, leading to a form of work that can be described as "compound non-standard work". With this in mind, since covering non-standard workers under labour and employment protection has traditionally been challenging, it is not surprising that the same happens with platform work. Many platform workers show features of non-standard work such as an unusual or dispersed workplace, short durations, irregular working hours, and piece-rate remuneration. Therefore, at first sight, their work arrangement may seem to have little in common with the traditional stereotype of a standard employment relationship, making it more difficult to argue in favour of their classification as employees (De Stefano 2021).

Nonetheless, as discussed in Section 4, over the last few years, courts and adjudicators worldwide have increasingly started to accept the claims of platform workers to be included in labour, employment, and social protection. Sometimes, these rulings minimise the importance of features that platform operators invoke as indicative of self-employment, such as flexibility of schedules and the nominal ability to be replaced by other workers. These bodies have also highlighted how technology has made it possible for platforms to surreptitiously give compelling instructions and directions to workers, monitor their actions at all times, and discipline them (through warnings, deactivations, etc.). Likewise, some decisions assign great importance to the fact that platform workers rarely have their own clientele and, in most cases, are essentially integrated into the business of the platform operator.

By balancing the weight of these various features in their rulings on platform work, courts and other adjudicating bodies may also further develop the legal principles and tests surrounding employment classification. Future research may be warranted to assess the extent to which this case law merely reflects already existing developments or is shaping the law of employment classification at large. Also, and most importantly, certain jurisdictions do not excel in the efficient administration of justice. Among other things, this contradicts Recommendation No. 198, which calls for "appropriate, speedy, inexpensive, fair and efficient procedures and mechanisms for settling disputes regarding the existence and terms of an employment relationship".[24] This is an issue for which researchers could aim at identifying best practices, also taking into account platform workers' limited income, frequent migrant background and so forth.

Focusing on legislative and regulatory changes, researchers may also consider exploring the effectiveness of legislative amendments, like the Californian ABC test, the Italian reforms, or the Spanish presumption, to grant access to labour and employment rights to platform workers adequately, and whether some of these actions engender unforeseen downsides.

Furthermore, as observed in Section 5, although some general measures could make a difference for every platform worker, many other actions may still predominantly serve only workers in transport and delivery. As noted, this does not seem to be the case with the recent EU proposed directive on platform work. This instrument would apply to all forms of digitally mediated platform work, for every working activity, regardless of whether it is performed online or is location-based. That said, it remains to be seen whether this legal development would be sufficient in practice to deal with platform work activities such as domestic work and online crowdwork. The effectiveness of the legal presumption proposed under this draft directive, which requires workers to litigate, is another crucial topic for future research. Finally, the adoption of a personal work approach, encompassing all persons who perform predominantly personal work for another party unless they constitute genuine businesses, can also be further assessed as a solution for the platform and other non-standard workers' quest for labour, employment, and social protection (see Countouris and De Stefano 2019). Additionally, some platforms arguably function similarly to private employment agencies (Wouters 2021; Ratti 2017). A legal solution to this issue, with unregulated platforms' activities threatening to undercut competition for the often better-regulated agencies, is likewise yet to be found.

To conclude, the multifaceted activism of judges and policymakers on platform work clearly reveals that the time of "platform work's exceptionalism" has started to fade away (De Stefano and Aloisi 2021). As this contribution shows, some significant steps forward have already been taken. However, as this volume attests to, the gig economy is a house of many rooms. The courts, policymakers, and scholars have already explored certain rooms extensively – others not so much. Legal researchers can make a valuable contribution by paying due attention to those rooms that have mostly been neglected. The other contributions in this volume are all excellent steps in that direction.

Notes

1. For instance in Spain, see Tribunal Supremo 25 septiembre 2020, Case No. ECLI: ES:TS:2020:2924; Tribunal Superior de Justicia núm. 1 de Madrid 27 de noviembre de 2019, Case No. ECLI: ES:TSJM:2019:11243, §38; and Tribunal Superior de Justícia de Catalunya 21 de febrer de 2020, Case No. 1034/2020.
2. For instance in Brazil, see Superior Tribunal de Justiça, 28 de agosto de 2019, Case No. 164.544 – MG (2019/0079952-0); Tribunal Superior do Trabalho, 5 de fevereiro de 2020, Case No. TST-RR-1000123-89.2017.5.02.0038.
3. A regional labour court in Brazil, for instance, has taken a different stance from the higher courts, see 33ª Vara do Trabalho de Belo Horizonte 13 de Fevereiro de 2017, Case No. 0011359-34.2016.5.03.0112, p. 26.
4. Cour de cassation du 4 mars 2020, Case No. ECLI:FR:CCAS:2020:SO00374.
5. Cour de cassation du 28 novembre 2018, Case No. ECLI:FR:CCASS:2018:SO01737.
6. Cour d'appel de Lyon du 15 janvier 2020, Case No. RG 19/08056.
7. Tribunale di Torino 11 aprile 2018, Case No. 778; Tribunale di Milano 10 settembre 2018, Case No. 1853.
8. Corte di Cassazione 24 gennaio 2020, Case No. 11629/2019.
9. Tribunale di Palermo 20 novembre 2020, Case No. 3570/2020.
10. Tribunal Supremo 25 de diciembre de 2020, Case No. ECLI:ES:TS:2020:2924.
11. Section 230, Employment Rights Act 1996.
12. The Supreme Court 19 February 2021, Case No. [2021] UKSC 5.
13. Court of Appeal 24 June 2021, Case No. [2021] EWCA Civ 952.
14. Supreme Court of California 30 April 2018, Case No. S222732.
15. California Assembly Bill No. 5, Chapter 296. An act to amend Section 3351 of, and to add Section 2750.3 to, the Labor Code, and to amend Sections 606.5 and 621 of the Unemployment Insurance Code, relating to employment, and making an appropriation therefor.
16. Real Decreto-ley 9/2021, de 11 de mayo, por el que se modifica el texto refundido de la Ley del Estatuto de los Trabajadores, aprobado por el Real Decreto Legislativo 2/2015, de 23 de octubre, para garantizar los derechos laborales de las personas dedicadas al reparto en el ámbito de plataformas digitales.
17. Proposal for a Directive of the European Parliament and of the Council on Improving Working Conditions in Platform Work, Brussels, 9/12/2021.
18. Ibid., article 2 1. (1).
19. Ibid., article 1 2.
20. Ibid., article 4.

21. Regulation (EU) 2019/1150 of 20 June 2019 of the European Parliament and of the Council on Promoting Fairness and Transparency for Business Users of Online Intermediation Services, OJ L 186.
22. Sections L7341-1 – L7345-6 Code du travail.
23. Закон України Про стимулювання розвитку цифрової економіки в Україні, No. 1667-IX from 15.07.2021.
24. Paragraph 4 (e) Employment Relationship Recommendation, 2006 (No. 198).

References

Aloisi, Antonio. 2018. "'With Great Power Comes Virtual Freedom': A Review of the First Italian Case Holding that (Food-delivery) Platform Workers are Not Employees". *Comparative Labor Law & Policy* Dispatch No. 13. Champaign: University of Illinois College of Law.

Aloisi, Antonio. 2021. "Demystifying Flexibility, Exposing the Algorithmic Boss: A Note on the First Italian Case Classifying a (Food-Delivery) Platform Worker as an Employee". *Comparative Labor Law & Policy* Dispatch No. 35. Champaign: University of Illinois College of Law.

Aloisi, Antonio, and Valerio De Stefano. 2020. "Delivering Employment Rights to Platform Workers" *il Mulino* (blog), 31 January 2020. https://www.rivistailmulino .it/a/delivering-employment-rights-to-platform-workers.

Atkinson, Joe, and Hitesh Dhorajiwala. 2021. "After Uber: Purposive Interpretation and the Future of Contract" *UK Labour Law* (blog), 1 April 2021. https://uklabourlawblog .com/2021/04/01/after-uber-purposive-interpretation-and-the-future-of-contract -by-joe-atkinson-and-hitesh-dhorajiwala/.

Barrio, Alberto. 2020. "Contradictory Decision on the Employment Status of Platform Workers in Spain". *Comparative Labor Law & Policy* Dispatch No. 20. Champaign: University of Illinois College of Law.

Cherry, Miriam A. 2021. "Proposition 22: A Vote on Gig Worker Status in California". *Comparative Labor Law & Policy* Dispatch No. 31. Champaign: University of Illinois College of Law.

Countouris, Nicola, and Valerio De Stefano. 2019. *New Trade Union Strategies for New Forms of Employment*. Brussels: ETUC.

Davidov, Guy, Mark Freedland, and Nicola Countouris. 2015. "The Subjects of Labor Law: 'Employees' and Other Workers". In *Comparative Labor Law*, edited by Matthew W. Finkin and Guy Mundlak, 115–31. Cheltenham:, UK and Northampton, MA, USA: Edward Elgar Publishing.

De Stefano, Valerio. 2021. "Not As Simple As It Seems: The ILO and the Personal Scope of International Labour Standards". *International Labour Review* 160(3): 387–486.

De Stefano, Valerio, and Antonio Aloisi. 2018. *European Legal Framework for "Digital Labour Platforms"*. Brussels: European Commission.

De Stefano, Valerio, and Antonio Aloisi. 2021. "The EU Commission Takes the Lead in Regulating Platform Work" *Social Europe* (blog), 9 December 2021. https:// socialeurope .eu/ european -commission -takes -the -lead -in -regulating -platform -work.

De Stefano, Valerio, and Mathias Wouters. 2021. "Embedding Platforms in Contemporary Labour Law". In *A Modern Guide to Labour and the Platform*

Economy, edited by Jan Drahokoupil and Kurt Vandaele, 129–44. Cheltenham, UK and Northampton, MA, USA: Edward Elgar Publishing.

De Stefano, Valerio, Ilda Durri, Charalampos Stylogiannis, and Mathias Wouters. 2021. "Platform Work and the Employment Relationship". ILO Working Paper No. 27. Geneva: International Labour Organization.

Doorey, David. 2009. "Who is the Employer of Temp Workers?" *Canadian Law of Work Forum* (blog), 27 October 2009. https://lawofwork.ca/who-is-the-employer-of-temp-workers/.

Dubal, Veena B. 2020. "An Uber Ambivalence: Employee Status, Worker Perspectives, and Regulation in the Gig Economy". In *Beyond the Algorithm: Qualitative Insights for Gig Work Regulation*, edited by Deepa Das Acevedo, 32–56. Cambridge: Cambridge University Press.

Eichhorst, Werner, Michela Braga, Ulrike Famira-Mühlberger, Maarten Gerard, Thomas Horvath, Martin Kahanec, Marta Kahancová, et al. 2013. *Social Protection Rights of Economically Dependent Self-Employed Workers*. Brussels: European Parliament.

Eurofound. 2020. *Labour Market Change: Trends and Policy Approaches towards Flexibilisation*. Luxembourg: Publication Office of the European Union.

Frouin, Jean-Yves, and Jean-Baptiste Barfety. 2020. *Réguler les plateformes numériques de travail*. Paris: Rapport au Premier Ministre.

ILO. 2016. *Non-Standard Employment around the World: Understanding Challenges, Shaping Prospects*. Geneva: ILO.

ILO Committee of Experts on the Application of Conventions and Recommendations. 2020. *Promoting Employment and Decent Work in a Changing Landscape*. Geneva: ILO.

Ilsøe, Anna, and Kristin Jesnes. 2020. "Collective Agreements for Platforms and Workers – Two Cases from the Nordic Countries". In *Platform Work in the Nordic Models: Issues, Cases and Responses*, edited by Kristin Jesnes, 44–55. Copenhagen: Nordic Council of Ministers.

Moore, Sian, and Kirsty Newsome. 2018. "Paying for Free Delivery: Dependent Self-Employment as a Measure of Precarity in Parcel Delivery". *Work, Employment and Society* 32(3): 475–92.

Pérez del Prado, Daniel. 2021. "The Legal Framework of Platform Work in Spain: The New Spanish 'Riders' Law'". *Comparative Labor Law & Policy* Dispatch No. 36. Champaign: University of Illinois College of Law.

Prassl, Jeremias. 2018. *Humans as a Service: The Promise and Perils of Work in the Gig Economy*. Oxford: Oxford University Press.

Ratti, Lucca. 2017. "Online Platforms and Crowdwork in Europe: A Two-Step Approach to Expanding Agency Work Provisions?". *Comparative Labor Law and Policy Journal* 38 (3): 477–511.

Sedacca, Natalie. 2022. "Domestic Work and the Gig Economy". In *A Research Agenda for the Gig Economy and Society*, edited by Valerio De Stefano, Ilda Durri, Charalampos Stylogiannis, and Mathias Wouters. Cheltenham: Edward Elgar Publishing.

Thörnquist, Annette. 2015. "False Self-Employment and Other Precarious Forms of Employment in the 'Grey Area' of the Labour Market". *International Journal of Comparative Labour Law* 31(4): 411–29.

Todolí Signes, Adrián. 2020. "Notes on the Spanish Supreme Court Ruling that Considers Riders to be Employees". *Comparative Labor Law & Policy* Dispatch No. 30. Champaign: University of Illinois College of Law.

Veneziani, Bruno. 2010. "The Evolution of the Contract of Employment". In *The Making of Labour Law in Europe*, edited by Bob Hepple, 31–72. Oxford: Hart Publishing.

Wouters, Mathias. 2021. *International Labour Standards and Platform Work*. The Hague: Wolters Kluwer.

3 The impact of the gig-economy on occupational health and safety: Just an occupation hazard?

Aude Cefaliello,[1] Cristina Inversi[2]

Introduction

The Fourth Industrial Revolution has brought the rise and the development of the so-called gig-economy, a new market which mostly makes use of on-demand self-employed workers. The development of mobile applications using AI and the spread of smartphones have been able to introduce significant changes in the way consumers are accessing services, with the most emblematic example being food delivery. Hand in hand with consumers' change, smartphones and apps have significantly changed the way work is performed and have a great impact on the health and the safety of workers. Apps are mostly valuable because they can generate data, and data can lead to a situation of control and surveillance by the platform (Srnicek, 2017).

Occupational Health and Safety (hereafter OSH) is one of the areas which suffer a huge impact from the increased presence on the labour market of companies that operate in the gig-economy. Even if riders' working conditions have always been known as dangerous, significant improvements have been made over the past decades through the adoption of an extensive protective legal framework. In Europe, the cornerstone of that legal framework is the Directive 89/391/EEC, and in the UK is the Health and Safety at Work Act 1974. Both include the general principles of prevention, and the basic employers' duties towards their workers. These principles are flexible and, so far, managed to adapt to new forms of work and new risks. New forms of work organisation and the use of modern technologies in the labour market are affecting many areas of employment regulation and their traditional rights and protections, in particular by influencing job security, working time patterns, and organisational structures (Stacey et al., 2018). There appears to be a "loophole" that some platforms are using to escape their responsibilities, both regarding the general labour law infrastructure, and the OSH legal framework in particular. The problem is twofold: not only the occupational hazard due to the nature of their work, but also because of their self-employed status, some gig-workers are in a situation of high precarity that can further place their health at risk. The present chapter will reflect on these two issues, to shed a light on the OSH perspective of gig-economy work and the UK legal framework. At first, in the following section, the chapter will present the current framework of risks and issues that gig-workers are facing in on-demand food delivery services, drawing from extensive qualitative research. In the third section, the chapter then presents and discusses the current UK legal framework for health and safety protection, with a special focus on gig-economy workers and recent legal challenges. Finally, in the fourth and fifth sections, the chapter will outline possible policy intervention for the UK context, to address regulatory change and enhance gig-workers' protections.

The gig-economy and the (new) occupational risks

The expansion of digital platforms has been described as a disruptive regulatory phenomenon that has affected many domains: production and distributions of goods and services, competition, social aspects of everyday life and, of course, labour markets (Weatherby, 2018). Platform work has been characterised under different typologies (European Parliament, 2017; Howcroft and Bergvall-Kåreborn, 2019): here, we mainly focus on "on-demand" work which "may utilise smartphones and mobile applications while the work is locally executed" (Howcroft et al., 2019, 216), in particular in the food delivery sector.[3]

The gig-economy, and in particular platform-based delivery services, combines two problematic aspects when it comes to considering OSH issues. First, labour regulation appears intrinsically nebulous when considering the business models adopted, which tend to neglect employment law and the application of OSH protections (Prassl, 2018a; Cherry and Aloisi, 2017; Todoli-Signes, 2017). Second, most businesses tend to adopt forms of casual and on-call types of work, with their well-documented problematic features when it comes to working conditions, precarity and uncertainty, and connected prevention frameworks (Burri et al., 2018).

In particular, if we consider the platform-based delivery industry, common hazards related to the tasks performed are well known and well characterised (Tran and Sokas, 2017). Because riders execute their work on the road, mainly by bikes or motorbikes, they are subject to an increased risk linked to accident and road safety, alongside the possibility of working in extreme weather conditions. The disruptive effect of these businesses has been mainly represented by the new approach to labour organisation, with the creation of a completely unregulated, extremely casualised type of work, or, as argued, the return to pre-industrial insecure forms of labour (Prassl, 2018a). It is thus the analysis of the combined effect of the "traditional" occupational risks of the tasks and the effect of the new approach to labour supply and demand, intensively using AI and algorithms (EU-OSHA, 2019), which is essential in order to assess the nature of the risks insightfully.

Workers in the gig-economy and generally platform workers are deemed more likely to experience work overload, extensive working times, and a difficult work–life balance (EU-OSHA, 2019). Furthermore, a main issue is the likeliness of experiencing isolation (HSE, 2020), individualisation (which is deemed to have a potential negative effect on collectivisation attempts and bargaining power; Graham et al., 2017) and communication issues with management, which might result in dissatisfaction and frustration, but also into an incentive to assume risks. When looking at the OSH risks that workers in the gig-economy are likely to be exposed to, it is arguable that the nature of these risks is neither indicative of a newly emerging type, nor a door to a new taxonomy of risks. The risks connected with these types of jobs are indeed not new in their substance: road accidents, fatigue, stress, attacks, job insecurity, and the (in some cases connected) poor mental health conditions. Instead, we argue that the new issues to be articulated and scrutinised mostly arise from the layering and the cumulation of risks created by new forms of work management through AI and online devices (INRS, 2018). In addition to the issues previously raised in the literature on telework and other forms of remote working (Sardeshmukh et al., 2012; Montreuil and Lippel, 2003; Mann and Holdsworth, 2003), what the gig-economy brings as a new OSH challenge for lone workers with no standard workplace resides in the novelty of the digital tools' design and data ownership from the platform organising the working activity, which allows for extensive power of control and data gathering on workers' tasks. Information represents here, once again, the contested terrain in which the regulatory game is played. Under these premises, we argue that an "OSH oriented" use of information is key to the design of a responsive system, with positive actions that could be taken when considering the re-building of an effective preventive and enforceable framework, as we will outline later.

In line with what has been highlighted by the 2019 EU-OSHA Report (EU-OSHA, 2019, 15),[4] our research findings illustrate that OSH is a predominant issue which affects both the temporal and the special organisation of riders' work. Within the on-demand delivery industry, working time is first characterised by being extremely flexible, and work/life boundaries are blurred. In some realities, riders often experience "hours famine" and uncertain shifts allocations; while in other cases, the oversupply of work by an uncontrolled labour offer increases the length of unpaid waiting time (Inversi, 2018). Both organising structures (hourly pay and piece-work pay) have the result of putting riders in uncertain working time patterns and irregular schedules. Online working platforms are, in general, currently not obliged to provide regular work, but have the flexibility of calling workers in on-demand (i.e., Deliveroo riders being called and given special offers and pay increase when it is raining or snowing to boost the offer of service, incentivising workers to work under extreme or undesirable weather conditions). Due to high competition and work offers, this often appears to be a forced flexibility. In these situations, the mental health of workers in poor-quality jobs has been found to be equivalent to or worse than that of those who are unemployed (Chandola, 2017). This has been even more evident during the COVID-19 sanitary emergency, when riders have been considered as "essential workers" to maintain food delivery services (Inversi et al., 2020).

Second, the performance pressures that the platform puts on workers are able to affect workers' physical and cognitive capabilities: riders revealed feeling incentivised to ride faster, in order to maximise income and rewards. This can generate a psychosocial risk in terms of working time intensity generated by the quantitative and qualitative requirements of the platforms (INRS, 2018). Within the qualitative data collection undertaken, riders testify feeling pressured by the fact that all their working activity is recorded and timed, with the knowledge of being constantly monitored and evaluated in all the tasks (from the time of acceptance of the delivery to the client's doorstep), with the further impact on the possibility to get more work (hours or deliveries) if times are not satisfactory. On this latter issue, riders also testified that good performances and especially constant work availability (no absences or interruptions due to holidays or sick leaves) were strongly perceived as a parameter to obtain and maintain working hours. Furthermore, taking time off due to work-related injuries may result in forms of punishment or detrimental conditions for riders.

Third, the constant oversight allowed to the management by the use of AI is documented to have an impact on workers in terms of uncertainty on the pervasiveness of control and the unilateral use of information, perceived to be made to restrain riders' agency and collective power. It is deemed, indeed, that these forms of monitoring can cause stress and anxiety, particularly if combined with a lack of control (real or perceived) of work pace and schedule (HSE, 2017).

Another element is that because the gig-economy work is coordinated and overseen by computer algorithms, and management of work relies heavily on AI; workers can lose control over work content, pace and schedule, and the way they do their work (Moore, 2018). Riders' autonomy appears to be limited, and platforms are often not supportive or communicative when the riders try to reach out. Despite companies claiming against it, a form of "middle management" does still exist, especially in the management of work offers: workers claim that the management is, in some areas, micromanaging hours, but the "frustration" comes from being just one-way communication.

A final but crucial issue that affects the OSH of riders at work is driven by the isolation of riders in "lone working" conditions. Riders are subject to increased risks because they do not enjoy assistance when they have an accident or a health problem. Lone workers in public space may also be vulnerable to physical violence or verbal abuse from third parties (HSE, 2020). Despite the recommendation of the HSE, when riders tried to reach out for help or assistance, the platform did not act to prevent risks or assist the rider. When referring to a series of assaults made through "fake orders", a rider from the Manchester area pointed out that the only way to prevent assaults was to ask another rider to join in the delivery as a helper, because the platform management decided not to help riders in any way. Riders in London Spitalfields and Camden Town highlighted the huge fear of acid attacks perpetrated on riders, which lead to forms of auto organisation and peer support.[5] Also, riders often expressed how they perceived the possibility of moving to a safer gig-economy job (such as working as a car driver for Uber) was considered a "career upgrade" because of the huge feeling of lack of safety in being a delivery rider.

The UK OSH Legal Framework put to the test of the on-demand gig-economy

According to the Health and Safety Executive (HSE)[6]: "For health and safety purposes, gig economy workers should be treated **no differently to other workers** and will often identify as agency or temporary workers, or self-employed. They may also be 'limb (b) workers' and entitled to certain employment rights as a result".[7]

The existing labour law legal framework in the UK is structured around the binary principle of the contract of service (i.e., employee–employer relationship) and the contract for services (i.e., independent contractor or "self-employed") (Barrett and Sargeant, 2008). Still, when there is a situation of significant dependency, an individual should be qualified as a limb(b) worker who has entered into or works under any other contract (i.e., not a contract of employment) whereby the individual undertakes to do or perform personally any work or services for another party to the contract (s.230(3)(b) ERA 1996). Therefore, in UK labour law, there are three categories (Figure 3.1): employee, limb(b) worker, and self-employed individual. However, the OSH legislation makes a distinction between employee and non-employee (e.g., limb(b) worker and self-employed). Thus, depending on the legal qualification of the contract, the protection and duties embodied by the OSH law change, as we will outline.

The Health and Safety at Work (HSW) Act is the cornerstone of the UK OSH Legal Framework and is completed by several Regulations.[8] The HSW Act is based on the philosophy of the Robens Report, which enshrines the basic enduring principle that OSH responsibilities lie *with those who create the risks and those who work with them* (Robens, 1972). Meanwhile, the European OSH Legal framework (in particular the Framework Directive 89/391/EEC), which has been implemented in the UK,[9] revolves around the concept of worker (Art. 3) that covers both employee and limb(b) workers.[10] There is, therefore, a "tension" between the national and European approaches and the boundaries of OSH protection, and the nature of that protection (see Figure 3.1).

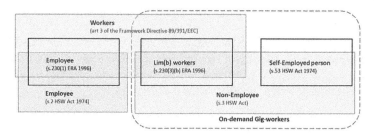

Figure 3.1   Personal scope of Occupational Health and Safety legislation in the United Kingdom and European Union

In the United Kingdom, the HSW Act 1974 provides a broad scope of the general duties that reaches beyond the employment relationship to protect persons other than employees. However, despite the broad theoretical coverage, the COVID-19 pandemic highlighted weaknesses in the current system – particularly regarding the protection of on-demand gig-workers such as food delivery riders (Robinson et al., 2020). Until recently, little attention has been given to the health and safety of on-demand gig-workers. Indeed, recent studies have underlined the risks they are exposed to (Wood, 2021) but not the legal consequences of their status regarding OSH legislation.

Prior to the highly commented *Uber BV v Aslam [2021] UKSC 5 ('Uber (SC)')* judgement, another important judgement significantly impacted the working conditions of on-demand gig-workers. In November 2020, *IWGB v SSWP and Others* ruled that the UK OSH legislation did not fully comply with the EU OSH Standards (Hobby, 2021). According to this ruling, for the purpose of health and safety legislation, "workers" (as defined in Dir. 89/391/EEC) should include employee and limb(b) workers as defined in s.230(3)(b) of the Employment Right Act 1996. It means that limb(b) workers should benefit from all the rights and duties originating from Dir. 89/391/EEC.

Considering that the status of the on-demand gig-workers can vary, the question of the OSH legal coverage takes place within the broader legal complexity and discrepancy between the national and European scope of OSH protection. Based on this idea, this section considers the implications and effects of the on-demand gig-economy on the coverage and effectiveness of the OSH Legal Framework in the UK. The effectiveness of OSH legislation in the UK relies on three main mechanisms: self-regulation from the employers, employee involvement, and enforcement agency (Epstein, 2012). We will focus on the first two mechanisms and examine whether they are adequate for the on-demand gig-economy.

Does broad employers' duty of care mean equal protection to non-employees?

At European level, Dir. 89/391/EEC provides that "the employer shall have a duty to ensure the safety and health of workers in every aspect related to the work" (Art. 5). The personal scope of the directive applies to workers defined as "any person employed by an employer" (Art. 3(2) Dir. 89/391/EEC). The Health and Safety at Work Act 1974 provides similar obligations for the employer but extends, to some degree, the employer's duty of care beyond the employment relationship. Indeed, there are two different provisions: section 2 is applicable to employees and section 3 to non-employees (including limb(b) workers and self-employed). Even if the two sections might appear similar, they, nevertheless, differ in their wording.

Employees[11] have their health, safety, and welfare ensured at work, meaning for all actions "throughout the time when [they are] in the course of [their] employment" (s.53 HSW Act 1974). Thus, the employer should guarantee the health and safety of her employees regardless of their work location.

However, the employer's obligation towards non-employees has a different legal grounding. The employer's obligation of s.3(1) is different and obliges them to conduct "his undertaking in such a way as to ensure, so far as is reasonably practicable, that persons not in his employment who may be affected thereby are not thereby exposed to risks to their health and safety". Reg. 3 of the Management of Health and Safety at Work (MHSW) Regulation 1999 draws a similar distinction between employee and non-employee (e.g., limb (b) workers). After assessment of the risks of their employee and persons who might be affected by the conduct of the undertaking, the employers shall apply the general principles of prevention as provided by Art. 6(2) Directive 89/391/ EEC if they implement any preventive or protective measures.[12] *IWGB v SSWP and Others* confirms that, in theory, these provisions should provide *equivalent* protection to employees and limb(b) workers (as persons not in their employment) (e.g., limb(b) workers).

One concern might be about the restriction to prevent the risks for non-employees only in the way the employer conducts their undertaking. *R v Associated Octel Co Ltd* rules that if the employee and the non-employee are working alongside each other, the protection is the same.[13] However, would the level of protection be the same if the employee and the non-employee do not share the same workplace? Particularly if non-employees are away from the premises of the undertaking but might still be affected by the conduct of this undertaking, as it is the case for riders. James et al. raised some concerns that section 3 of the HSW Act might not extend protections in situations where work is undertaken away from an employer's premises[14] (James et al., 2007). The HSE published guidelines to help employers to manage the risks for employees and non-employees who are drivers, providing some elements of answers.

> Managing the risks to employees who drive at work requires more than just compliance with road traffic legislation. The Health and Safety at Work etc Act 1974 requires employers to take appropriate steps to ensure the health and safety **of their employees and others who may be affected by their activities when at work. This includes the time when they are driving or riding at work, whether this is in a company or hired vehicle, or in the employee's own vehicle**. There will always be risks associated with driving. Although these cannot be completely controlled, an employer has a responsibility to take all reasonable steps to manage these risks and do everything reasonably practicable to protect people from harm in the same way as they would in the workplace.[15]

Thus, **if** the on-demand gig-workers are considered as limb(b) workers by the platforms, the said-platform should apply the following considerations in the journey planning:[16]

- take account of appropriate routes;
- incorporate realistic work schedules;
- not put drivers at risks from fatigue;
- take sufficient account of adverse weather conditions.

It is fundamental that the effect of the *conduct of the undertaking* is understood broadly. The purpose of extending labour law protection to limb(b) workers is because they are, substantively and economically, in a subordinate and dependent position towards their employers, similarly to employees. According to Davidov, a purposive approach of health and safety legislation would justify its extension to all of those working for others (Davidov, 2016). The '*Uber (SC)*' judgement of the Supreme Court illustrates the various degrees of control exercised by the platform while the drivers are logged onto the app. Even if the on-demand gig-workers are away from the main undertaking, they are still considerably affected by the way Uber is conducting its business. Similarly, the conduct of the undertaking creates risks for non-employees (limb(b) workers and self-employed) that should be assessed and prevented as far as reasonably practicable. It is the reason why recognising the status of limb(b) workers to on-demand gig-workers is fundamental to guarantee them adequate minimal protections. Unfortunately, *Uber (SC)* is an ad hoc judgement, and many workers in rather similar situations still do not benefit from the limb(b) worker status that the decision has granted to drivers; in fact, many on-demand gig-workers are still classified as self-employed. The employer's duty of care should cover all non-employees impacted by the conduct of the undertaking (s.3(1) HSW Act 1974). As pointed out earlier, regardless of their status, riders are impacted by platforms' managerial practices, accordingly, the platform should be obliged not to expose self-employed riders to the risks arising from the way it conducts the undertaking. However, one can argue that OSH obligations of the self-employed to assess their own risk (s 3(2) HSW Act 1974) could counterweight the employer's obligation, and thus its responsibility in case of accidents. According to s.3(2) of the HSW Act 1974, "it is the duty of every self-employed person to conduct his undertaking in such a way to ensure, so far as is reasonably practicable, that he and other persons (not being his employees) who may be affected thereby are not thereby exposed to risks to their health and safety".

When on-demand gig-worker riders are classified as self-employed, they are responsible for their own health and safety, and for people in the public sphere that they might encounter during their rides/deliveries. The self-employed are expected to take reasonable steps to identify risks adequately.[17] In these circumstances, the employer/platform and the self-employed rider share the obligation to assess and prevent the risks. This raises the question of shared responsibility between the platform and the self-employed if an accident occurs while the rider is logged on the app. One might wonder if in cases where the platform fails to assess the risk adequately for the self-employed, the riders will be entitled to any compensation under tort law for breach of the duty of care considering that the rider should have assessed and prevented the risk.

Similarly, even if the OSH provisions have been amended so limb(b) workers cannot be subject to a penalty by their employer for leaving or refusing to return to their workplace or for taking steps to protect themselves in circumstances of danger which the worker reasonably believes to be serious and imminent, this is not the case for self-employed workers.[18] Currently, there is nothing stopping platforms from deactivating – even unfairly – riders if they left or refused to work to protect themselves from serious and imminent danger. It means that even if the platform failed not to expose them to such risk, the riders could still be subject to detrimental treatment if they took precautionary measures.

To conclude, even if at first the broad employer's duty of care seems to provide an equivalent level of protection to employee and non-employees, when we test these provisions in gig-economy settings there is still a significant risk that the employer will not assess and prevent the risks properly. The only way to guarantee minimum effective safety measures is to guarantee the limb(b) worker status to on-demand gig-workers to promote employers' OSH compliance. In addition, we believe that focusing only on the employer's duty of care overlooks other substantive parts of the OHS principles: workers' involvement and participation.

Beyond the duty of care: The imbalance between employees and non-employees OSH participation

The object of the Framework–Directive reaches beyond the employer's obligation to ensure the safety and health of workers in every aspect related to work. The improvement of workers' health and safety also relies on workers' involvement with information, consultation, and balanced participation (Art. 1(2) Dir. 89/391/EEC). As soon as on-demand gig-workers are qualified as limb(b) workers and fall within the scope of Art. 3(2) of Dir. 89/391/EEC, they should also be involved in the development of a preventive plan. However, the current UK legal framework excludes limb(b) workers from the participatory mechanisms.

Dir. 89/391/EEC places a lot of importance on the workers' representation with health and safety representatives to participate in OSH prevention. This is illustrated in Art. 11(1) of Dir. 89/391/EEC, which provides that "employers shall consult workers and/or their representatives and allow them to take part in discussions on all questions relating to safety and health at work". The employer should consult workers and their representatives but should also give them the possibility to make proposals on "any measure which may substantially affect safety and health". A broad understanding of health and safety can lead to mandatory consultation of the health and safety representatives when there is a significant organisational change.

Applied to the on-demand platform economy, a change in the programming of the algorithm management software can modify the condition to allocate shifts. This modification could lead to work-related stress (or psychosocial risks) and should therefore be discussed with their health and safety representatives. On-demand gig-workers, if considered as limb(b) workers, should have the right to be consulted and to have health and safety representatives (Art. 7(1) Dir. 89/391/EEC). However, domestic law under its current form implements these rights only for employees and still excludes limb(b) workers (Johnstone et al., 2005).

Currently, health and safety representatives are appointed by recognised trade unions amongst employees and those representatives represent employees' interests when consulted (s. 2 HSW Act 1974). Similar restrictions to employees' interests and to measures affecting "the health and safety of employees represented" can be found in the Regs 3, 4A of the SRSC Reg 1977. Similarly, the Health and Safety (Consultation with Employees) Regulations 1996 (Reg. 3) gives the employer the possibility to directly consult employees not represented by a recognised union on matters that may substantially affect the employees' health and safety. Even the official code of conduct recommends focusing the risk assessment on **employees' needs**.[19] All of these provisions are centred around the employees and do not recognise the limb(b) workers as part of the undertaking, which is in breach of the Framework Directive. Previous studies have underlined that OSH legal provisions cannot "cope with more fragmented organisational structures (e.g., platform economy)" (James et al., 2007, 174). The exclusion of the gig-workers from the consultation process on OSH issues might represent one of the most significant gaps in the OSH legal provisions. This issue relates to the broader question of gig-workers' voices and collective representation/organisation (Prassl, 2018b; Aloisi, 2019).

Time for a regulatory change?

Since technological developments and their business implications run at a very high speed and, to some extent, they are unpredictable and thus difficult to anticipate for regulators, it is important to understand which are the policy gaps that we are experiencing today and how it can be possible to address them in a timely and comprehensive manner (Stacey et al., 2018). Although the adoption of new legislative measures to address loopholes and flaws in legal provisions represents one of the desirable regulatory strategies, we believe that they would be ineffective if not combined with a broader range of interventions. We argue that the role of the state and its potential for intervention through prescriptive and proscriptive regulation are of fundamental importance. In this sense, purely voluntary–based approaches or regulatory frameworks that overwhelmingly emphasise the self-regulating role of businesses are deemed to be ineffective (Bales et al., 2018). In order to provide a cornerstone to the OSH discipline for platform work, it is important to develop a coherent and comprehensive ethical framework for the digitalisation of work, engaging with two main streams that we consider fundamental to OSH regulation.

The first stream engages with a "decent work agenda" on the future of work and its principles, which have been recognised both in the literature and through the work of labour institutions, such as the ILO and the European Union (De Stefano and Aloisi, 2018; Aloisi et al., 2017). "Seizing the moment" in recognising the importance of the principles contained in the ILO's Report of the Global Commission on the Future of Work, fundamental principles of the ethical framework will have to engage with the promotion of investment in decent and sustainable work, including standards in OSH measures, as well as promoting responsibility of private and public actors in regulating for it. Furthermore, in line with the Global Commission's view on the necessity to universalise OSH protections, thus going beyond employment status (ILO, 2019), the decent work agenda will serve as fundamental to build and develop workers' protection, and a global approach to fairness and security at work, in any type of work.

The second stream of fundamental principles revolves around the ethical perspective, which is able to ensure proper governance on AI, networks, algorithms, or, broadly speaking, information. This would engage with the ethics of information and business ethics approach (Floridi, 2009), reflecting on how (and when) to protect the information (personal and public) produced and available through working via online platforms and how (and why) these can be used for OSH purposes. Issues of data collection, transparency, accessibility, and protection need to also be addressed also from a labour law perspective, converging into an ethical framework able to reflect on the fundamental principles that support subsequent regulation such as primary legislation, codes of conduct, practices, and industrial relations instruments. This approach is deemed to be an efficient supporting measure to sustain employment law reforms, with the specific objective to force information disclosure on for OSH purposes to re-address and minimise information asymmetry, which is one of the barriers to effective voluntary regulation (Collins, 2000). In this sense, we support the idea of integrating both platforms and workers' agency supported by a regulatory framework to clarify OSH liabilities and responsibilities in platform work. The issue of a regulatory framework that can shed clarity on OSH liabilities and responsibilities in relation to new systems and new ways of working is one of the fundamental instruments that would enhance the creation of a legal comprehensive OSH response to digitalisation at European level (EU-OSHA, 2019). The availability of information could, for instance, help in developing a prompt and efficient prevention model, which could support, especially if recognised under the umbrella of employment protections, risk assessments and synchronised control of OSH issues. Consequently, platform data could inform the elaboration of codes of conduct, by providing at first useful information to set standards through the analysis of past OSH-related cases, qualitative and quantitative data on risks, accidents, workers' perceptions and compliance.

Furthermore, information ownership could impose liability on platforms that, for instance, had access to the information and did not act to prevent the OSH hazard, thus reflecting on the purposive use of information. This could also help tackling those contested practices that encourage and incentivise riders to work under extreme or unsafe working conditions.[20] In addition, it would promote effective cooperation between riders and managerial platform services, imposing necessary and immediate handling of OSH risks and support to avoid situations where the riders are left alone to deal with potentially dangerous situations, as previously pointed out.

On the specific issue of working time regulation in platform work, we recognise the value of previous propositions to support transparent workplace policies in terms of hours security and job stability, to contract extreme precarious work and promote transparent and predictable working conditions (Aloisi et al., 2017). In order to guarantee the functioning of the regulatory framework proposed earlier, the fundamental role of the state has to be recognised as a bearer of regulatory power and as a democratic public interest facilitator. The state should intervene because of a range of public-relevant issues, which can be briefly summarised here:

- Harmonising and clarifying regulation would help to avoid "freeriding" issues and the creation of a difficult competitive environment for firms that adopt traditional employment models and firms that profit from the misclassification; another reason could be to fight the "race to the bottom effect".
- Improving social and job security for all workers is a wider societal issue and taking steps to expand OSH protection following the example of other European countries would help address basic OSH issues to include self-employed workers – e.g., the French case.[21]

Importantly, State legislative intervention is not the only way to address the regulatory challenge of platform work, and, at the same time it is important to recognise the difficulties in regulating quasi self-employment without harming "voluntary" forms of enterprise and inter-firm cooperation at the same time (Kautonen et al., 2010). Here, once again, the need to find a balance between "basic protection" and respect of the contractual will is still at the heart of the discussion, and the possibility of having a facilitative role for legal provisions to support forms of balanced voluntarism is very welcome. Accordingly, the extension of basic social protection to all forms of self-employment might be one way to respect this balance. In parallel, another way must consider supporting voluntary regulatory instruments already available for workers and employees, such as union representation and the possibility of engaging in collective bargaining.

Conclusion

As underlined in the chapter, the OSH challenges for on-demand gig-workers are twofold. First, these workers are facing a "new" combination of risks arising from the layering and the accumulation of old/traditional risks and risks created by new forms of work management through AI and online devices. Indeed, using algorithmic management software to organise work has a detrimental impact on riders' health and safety. The allocation of shifts by the app places the riders in uncertain working time patterns and irregular schedules, which is coupled with performance pressures. Additionally, the constant oversight allowed to the management by the use of AI can have a detrimental impact on workers' health.

Second, these risks are not adequately assessed by the platform due to the inadequacy of the OSH legal framework to the "reality" of the on-demand platform economy. Here, there is a paradox between the legal principles and its application. On one side, the employer's duty of care and their obligation to prevent the risks arising from the conduct of the undertaking is also extended to the non-employee. On the other side, an examination of the details of the legal framework showed significant differences between employees, limb(b) workers, and the self-employed. Indeed, the protective effect of the employer's duty of care is limited to the employee and the limb(b) workers and excludes the self-employed (which in practice represents the vast majority of on-demand gig-workers). Thus, it is fundamental for on-demand gig-workers to be qualified as limb(b) workers to be adequately protected. Still, it is important to stress that the status of limb(b) workers would only give on-demand gig-workers partial access to the OSH prerogatives they are entitled to. As workers under Art. 3 of Dir. 89/391/EEC, limb(b) workers should have the right to workers representation and to be consulted on work matters affecting their health and safety. One idea for future research would be to investigate ways to ensure the active participation of on-demand gig-workers (as limb(b) workers) on health and safety issues.

Finally, in the last part of this chapter, we outlined some points to address the policy gaps emphasised in the discussion. One way, which should be explored further, would be to develop a strong "prevention through design" approach integrating both platforms and workers' agency and a regulatory framework to clarify OSH liabilities and responsibilities in platform work. Indeed, new legislative measures should be combined with a broader range of interventions such as comprehensive ethical frameworks for the digitalisation of work. This approach could be an effective means to sustain employment law reforms, with the specific objective to force information disclosure on the OSH purposes to re-address and minimise information asymmetry.

Notes

1.   Researcher at the European Trade Union Institute, Belgium.
2.   Lecturer in Employment Law at the University of Manchester, Research Fellow at Università degli Studi di Milano.
3.   For the elaboration of this paragraph we draw from the empirical research conducted as part of a PhD dissertation (Inversi, 2018). The research has been conducted through semi-structured interviews (in the number of 40) with riders and their unions in three UK cities (London, Brighton, and Manchester) working for (or 'with') the same delivery company, which is Deliveroo. The use of interviews

and primary qualitative data is of fundamental importance to identify the risks and occupational hazards, (and very importantly also to understand workers' perceptions of risks), while at the same time being able to investigate how these are managed and dealt with, both by the companies and the workers themselves, in a unilateral or self-regulatory perspective.

4. Which states that "Risks are likely to be aggravated by the specific features of online platform work. These include work requests issued at short notice, penalisation for not being available, the fragmentation of jobs into tasks with narrower job content and subject to continuous evaluation and performance rating. Further pressures result from increasing competition as the online labour market becomes global accessible to more workers, irregular working hours, blurred boundaries between work and private lives, unclear employment status, insecure income, no training opportunities, no social entitlements such as sick pay and holiday pay, poor worker representation and lack of clarity in terms of who is responsible for OSH. Online platform work offers the benefits of flexibility in terms of working time and place of work, but, in many cases, this flexibility is imposed on the worker. Workers in non-standard, poor-quality forms of work tend to have poorer physical and mental health".

5. Especially during the summer months of 2017; see for instance https://www .standard.co.uk/news/london/deliveroo-riders-refuse-work-in-parts-of-london -after-acid-attacks-and-thefts-a3602716.html.

6. The Health and Safety Executive (HSE) is Britain's national regulator for workplace health and safety. It prevents work-related death, injury and ill health. It is an executive non-departmental public body, sponsored by the Department for Work and Pensions. The HSE can be described as a specialist inspectorate mainly responsible for securing compliance with OSH requirements, and sometimes with certain requirements on general working conditions (Walters, 2017).

7. As reported in the Official HSE website: see https://www.hse.gov.uk/vulnerable -workers/gig-agency-temporary-workers/employer/index.htm (last access on 26 January 2022).

8. E.g., the Safety Representative and Safety Committee Regulation 1977, and the Management Health and Safety Regulation 1996 and 1999.

9. Dir. 89/391/EEC has still some authority in the United Kingdom, even after Brexit, as part of "retained European Labour Law".

10. See below explanation regarding *IWGB v SSWP and Others*.

11. S.53 of the HSW Act 1974 – "employee" means an individual who works under a contract of employment (similar definition that the one provided at s.230(1) ERA 1996).

12. Reg. 4 MSH Reg 1999.

13. *(1996) 4 ALL ER 846.*

14. S.53 of the HSW Act provides that "premises" *includes any place and, in particular, includes any vehicle.*

15. See https://www.hse.gov.uk/roadsafety/employers.htm.

16. See https://www.hse.gov.uk/roadsafety/practical.htm.

17. Point 13(b) MHS Reg 1999 about Reg. 3.

18. The Employment Right Act 1996 (Protection from Detriment in Health and Safety Cases) (Amendment) Order 2021.

19. ACOP point 15 about Reg. 3 MHS Reg 1999.

20. See for instance https://www.independent.co.uk/life-style/food-and-drink/deliveroo-driver-safety-uk-weather-snow-criticism-extra-charge-delivery-a8236966.html (last access on 2 March 2020).
21. Loi n° 2017-1836 du 30 décembre 2017 de financement de la sécurité sociale pour 2018. This law abolished the social security scheme for the self-employed (RSI) created in 2006. Social protection for the self-employed was entrusted to the general social security system. A two-year transitional phase was necessary for the general scheme funds to be able to take over the various tasks of the RSI (retirement pensions, health insurance, collection of contributions, etc.).

References

Aloisi, Antonio. 2019. "Negotiating the Digital Transformation of Work: Non-Standard Workers' Voice, Collective Rights and Mobilisation Practices in the Platform Economy". *EUI Working Paper MWP*, 2019/03.

Aloisi, Antonio, De Stefano, Valerio, and Silberman, M. 2017. "A Manifesto to Reform the Gig Economy". *Pagina99*. https://www.eurofound.europa.eu/is/data/platform-economy/records/a-manifesto-to-reform-the-gig-economy.

Bales, Katie, Bogg, Alan and Novitz, Tonia. 2018. "'Voice' and 'Choice' in Modern Working Practices: Problems with the Taylor Review". *Industrial Law Journal*, 47(1): 46–75.

Barrett, Brenda, and Sargeant, Michael. 2008. "Health and Safety Issues in New Forms of Employment and Work Organisation". *International Journal of Comparative Labour Law and Industrial Relations*, 24(2): 243–61.

Burri, Susanne, Heeger-Hertter, Susanne, and Rossetti, Silvia. 2018. "On-Call Work in the Netherlands: Trends, Impact and Policy Solutions". *ILO, Conditions of Work and Employment Series 103*. Geneva: ILO.

Chandola, Tarani. 2017. "Is Any Job Really Better Than No Job At All?". *British Politics and Policy at LSE*. http://eprints.lse.ac.uk/85292/1/politicsandpolicy-is-any-job-really-better-than-no-job-at.pdf.

Cherry, Miriam, and Aloisi, Antonio. 2017. "'Dependent Contractors' in the Gig-Economy: A Comparative Approach". *American University Law Review*, 66: 635–89.

Collins, Hugh. 2000. "Justifications and Techniques of Legal Regulation of the Employment Relation". In Hugh Collins, Paul Davies, and Roger Rideout (eds.), *Legal Regulation of the Employment Relation*, 3–27. Alphen aan den Rijn: Kluwer Law International.

Davidov, G. 2016. *A Purposive Approach to Labour Law*. Oxford: Oxford University Press.

De Stefano, Valerio, and Aloisi, Antonio. 2018. *European Legal Framework for 'Digital Labour Platforms'*. Luxembourg: European Commission.

Epstein, David G. 2012. "Does UK Health and Safety Legislation Rely Upon a Poorly-Resourced Enforcement Agency, a Limited Scheme for Employee Involvement, and a Misplaced Emphasis on Self-Regulation?". Public Personnel Management, 41(1): 61–77.

European Agency for Safety and Health at Work (EU-OSHA). 2019. *Foresight on New and Emerging Occupational Safety and Health Risks Associated with Digitalisation by 2025.* https://data.europa.eu/doi/10.2802/515834.

European Parliament, Directorate-General for Internal Policies of the Union, Schmid-Drüner, M. 2017. *The Social Protection of Workers in the Platform Economy.* https://data.europa.eu/doi/10.2861/976178.

Floridi, Luciano. 2009. "Network Ethics: Information and Business Ethics in a Networked Society". *Journal of Business Ethics*, 90: 649–59.

Graham, Mark, Hjorth, Isis, and Lehdonvirta, Vili. 2017. "Digital Labour and Development: Impacts of Global Digital Labour Platforms and the Gig Economy on Worker Livelihoods". *Transfer*, 23(2): 135–62.

Hobby, Catherine. 2021. "Workers' Rights: A Public Health Issue: R (on the application of The Independent Workers' Union of Great Britain) v The Secretary of the State for Work and Pensions". *Industrial Law Journal*, 50(3): 467–91.

Howcroft, Debra, and Bergvall-Kåreborn, Birgitta. 2019. "A Typology of Crowdwork Platforms". *Work, Employment and Society*, 33(1): 21–38.

Howcroft, Debra, Dundon, Tony, and Inversi, Cristina. 2019. "Fragmented Demands: Platform and Gig-Working in the UK". In Michelle O'Sullivan et al. (eds.), *Zero Hours and On-call Work in Anglo-Saxon Countries*, 216–32. Singapore: Springer.

HSE. 2017. *Tackling Work-Related Stress using the Management Standards Approach: A Step-By-Step Workbook.*

HSE. 2020. *Protecting Lone Workers – How to Manage the Risks of Working Alone.* https://www.hse.gov.uk/pubns/indg73.pdf.

ILO. 2019. *Report of the Global Commission on Future of Work.* https://www.ilo.org/global/topics/future-of-work/publications/WCMS_662410/lang--en/index.htm.

INRS. 2018. *Plateformisation 2027. Conséquences de l'ubérisation en santé et sécurité au travail.* Institut National de la Recherche et de la Securité, Paris. https://www.inrs.fr/media.html?reflNRS=PV%208.

Inversi, Cristina. 2018. *Exploring the Concept of Regulatory Space: Employment and Working Time Regulation in the Gig-economy.* PhD Dissertation, University of Manchester, Alliance Manchester Business School.

Inversi, Cristina, Cefaliello, Aude, and Dundon, Tony. 2020. *#Heretodeliver: Valuing Food Delivery Workers in the Future.* Policy at Manchester Blog. http://blog.policy.manchester.ac.uk/health/2020/06/heretodeliver-valuing-food-delivery-workers-in-the-future.

James, Philip, Johnstone, Richard, Quinlan, Michael, and Walters, David. 2007. "Regulating Supply Chains to Improve Health and Safety". *Industrial Law Journal*, 36(2): 163–87.

Johnstone, Richard, Quinlan, Michael, and Walters, David. 2005. "Statutory Occupational Health and Safety Workplace Arrangements for the Modern Labour Market". *The Journal of Industrial Relations*, 47(1): 93–116.

Kautonen, Teemu, Down, Simon, Welter, Friederike, Vainio, Pekka, Palmroos, Jenny, Althoff, Kai, and Kolb, Susanne. 2010. "'Involuntary Self-Employment' as a Public Policy Issue: A Cross-Country European Review". *International Journal of Entrepreneurial Behavior & Research*, 16(2): 112–29.

Mann, Sandi, and Holdsworth, Lynn. 2003. "The Psychological Impact of Teleworking: Stress, Emotions and Health". *New Technology, Work and Employment*, 18(3): 196–211.

Montreuil, Sylvie, and Lippel, Katherine. 2003. "Telework and Occupational Health: A Quebec Empirical Study and Regulatory Implications". *Safety Science*, 41(4): 339–58.

Moore, Phoebe V. 2018. *The Threat of Physical and Psychosocial Violence and Harassment in Digitalized Work*. Geneva: International Labour Office. http://www. ilo. org/wcmsp5/groups/public/---ed_dialogue/---actrav/documents/publication/ wcms_617062.

Prassl, Jeremias. 2018a. *Humans as a Service: The Promise and Perils of Work in the Gig-Economy*. Oxford: Oxford University Press.

Prassl, Jeremias. 2018b. "Collective Voice in the Platform Economy: Challenges, Opportunities, Solutions". Report to the European Trade Union Congress. https :// www. Etuc. Org/sites/default/files/publication/file/2018-09/Prassl%   20report% 20maquette.

Robens, Alfred. 1972. *Safety and Health at Work: Report of the Committee, 1970–72*. Vol. 1. HM Stationery Office.

Robinson, Laura, Schulz, Jeremy, Khilnani, Aneka, Ono, Hiroshi, Cotton, Sheila R., Mcclain, Noah, Levine, Lloyd, Chen, Wenhong, Huang, Gejun, Casilli, Antonio A., and Tubaro, Paola. 2020. "Digital Inequalities in Time of Pandemic: COVID-19 Exposure Risk Profiles and New Forms of Vulnerability". *First Monday*, 25(7).

Sardeshmukh, Shruti R., Sharma, Dheraaj, and Golden, Timothy D. 2012. "Impact of Telework on Exhaustion and Job Engagement: A Job Demands and Job Resources Model". *New Technology, Work and Employment*, 27(3): 193–207.

Srnicek, N. 2017. *Platform Capitalism*. Hoboken, NJ: John Wiley & Sons.

Stacey, N., Ellwood, P., Bradbrook, S., Reynolds, J., Williams, H., and Lye, D. 2018. *Foresight on New and Emerging Occupational Safety and Health Risks Associated with Digitalisation by 2025*. Luxembourg: European Agency for Safety and Health at Work.

Todoli-Signes, Adrian. 2017. "The 'Gig-Economy': Employee, Self-Employed or the Need for a Special Employment Regulation?". *Transfer*, 1–13.

Tran, Molly, and Sokas, Rosemary. 2017. "The Gig Economy and Contingent Work: An Occupational Health Assessment". *Journal of Occupational and Environmental Medicine*, 59(4): e63–e66.

Walters, David. 2017. "Labour Inspection and Health and Safety in the EU". *Health and Safety at Work Magazine*, 14: 12–17.

Weatherby, Leif. 2018. "Delete Your Account: On the Theory of Platform Capitalism". *Los Angeles Review of Books*, April 24, 2018. https://lareviewofbooks .org/ article/ delete-your-account-on-the-theory-of-platform-capitalism.

Wood, Alex J. 2021. "Algorithmic Management Consequences for Work Organisation and Working Conditions". *JRC Working Papers Series on Labour, Education and Technology*, 2021/07.

4 Algorithmic discrimination, the role of GPS, and the limited scope of EU non-discrimination law

Elena Gramano, Miriam Kullmann[1]

Introduction

The gig economy brought about another change to work relations: by employing workers hired to provide piecemeal jobs or tasks, a new form of atypical employment was added to the plethora of non-steady work, e.g., fixed-term and part-time work, temporary agency work, and teleworking. Gig work, with its fragmented work patterns and shift from pay per hour to pay per task, most prominently raises two interrelated issues: (a) it challenges existing legal notions of employee and employment contract/relationship, a classification issue that is still key to accessing labour protection, and (b) it forces a debate, linked to the classification of workers' issues, on the role, power dynamics, and legal consequences of algorithmic management,[2] i.e., platform or gig companies using algorithms to manage work and the workforce. The question is whether and to what extent employing companies indirectly give instructions and determine, e.g., who will be offered the next gig and who will be removed from the workforce altogether, by using the technology at their disposal. The latter issue brings up questions relating to workers' discrimination, not only when it comes to allowing individuals access to find work through the platform, but also when decisions are made pertaining to whether workers will be receiving additional job offers or not.

After decades of statutory sources, case law, and legal writing, it is somewhat clear that employers are ultimately responsible for managing the workforce, and that their prerogatives must be limited to some extent – and the limitation enforced – to safeguard the freedom, dignity, personal life, and economic, personal, and social rights of workers. Algorithms blur the boundaries of employers' liability, and companies take advantage of this technology to manage workers. Somehow, algorithms shelter employers from having direct contact with workers and make it more difficult to: (a) verify the lawfulness of the impact algorithms have on workers, and (b) ascertain the true dynamics that occur behind the curtains of what often appears – or is presented – as a neutral artificial system, within which human interaction is absent or reduced to the very minimum.

Over the past few years, courts in different jurisdictions were asked to classify the relationship between platform companies and platform workers (Hiessl, 2021a). Lately, courts have been seized also with questions on the discriminatory potential of algorithms that platforms employ to manage the workforce (Hiessl, 2021b). These cases are rich with implications at national and EU level and might be of help to build a research agenda on algorithmic discrimination.

We draw from two national cases to illustrate discrimination through algorithmic decision-making, the role EU non-discrimination law plays in protecting platform workers (or not) and the related classification of platform workers' relationship with the platform, a question that is also key to determining whether EU non-discrimination laws apply to all workers or standard employees only. The first case was decided by the Court of Bologna on December 31, 2020, and the second was decided by the Amsterdam Court of Appeal on February 16, 2021, both decisions involving the food delivery platform Deliveroo.

This chapter investigates the potential discriminatory outcome of algorithmic decision-making and the effectiveness and suitability of the current legal framework in preventing and sanctioning discrimination perpetrated through algorithms. This matter has caught the attention of legal scholars for some time now (Kullmann, 2018). However, we would like to go a step further and build a research agenda by drawing on the concrete implications and issues that stem from the abovementioned cases, which happen to be the first court decisions on this matter. We believe that adopting a practical approach by analysing how the two courts use the existing legal sources could reframe the debate and call attention to this matter's most problematic aspects.

Our focus and thus our core argument is that algorithms could bring about direct, or more often indirect (Kullmann, 2018, 19), discrimination. In doing so, we will assess the decision-making process on the basis of neutral factors, which does not attribute any significance to workers' personal aspects or conditions, at least in theory. Moreover, GPS (Global Positioning System), as an instrument used by businesses, including platforms, to gather data unrelated or not directly relating to work performance, can be used to discriminate or to produce discriminatory effects. In doing so, we focus on how GPS is being repurposed by platform companies that offer on-location services[3] and to what extent GPS usage can be covered by EU non-discrimination law. It will become increasingly clear that, even if GPS were brought within the scope of one or more of the protected grounds, as the data collected by GPS can be regarded as "proxy discrimination" for race or ethnic origin, age, or even gender, we face a second challenge: the substantive scope of most EU non-discrimination laws. This shows the perils of the gig economy can be that workers, as defined by EU case law, are protected by EU law against discrimination, but the self-employed, or contractors, as platform companies often classify their workforce, are not or not entirely protected.

The chapter ends with a discussion rooted in the premise that algorithms do not differentiate between different contractual underpinnings and thus are "blind" to some extent: we discuss whether EU non-discrimination law needs broadening to protect a larger group of platform workers, especially when distinguishing between self-employed and employee platform workers is not possible.

The questions raised at national level

The Court of Bologna case

Three trade unions, all based in Bologna, Italy, lodged a claim with the Court of Bologna, Labour Division, to have the court ascertain the discriminatory nature of work access conditions for Deliveroo riders. The claimants alleged that the algorithm used by Deliveroo – "Frank" – indirectly discriminated against workers who, after having booked a certain working slot through the algorithm, later decided to cancel and abstain from work for justifiable reasons.

Based on the description in the decision, the algorithm under scrutiny works as follows. Each rider is periodically rated by the system. The rating depends, at least partly, on the number of tasks completed and the number of tasks booked by the rider but then cancelled less than 24 hours before the scheduled time of work. The more often riders book and cancel without giving 24 hours' notice, the worse the rating gets, which in turn impacts future work opportunities: high-rated riders have priority booking and can book their working slots early in the morning as soon as the platform makes them available; the last time-frame to book working slots (from the afternoon onwards) is open to low-rated riders and most slots are already taken.

According to the claimants, the abovementioned system discriminated, at least indirectly, against workers who decided to abstain from work by cancelling previously booked slots to go on strike or who had to cancel on short notice for family or just as legitimate reasons, because it meant that they would be offered fewer opportunities to work in future.

Deliveroo defended itself by claiming that no correlation existed between the number of deliveries completed and future opportunities to do so. However, the court held that its defence was too generic and that the company had failed to detail the algorithm's inner workings, more specifically the exact parameters the algorithm used to assign work.

The court held that anti-discrimination laws were fully applicable to the case at hand for a number of reasons. Under Italian law, riders might be classified as hetero-organised workers and, in this case, laws on subordinate employees thus apply to them in full. Even if that were not the case, a specific legislation introduced in 2019[4] stipulated that anti-discrimination laws apply to riders who deliver goods or food for platforms, even if classified as self-employed workers. Furthermore, Directive 2000/78/EC, implemented in Italy through Legislative Decree 216/2003 on discrimination with regard to "access to employment, self-employment or occupation" applies also to self-employed workers. Finally, the court relied on previous national decisions to state that, according to Directive 2000/78/EC, discrimination based on personal beliefs also includes trade union affiliation and activities.

That said, the court ascertained that the system that allowed riders to pre-book slots depended on their "statistics", defined by the trade unions/claimants as "reputational ranking", and that said statistics depended also on the number of pre-booked and then cancelled slots and on the number of times when riders made themselves available on high-demand days, e.g., weekends. Consequently, according to the court, the system discriminated against riders who went on strike or attended protests, as they would have fewer opportunities to work in future.[5]

In this regard, the claimants had to merely document their claims, whereas Deliveroo had to prove that the algorithm was not producing any discriminatory effects or that the effects were lawful. The court held that Deliveroo failed to specifically illustrate how the algorithm worked, thus failing to discharge its burden of proof. The court thus relied on the claimants' arguments, witness evidence, and the available documentation, including information published on Deliveroo's website. That was enough, as the burden of proof relies on the defendant and this was essential for the success of the claim as asymmetry information on the functioning of the algorithms is one of the key problematic elements.

According to the court, the fact that the algorithm included delayed cancellations in calculating the riders' statistics without considering the reasons for cancelling brought about the discriminatory effect. In other words, the algorithm did not consider whether cancellation was due to legitimate personal reasons (sickness, maternity, childcare, etc.) or workers' rights (right to strike and right to protest) being exercised, and its "blindness" resulted in discriminating against workers who were unable or unwilling (for legitimate reasons) to make their services available to the platform.

The Amsterdam Court of Appeal case[6]

The Dutch case dealt with whether Deliveroo riders, who before a change in policy had an employment contract with Deliveroo, could and should be considered employees. Although classifying work is key for most EU non-discrimination laws, this chapter seeks to investigate the role algorithms play in the gig economy, specifically in platform work. In the Dutch case, lodged by FNV (the Dutch trade union federation) under the collective action procedure under Art. 3:305a of the Civil Code, the role of Frank, Deliveroo's algorithm, was only taken into consideration when assessing how Deliveroo's core business, i.e., delivering food from restaurants to the customers, was organised.

This case showed that the algorithm Frank is at the core of Deliveroo's operation because it pinpoints riders' locations in relation to the pick-up and delivery addresses, and selects the most efficient rider by taking the following aspects into consideration: location in relation to the restaurant, type of vehicle used, estimate of when the order will be ready for delivery, and the estimated delivery time. For this reason, riders' GPS location is continuously tracked as soon as they log in.

Deliveroo needs to know where a rider who is logged in but not making a delivery is located so that they can be called. When the rider is close to the restaurant (less than 80 metres away based on GPS data), the restaurant is automatically notified. When the order is out for delivery, the customer can track the rider through their GPS data. Furthermore, the customer expects delivery at a certain time. If, for example, a rider slows down, the customer (and Deliveroo) will know, which the rider likely wishes to avoid. GPS thus allows Deliveroo far-reaching monitoring, which can be regarded as a form of authority or subordination. GPS data is crucial for the service, yet it tracks the rider's location, evaluations, and driving. Once collected, the information may be stored and used in future. Given that timely delivery is a selling point for food delivery services, tracking riders can be seen as crucial. However, geo-location technologies such as GPS may not always be as reliable as one would assume, and GPS may be manipulated through location-masking tools; the resulting data is then considered by the algorithm to assign work.

In the case at hand, Deliveroo emphasised that the algorithm did not and could not distinguish a rider from the way he/she works. The data is neither available nor of interest to Frank. Yet, as Edwards and Vaele argue, "[d]ata we would once have regarded as obviously non-personal such as raw data from home energy meters or location data from GPS devices is now, often through ML techniques, can be re-connected to individuals, and identities established from it". Therefore, individuals may "leave trails of potentially sensitive latent personal data in the hands of controllers who may be difficult to identify". The question is whether this is relevant to a discrimination case. It seems to be, when it comes to indirect discrimination, when, e.g., at a certain time of the day women are unable to offer immediate availability for deliveries due to child care obligations, that proof that women are at a disadvantage is likely to emerge. For indirect discrimination, this seems sufficient.

The Court of Appeal held that Deliveroo organised its business in such a way as to affect how the work was performed. The criteria according to which the algorithm Frank assigns deliveries are somewhat unclear. Deliveroo designed Frank and continuously updates it, and thus the court held that it was greatly involved in the way work was performed.

In addition to its observations on Frank and the role of GPS, the court classified the contractual relationship between riders and Deliveroo and, after a thorough investigation, concluded that it met all the criteria of an employment contract as defined under Art. 7:610 of the Civil Code, i.e., work, remuneration, and subordination. The court stressed that although riders were allowed some freedom to not accept deliveries, which would suggest no employment contract, the level of freedom was not such as to make the relationship incompatible with an employment contract. As to remuneration, which is set by Deliveroo alone and was not subject to bargaining with riders, there was reason for the Appeals Court to rule that the Civil Code criterion was met. As to subordination, the court emphasised that only minor instructions were needed for the type of work performed, i.e., picking up food at restaurants and delivering to customers. Therefore, the kind of activities hardly say anything about whether there is an employment contract. That riders use their own vehicles, mostly bicycles, does not indicate that investments have been made by Deliveroo as entrepreneur and that they do not manifest themselves as entrepreneurs (also because two-thirds of the riders do not pay value added tax) does point towards the existence of an employment contract. Also, Deliveroo took out insurance against accidents at work for its riders.

In adopting a holistic approach, the court concluded that, given all the circumstances, only the freedom to work riders enjoy points to no employment. All other elements, including remuneration, supervision, the time rather suggest employment. In any case, the freedom to work is not incompatible with the employment contract.

Acceptance rate and GPS as a discriminatory device and the role of proxy discrimination

Connecting the two court decisions: The use of acceptance rates and GPS by platforms

Even though the two cases differ in the claims lodged, there seems to be an important connecting factor that potentially links the two cases, namely the relevance accorded to riders' ranking, specifically the acceptance rate that feeds into the rider's rating and thus access to work (Italian case) and use of the exact location fed to the algorithm through GPS tracking to offer work (Dutch case). Both are crucial data in determining whether requests are seen – and thus can be accepted – by riders. Acceptance of requests is also relevant information possibly affecting the algorithm's evaluation of a rider. Rating or "digital reputation" mechanisms may lead to lower remuneration or other adverse work-related outcomes for affected riders, e.g., de-activation of the rider's account (De Stefano, 2016). Therefore, rating systems should not be underestimated, as riders' livelihoods depend on positive feedback. Most importantly, not being logged into the system basically means being unavailable to work.

Both cases offer an opportunity to investigate the potential discriminatory effects of algorithmic management and to assess whether the current legal framework can effectively tackle discriminatory dynamics and effects brought about through AI. The overall legal framework affects how the potential discriminatory effects of an algorithm are classified, which is the core issue and the connecting dot between the Dutch and Italian cases.

First, AI changes the quality of the decisions and the concrete methods of workforce management in practice. This leads to new problems and risks, also from a legal point of view. The quality of the instrument used by platforms to connect and "communicate" with workers, far from being neutral or irrelevant in the contractual relationship and power dynamics between the parties, influences their core legal implications, classification under law, and evaluation in terms of discrimination on grounds protected under law. Indeed, the Artificial Intelligence Act proposal of the European Commission ("AI Act") states that "[t]he use of AI with its specific characteristics (e.g., opacity, complexity, dependency on data, autonomous behaviour) can adversely affect a number of fundamental rights enshrined in the EU Charter of Fundamental Rights ('the Charter')".[7]

AI is a source of risk that requires legislative intervention, all the while building on existing legislation and worker protections. Decisions made by algorithms can be replicated on a large scale and, therefore, AI and algorithms dramatically increase information asymmetries between the parties; the opacity of the system, processes, and data that produce the final output make workers unaware of the discriminatory effects the system may produce, and the system is thus able to hide the power (in)directly exercised by employers (with subsequent difficulties in classifying the contractual relationship between the parties). The European Commission proposal on platform work acknowledges that algorithmic management poses a risk of offering insufficient transparency as to monitoring and decision-making systems.[8] The proposal seeks to improve transparency by obliging digital labour platforms to inform platform workers (electronically) of automated monitoring systems used for monitoring, supervisory, or evaluation purposes, and automated decision-making that significantly affects platform workers' working conditions (Art. 6(1)). As regards the latter, platforms have to share information on the main parameters used by automated decision-making systems and how they work, including how platform workers' personal data or behaviour influences the decisions (Art. 6(2)(b)).

Significantly, a regulation on promoting fairness and transparency for business users of online intermediation services has also recently been enacted;[9] it represents a step forward in ensuring full transparency of contractual terms, ranking, and procedural safeguards in contractual relationships between business users, including self-employed and solo self-employed workers (which platform workers could be classified as) and online platforms. The regulation partially meets the same need for fairness and transparency spelled out in the proposal on improving working conditions in platform work, which also extends the proposed measures on algorithmic management to self-employed workers.

Second, the main issues relating to algorithmic management and discrimination become clear following the national cases' finding that the core instrument with which work and workers are managed is the algorithm Frank. Frank performs different, albeit related, tasks that were traditionally performed by human employers, namely scheduling work and working hours, paying workers, monitoring and evaluating workers' performance, and coordinating where workers have to be for work purposes. Not only is automated management closely linked to the subjective scope of the contractual relationship – whereby the more instructions are given and the less freedom there is, the more likely an employment contract is in place – but is also closely linked to discrimination issues, as the information collected through algorithms may result in discriminatory outcomes that would need to be justified by employers. The subjective scope becomes even more crucial when investigating the regulatory scope of non-discrimination regulations.

Scope of application and discrimination grounds

EU non-discrimination law protects workers against discrimination on different grounds: sex (Art. 157 TFEU, Directive 2006/54/EC), race and ethnic origin (Directive 2000/43/EC), religion or belief, disability, age, or sexual orientation (Directive 2000/78/EC).[10] Although Art. 51(2) of the EU Charter does not extend the EU's legislative competence, Art. 21 lists additional grounds relevant to algorithmic management and its discriminatory impact, e.g., colour, social origin, genetic characteristics, language, political or other opinions, membership of a national minority, property, and birth. Arts. 3 of Directives 2000/43/EC and 2000/78/EC apply to all individuals and to the public and private sectors, including public bodies, in relation to, among other things, the conditions to access employment, self-employment, and occupation, including selection criteria and recruitment conditions, employment and working conditions, dismissal and remuneration, and membership and involvement in an organisation of workers or employers, or any professional association, whatever the branch and at all levels of the professional hierarchy, including through promotion. Similarly, Art. 1(a) of Directive 2006/54/EC spells out the principle of equal treatment in relation to access to employment, including promotion, and vocational training and working conditions, including remuneration.

The abovementioned EU directives show that individuals can rely only on a limited number of grounds to seek protection against discriminatory decisions or outcomes. Algorithmic decision-making depends on the information (i.e., the data) it bases its decisions on or it makes inferences and assumptions on. As mentioned, a residential address might be an indication of race or ethnic origin if the area is known to accommodate people of a certain race or ethnic origin. People riding (e-)bikes for deliveries might be on the younger side, thus the workforce's average age might be inferred or assumed. Thus, a member of a protected group might end up being discriminated against by proxy. The difficulty is having a set of limited grounds to unmask proxies.

Whereas Art. 157 TFEU on the right to equal pay for men and women applies to individuals who meet the conditions applicable to a union worker, as the notion of worker developed by the ECJ (European Court of Justice) is a means to determine the scope of application of Art. 157 TFEU (Kullmann, 2018; Countouris, 2018), the other EU instruments apply to individuals who find themselves in one of the circumstances defined by the directives. Self-employed workers are, to a limited extent, included within the scope of EU equal treatment law.[11] Notably, they may experience the consequences of a discriminatory or biased algorithm.[12] Discrimination entails the exercise of power and is clearly not limited to the relationship between an employer and an employee.[13] Therefore, individuals who work or want to work as self-employed workers may be subject to discriminatory decisions. This makes a broad subjective scope of EU non-discrimination law all the more important, perhaps even more so when workers such as those in the gig economy are in a weaker bargaining position compared to employers who delegate (some of) their decision-making to an algorithm. If platform workers are classified as employees within a contractual relationship that can be classified as meeting all the conditions of an employment contract, they would be covered by protected non-discrimination grounds.[14] National legal systems are in a position to broaden the scope of anti-discrimination law beyond the limits set at EU level. Still, this is not the case in most Member States and the EU's leadership appears still essential in triggering protection also at national level.

Both direct and indirect discrimination are protected against. Direct discrimination occurs when a group is, has been, or would be treated less favourably, on grounds of sex or race for instance, as regards access to employment. To prove direct discrimination, it is necessary to identify an actual or hypothetical group in a comparable position that has been treated more favourably. The motive behind or intent of the discrimination is not relevant: it is sufficient to show that the disadvantageous treatment is based on, or caused by, application of a protected ground of discrimination. Indirect discrimination concerns provisions, criteria, and practices that appear neutral but de facto discriminate against, e.g., a considerably higher percentage of women or job candidates of a particular age. In such cases, the discriminatory effect must be shown either by statistical evidence or any other means, by pooling individuals/groups to serve as comparators. As Xenidis and Senden stress, "the concept of indirect discrimination allows shifting the focus of the analysis onto the effects of algo-rithms, instead of their rules, parameters and content" (Xenidis and Senden, 2020, 172).

Both national cases force an assessment of the suitability of the unlawful grounds of discrimination identified by law. In the Italian case, the court was able to include trade union affiliation and activities attributable to personal belief. On different occasions, the Court of Justice of the European Union (CJEU) stressed the broadness of the discriminatory grounds and their capac-ity to include proxy discrimination (the link between discrimination due to pregnancy/maternity and sex-based discrimination as identified by the CJEU is well known). AI shows that the greatest concerns in terms of protection against discrimination trail the line between different grounds; thus, investi-gating proxy discrimination is more essential than ever.

This leads our investigation to a related matter: the complexity (and therefore opacity) of AI systems and algorithms. In both cases, the courts struggled to understand the real mechanisms underpinning algorithm Frank. This raises a number of important questions that a research agenda on the topic must include: How was the algorithm designed? Was it tailored to the Italian or the Dutch market? Which data was processed and what was the underlying logic?

Quality of the data used for and by the algorithm

For the algorithm to work how Deliveroo intends it to, i.e., ensuring timely deliveries to customers, Deliveroo set certain criteria to be taken into account in the decision-making process and that impacts the decision whether and to what extent a rider sees delivery requests. By processing data in accord-ance with Deliveroo's criteria, decisions are ultimately made. In Italy, rating influences future possibilities to work, meaning that highly rated riders (i.e., riders who cancelled previously booked slots on very few occasions at most) can pre-book timeslots, whereas only the last timeslots (from the afternoon onwards) are open to low-rated riders, meaning they have fewer opportunities to work, as usually better-rated workers have already booked the attractive timeslots. In the Dutch case, GPS data was part of the court's assessment, although the court had been asked only to classify the contractual relationship between riders and Deliveroo.

Selecting the criteria is linked with data with which the algorithm is being trained, tested, and, ultimately, deployed, that is the moment the system goes live for use in real cases. As to acceptance rate and GPS, i.e., the two criteria considered in both decisions, riders need to be registered and logged into the system to show that they are available to work and, on top of that, they have to share their location so that the system can determine who is close to the restaurant to pick up the order. Therefore, the system knows when riders are logged in and where they are. Either indicator could say a lot about a rider's private circumstances. For instance, not being available in the evenings might indicate having a family or a hobby or another job. GPS could pinpoint where a rider lives based on where they await requests, e.g., areas where many restaurants offer delivery through Deliveroo and other places that say something about the rider's private life, most notably whether the rider is still a student and frequently goes to university or public libraries or whether the rider has caring duties and thus visits a parents' home or care facility.

The AI Act is relevant to the above for the following reason:

> [It] complements existing Union law on non-discrimination with specific requirements that aim to minimise the risk of algorithmic discrimination, in particular in relation to the design and the quality of data sets used for the development of AI systems complemented with obligations for testing, risk management, documentation and human oversight throughout the AI systems' lifecycle.[15]

Recital 36 stresses that AI systems used in employment, workers' management, and access to self-employment, among other things, to make decisions on work allocation, promotion and termination, and monitor or evaluate workers in work-related contractual relationships, are classified as high-risk. Those systems "may appreciably impact future career prospects and livelihoods of these persons". Moreover, the AI Act highlights that work-related contractual relationships concerning services provided through platforms, as described in the Commission Work Programme 2021, should be covered. These workers should in principle not be considered users within the meaning of this Regulation. AI systems may perpetuate historical patterns of discrimination against women, certain age groups, individuals with disabilities, or individuals of certain racial or ethnic origins or sexual orientation. AI systems used to monitor performance and behaviour of these individuals may also impact their data protection and privacy rights.

As to AI development, Art. 10(1) of the AI Act identifies high-risk AI systems, i.e., systems to recruit or select individuals and make decisions on promotion and termination of work-related contractual relationships, assign work, monitor, and evaluate performance and behaviour.[16] These systems use models developed on the basis of training, validation, and testing data sets that meet the quality criteria under paras 2–5. Training, validation, and testing data sets have to be relevant, representative, free of errors, and complete (Art.

10(3)). Art. 10(1) of the AI Act on data and data governance lists quality criteria that high-risk AI systems must meet, which includes design choices and data preparation processing operations (e.g., annotation, labelling, cleaning, enrichment, and aggregation); assumption formulation; assessment of the availability, quantity, and suitability of the data sets; biased-data assessment; and data gap identification and related solutions. Moreover, the data needs to have the appropriate statistical properties, including with regard to any individuals or groups on which the high-risk AI system will be used. These characteristics may concern individual data sets or a combination thereof. Adams-Prassl stresses the following:

> Early empirical work has clearly demonstrated that automated decision making can replicate – or even bolster – patterns of discriminations prevalent in the labour market. At the same time, however existing legal categories, including notably indirect discrimination/ disparate impact, may well be insufficient to hold employers accountable for algorithmic control resulting in such discriminatory outcomes. (Adams-Prassl, 2020, 123)

High-quality data appears to be one of the main concerns of the AI Act to ensure that a high-risk AI system does not bring about discrimination prohibited by EU law. Recital 44 suggests that also special categories of personal data (Art. 9 GDPR) "as a matter of substantial public interest" should be used "to ensure the bias monitoring, detection and correction in relation to high-risk AI systems". Personal data processing means revealing racial or ethnic origin, political opinions, religious or philosophical beliefs, or trade union membership, and processing genetic or biometric data to univocally identify an individual, data concerning health, sex life, or sexual orientation. Some data concerns protected/non-discrimination grounds. As a general rule, processing special categories of personal data is not permitted, except as follows: (1) if (prospective) employees give their consent (Art. 7(3)(a) GDPR); (2) if employers/users exercise their rights and obligations under labour and welfare law and fulfil their legal obligations (Art. 7(3)(b) GDPR); or (3) if (prospective) employees make personal data publicly available to others. The high-quality data requirement/criterion falls under the second exception, as employers are required to make sure that they do not violate labour law, including the right of non-discrimination. In general, data processing must be adequate, relevant, limited to what is necessary to reach the purpose for which it is processed (Art. 5(1)(c) GDPR), accurate, and up to date (Art. 5(1)(d) GDPR).

In accordance with Art. 15 GDPR, platform workers have the right to know whether the platform processed their personal data, and if so, the purpose of the processing, the categories of personal data concerned, and any recipient to whom personal data has been disclosed, among other things. Platforms may reject a platform worker's request if the rights and freedoms of others are involved; "others" may include the platform and its customers (para 4). However, reducing access to personal data might be limited and thus platform workers may not be in a position to investigate how their data resulted in a decision taken by the algorithm deployed by the platform. In a decision issued on March 11, 2021, the Amsterdam Court of Appeal decided on a claim lodged by Uber drivers, concerning the information processed by Uber. The claim was rejected on two grounds: first, as Uber processes a huge amount of data, the claimants should have specified the data they wished to obtain. Second, the court ruled that the right of access was limited to the period during which the claimants used the Uber Driver app.[17] In another case, the same court ruled that access to GPS data could be limited to the date and time, start and end location, distance travelled, and price of the ride.[18] Both cases came to the conclusion that requests for additional information must be properly substantiated. Art. 7 of the proposed Directive on improving working conditions in platform work requires digital labour platforms to inform platform workers and "persons performing platform work" of: (a) automated monitoring systems, including the categories of actions monitored; (b) automated decision-making systems, including the main parameters that these systems take into account and their relative importance; and (c) the grounds for decisions to restrict, suspend, or terminate platform workers' accounts, refuse remuneration, change platform workers' contractual status, and similar decisions.[19] This obligation goes beyond what is required under Art. 15 GDPR; if the directive is enacted, it could be a useful instrument for platform workers or those who perform platform work and/or their representatives to assess the decision-making process at their request (Arts. 7(4) and 10)).

Enforcement and the role of trade unions

One of the challenges, from a worker's perspective at least, is knowing whether a decision has the effect of discriminating based on certain (hidden) protected grounds (Wachter, Mittelsdadt, and Russell, 2020). Algorithms are often designed to work based on criteria that, instead of directly relating to a protected ground, can be seen as proxies. Someone's location, for instance, may offer insights into where a platform worker lives. Acceptance rates might show that a platform worker is available online to accept any job that pops up on their phone screen. Thus, a platform worker would first need to suspect that the decision-making process, specifically the criteria combined with the data used, likely results in discriminatory outcomes. Given these circumstances, the role of trade unions becomes clear: not by chance in both cases, trade unions were the claimants, acting on the platform workers' behalf.

Monitoring and enforcement issues are, with few exceptions, left to the Member States.[20] To the extent matters are not regulated at EU level, it is for Member States, by taking into account the conditions of equivalence and effectiveness, to establish effective enforcement mechanisms to protect platform workers, including when it comes to classifying platform workers' status.[21] In enforcing EU non-discrimination law, there is a reverse burden of proof that alleviates the burden on workers (and their representatives), allowing them to make believable that the automated decision-making resulted in a discriminatory decision. Crucially, the focus is on the effects of the decision and not on the wilful intent to discriminate on the employer's part.

Apart from enforcing compliance with EU non-discrimination law through the traditional method, i.e., judicial enforcement, whereby a lawsuit is brought before a (national) court, trade unions have their own industrial relations enforcement method. This not only enables trade unions to initiate proceedings in their own interest, usually by seeking compliance with (presumably) applicable collective agreements, but also involves more traditional trade union engagement, i.e., collective bargaining and the subsequent collective bargaining agreements. In some Member States, like Italy, trade unions act as claimants in all cases in which a number or a group of workers, whether identifiable or not, are discriminated against. This collective claim impacts not only workers who are directly involved in the lawsuit, but also many platform workers whose working conditions are bound to improve.[22]

A number of reasons justify including workers' representatives in monitoring potential discriminatory effects through AI and algorithms, and they all have to do with the abovementioned unresolved issues relating to AI.

As anticipated, individual workers might not be in a position to know or fully understand that discriminatory effects are the result of the decision-making process implemented by the algorithm. Workers' representatives having a collective view might have better tools or be better equipped to understand the process or access useful information. Unions might have a comprehensive vision of how workers are treated within organisations, although they might not focus on the individual position of individual workers. Algorithms repeat the same processes, all the while partially improving them by including new data and patterns; nonetheless, employing the same algorithm within an organisation might help unions and workers' representatives detect discriminatory effects and patterns.

Second, unions could shoulder the costs of understanding the process. That said, the cost should not fall on individual workers, given that – despite unions being better positioned than workers – a deep information asymmetry between unions and companies remains. In this regard, a whole new set of information and consultation rights must be acknowledged as essential to guarantee the essential rights of unions and workers (i.e., the right not to be discriminated against). The Italian legal system offers a good example of improving on legal procedures offered to unions and workers' representatives to effectively fight discrimination in court with a speedy and simplified procedure, especially when discrimination is indirect and widespread, and, paradoxically, more difficult to detect with regard to individual workers.

Outstanding issues

We draw some conclusions by listing some of the issues that still need to be regulated to avoid discrimination.

The first and preliminary issue depends on the almost complete opacity of the decision-making process implemented by an algorithm. Employers, who are ultimately responsible for their businesses, manage decision-making processes, one might argue. One might also argue that information and consultation rights already exist in certain areas. However, while not shifting employers' liability, as they are fully responsible for the process and outcomes of the decision-making processes (be it entrusted to humans or technologies), it is no longer deniable that AI and algorithms qualitatively change the process and might not only exacerbate existing discriminatory effects but also create new ones. The EU itself, in the AI Act proposal, stressed the high risk these systems pose.

The core issue, then, is lack of monitoring of the decision-making processes, which forces the affected parties or their representatives to wait for the damaging and discriminatory effects to be in place to be able to fight them. The quantity and quality of the data, the patterns followed and the desired outcomes must be transparent and readable by those affected, who may legitimately demand such transparency. Knowledge of how decisions are made is a legitimate interest.

It is undeniable that fully understanding the system requires specific technical knowledge and skills that not everyone has. As mentioned, workers' representatives must be supported. Some legal systems (e.g., Germany) involve workers' representatives to a certain extent in managing the workforce, but that is definitely not the sole model of workers' representation or participation. A partial solution could be granting unions the right to access information (and establishing obligations on employers to disclose it), be informed and consulted, and be entitled to take action through rapid judicial procedures. Constant monitoring of the decision-making process and collection of data, through a bipartisan body could intersect discriminatory outcomes before they affect individual workers. Still, this process would be largely limited by the fact that platform workers are often not classified as employees, nor collectively organised and represented. In most cases, they are not even entitled to exercise fundamental collective rights. Lacking a collective dimension of work, platform workers' capacity to understand and react against discrimination is diminished.

The AI Act proposal ignores the above aspects; similarly, the proposal for a directive on platform work submitted by the European Commission barely addresses them. This is symptomatic of the fact that lawmakers must adopt a different approach when regulating AI in work-related contractual relationships, including its power dynamics and specificities, by tackling the need to involve workers' representatives.

Notes

1. Assistant Professor at Bocconi University Milan/ Associate Professor at Radboud University Nijmegen, member of the European Committee of Social Rights. ORCID 0000-0002-0365-4566.
2. European Union, Commission, "Proposal for a Directive of the European Parliament and of the Council on improving working conditions in platform work", COM (2021) 762 final, 2. https://ec.europa.eu/commission/presscorner/detail/en/ip_21_6605. Regarding algorithmic management, see also Adams-Prassl, 2020 and Wood, 2021.
3. This includes ride-hailing, delivery of goods, cleaning and care services. See COM (2021) 762 final, 1.
4. Law Decree 101/2019, which modified Legislative Decree 81/2015, specifically by introducing Arts. 47-*bis* et seq. on digital platforms.
5. Under Italian law, trade unions or associations may bring a claim concerning discrimination (through a faster procedure compared to labour proceedings) even when the target of the discrimination has not been identified but a certain behaviour is regarded as discriminating against a certain group of workers on the basis of one of the protected grounds. The "urgent" procedure aims to remove the discriminatory effects in the shortest possible time.

    Therefore, in the case at hand, unions did not need to prove that certain workers who were on strike were concretely affected by the algorithm but merely that, in general, the algorithm was producing indirect discriminatory effects on all workers who did not work in given timeslots or cancelled their previously booked slots. These workers could include workers on strike but also workers with family or child care duties, sick workers, and workers who had any other legitimate reason not to work.

6.   Hof Amsterdam 16 februari 2021, ECLI:NL:GHAMS:2021:392.
7.   European Union, Commission. 2021. "Proposal for a Regulation of the European Parliament and of the Council Laying Down Harmonised Rules on Artificial Intelligence (AI Act)". COM (2021) 206 final, 11.
8.   COM(2021) 762 final, 3.
9.   Council Regulation (EU) 2019/1150 of the European Parliament and of the Council of 20 June 2019 on promoting fairness and transparency for business users of online intermediation services [2003] OJ L 186/57. https://eur-lex.europa .eu/eli/reg/2019/1150/oj.
10. On the right not to be discriminated under the ECHR, see Zuiderveen Borgesius, 2020.
11. Case C-177/88 Elisabeth Johanna Pacifica Dekker v Stichting Vormingscentrum voor Jong Volwassenen (VJV-Centrum) Plus [1990] ECR I-03941 (sex/pregnancy); Case C-109/00 Tele Danmark A/S v Handels- og Kontorfunktionærernes Forbund i Danmark (HK) [2001] ECR I-06993 (sex/pregnancy); and Case C-54/07 Centrum voor gelijkheid van kansen en voor racismebestrijding contro Firma Feryn NV [2008] ECR I-05187 (race/ethnic origin).
12. For a critical view on excluding self-employed persons from equal treatment laws, see Fredman, 2015, and Barnard and Blackham, 2017.
13. Ibid.
14. On the notion of "worker" for the purpose of applying Art. 45 TFEU and EU law in general, including anti-discrimination law, see Countouris, 2018, 192; Menegatti, 2019, 2020; Giubboni, 2018; and Sagan, 2019.
15. COM (2021) 206 final.
16. See Annex III, point 4.
17. Rb. Amsterdam 11 maart 2021, ECLI:NL:RBAMS:2021:1020 [Uber].
18. Rb. Amsterdam 11 maart 2021, ECLI:NL:RBAMS:2021:1019 [Ola].
19. COM (2021) 762 final, 37.
20. Notable exceptions are Council Directive 2014/67/EU of the European Parliament and of the Council of 15 May 2014 on the enforcement of Directive 96/71/EC concerning the posting of workers in the framework of the provision of services and amending Regulation (EU) No 1024/2012 on administrative cooperation through the Internal Market Information System ("the IMI Regulation") [2014] OJ L 159/11 (posted workers), https://eur-lex.europa.eu/legal-content/EN/TXT/PDF/ ?uri=OJ:L:2014:159:FULL&from=DE; and Council Directive 2014/54/EU of the European Parliament and of the Council of 16 April 2014 on measures facilitating the exercise of rights conferred on workers in the context of freedom of movement for workers [2014] OJ L 128/8 (Union workers), https://eur-lex.europa.eu/legal -content/EN/TXT/?uri=OJ:L:2014:128:TOC.
21. See Case 33/76 Rewe-Zentralfinanz eG and Rewe-Zentral AG v Landwirtschaftskammer für das Saarland [1976] ECR 1976–01989; and Case 45/76 Comet BV v Produktschap voor Siergewassen [1976] ECR 1976–02043.
22. See COM (2021) 762 final, 34, specifically Art. 5, whereby platform workers may rebut the legal presumption under Art. 4.

References

Adams-Prassl, Jeremias. 2020. "What if Your Boss was an Algorithm? Economic Incentives, Legal Challenges, and the Rise of Artificial Intelligence at Work". *Comparative Labor Law & Policy Journal* 41(1): 123.

Barnard, Catherine, and Alysia Blackham. 2017. "Discrimination and the Self-employed: The Scope of Protection in an Interconnected Age". In *European Contract Law and the Charter of Fundamental Rights*, edited by Hugh Collins, 197–218. Cambridge: Intersentia.

Countouris, Nicola. 2018. "The Concept of 'Worker' in European Labour Law: Fragmentation, Autonomy and Scope". *Industrial Law Journal* 47(2): 192–225.

De Stefano, Valerio. 2016. "The Rise of the 'Just-In-Time Workforce': On-Demand Work, Crowdwork and Labour Protection in the 'Gig-Economy'". *Comparative Labor Law & Policy Journal* 37(3): 471–504.

Edwards, Lilian and Veale, Michael. 2017. "Slave to the Algorithm? Why a 'Right to An Explanation' Is Probably Not the Remedy You Are Looking For". *Duke Law & Technology Review* 16(1): 18–84.

Fredman, Sandra. 2015. "Equality Law: Labour Law or an Autonomous Field?". In *The Autonomy of Labour Law*, edited by Alan Bogg, Cathryn Costello, ACL Davies and Jeremias Prassl, 257–74. Oxford: Hart Publishing.

Giubboni, Stefano. 2018. "Being a Worker in EU Law". *European Labour Law Journal* 9(3): 223–35.

Hiessl, Christina. 2021a. "The Classification of Platform Workers in Case Law: A Cross-European Comparative Analysis". *Comparative Labor Law & Policy Journal* (forthcoming). https://papers.ssrn.com/sol3/papers.cfm?abstract_id=3839603.

Hiessl, Christina. 2021b. "Case Law on Algorithmic Management at the Workplace: Cross-European Comparative Analysis and Tentative Conclusions". https://papers.ssrn.com/sol3/papers.cfm?abstract_id=3982735.

Kullmann, Miriam. 2018. "Platform Work, Algorithmic Decision-Making, and EU Gender Equality Law". *International Journal of Comparative Labour Law and Industrial Relations* 34(1): 1–21.

Menegatti, Emanuele. 2019. "The Evolving Concept of 'Worker' in EU Law". *Italian Labour Law e-Journal* 12(1): 71–83.

Menegatti, Emanuele. 2020. "Taking EU Labour Law beyond the Employment Contract: The Role Played by the European Court of Justice". *European Labour Law Journal* 11(1): 26–47.

Sagan, Adam. 2019. "The Classification as 'Worker' under EU Law". *European Labour Law Journal* 10(4): 353–361.

Wachter, Sandra, Brent Mittelsdadt, and Chris Russell. 2020. "Why Fairness Cannot be Automated: Bridging the Gap Between EU Non-Discrimination Law and AI". https://papers.ssrn.com/sol3/papers.cfm?abstract_id=3547922.

Wood, Alex. J. 2021. "Algorithmic Management: Consequences for Work Organisation and Working Conditions". JRC Working Papers Series on Labour, Education and Technology 7: 1–26. Seville: European Commission.

Xenidis, Raphaële, and Linda Senden. 2020. "EU Non-discrimination Law in the Era of Artificial Intelligence: Mapping the Challenges of Algorithmic Discrimination". In *General Principles of EU Law and the EU Digital Order*, edited by Ulf Bernitz, Xavier Groussot, Jaap Paju and Sybe de Vries, 151–182. Alphen aan den Rijn: Kluwer Law International.

Zuiderveen Borgesius, Frederik J. 2020. "Strengthening Legal Protection against Discrimination by Algorithms and Artificial Intelligence". *The International Journal of Human Rights* 24(10): 1572–93.

5   The law and worker voice in the gig economy

Alan Bogg, Ricardo Buendia

Introduction

This chapter will examine the role of law in supporting (and obstructing) worker voice in the gig economy. The first section will distinguish three normative approaches to worker voice as they relate to the gig economy, rooted in the popular republican account of freedom as non-domination. These can be described as the exit, constitutional rights, and radical models. We reject the 'exit' model as risking a form of deregulatory discourse that will be damaging to the interests of workers in the gig economy. We then consider the strengths and weaknesses of the 'constitutional rights' and 'radical' models. While we would expect workers and unions to pursue both strategies in tandem, there is a value in understanding the differences between them as ideal-types. We also acknowledge that the gig economy context has revealed some weaknesses of the 'constitutional rights' strategy in a particularly acute way. In the final section, we reflect on the significance of this typology for the future research agenda on law and worker voice in the gig economy.

Theoretical foundations of voice in the gig economy: Exit, constitutional rights, radical resistance

Disrupting the normative foundations of worker voice: The challenges of the gig economy

Historically, the justifications for worker voice were aligned with broader theories of democracy in the polity, such as pluralist theories of interest-group democracy through competitive bargaining (Bogg 2009, chap. 1). These pluralist theories provided an elegant rationalisation of the existing institutions of industrial democracy, collective bargaining through stable and independent trade unions. Trade unions usually operated as exclusive bargaining agents for relatively homogenous groups of workers employed by large vertically integrated employers in a 'standard employment relationship'. Collective bargaining mirrored the democratic process of interest-group bargaining and the civic culture of pressure groups, with the trade union operating as a democratic opposition to the employer in a model of competitive democracy. This 'standard employment relationship' was underpinned by a stable and open-ended employment contract, based upon reasonable expectations of long-term and full-time employment in a specific geographical location. In certain respects, the stability of these institutions of joint rule-making were so taken for granted that the normative questions tended to be treated as peripheral to empirical enquiries into the sociological aspects of these institutions of voice (Collins 1997).

In many countries around the world, these institutional arrangements of worker voice are now under severe pressure. This untethering of labour law from its institutional moorings has led to fresh interest in the philosophical foundations of worker voice. While the erosion of the 'standard employment relationship' preceded the emergence of the gig economy, the disintegrative forces operating upon standard employment have certainly accelerated in contexts of gig work. Gig work displays a rich variety of forms, but there are certain general features that recur in the literature on the gig economy.

The most important feature is that the platform tends to operate as a vector of casualisation (Woodcock and Graham 2020, 16–18). In many situations where there is platform intermediation, workers are free to 'log on' to the app and accept work to suit their lifestyle preferences. In turn, employers are under no continuing duty to offer work as in a standard employment arrangement. In English labour law, we would say that there is an absence of 'mutuality of obligation', in the sense of ongoing reciprocal offers to offer and accept work. This is significant because 'mutuality of obligation' remains an important feature of the legal test to identify an 'employee' in the UK. This has led to a strong reliance on 'zero hours' contracts in the UK gig economy, as reflected in many of the contractual arrangements scrutinised in the employment status litigation in the gig economy. Platform companies have also acquired great monopoly powers, investing huge subsidies to attract new customers to their networks and augmenting their structural market power in the process (Prassl 2018, 22–24). This has intensified the dominating power of companies in designing and enforcing one-sided written contractual arrangements that exclude employment status for workers, while also ratcheting control over the labour process through surveillance technology. However, there is an increasing recognition that these problems flow from structural features of gig labour markets, rather than discrete instances of inequality of bargaining power in individual transactions between workers and employers. The outstanding work of legal scholars like Veena Dubal has identified how the breakdown in municipal regulation of transportation allowed platforms such as Uber to enter the local labour market. In what she describes as a 'political bargain' in the San Francisco context, 'the Chauffeurs' Union shaped business models, set prices, and effected public policy, establishing strong municipal regulation of a once unregulated industry' (Dubal 2017, 79). The collapse of this 'political bargain' allowed Uber to exploit the economic conditions created by an oversupply of labour.

These contracting practices, where gig employers leverage their structural dominance in the unilateral design of written contracts, have also led to a significant growth in self-employment among gig workers. These contractual arrangements often present a picture of workers as independent entrepreneurs exercising their autonomy and commercial judgment to 'grow' their own businesses (Prassl 2018, 52–55). The stark reality is that economically dominant companies create and sustain structures of extensive direct and indirect legal control, fixing payment rates, specifying delivery routes, utilising systems of algorithmic discipline based upon customer ratings, and collecting data (De Stefano 2016). Despite formal contractual appearances, gig workers experience high levels of dependence, subordination, and vulnerability to contractual exploitation. In legal terms, however, the absence of employment status may lead to the exclusion of important statutory rights that depend upon an employment contract as a basis of legal entitlement. In UK law, for example, the main legal rights of freedom of association all depend upon 'worker' or 'employee' status. Even those legal rights not linked specifically to the institutionalisation of voice, such as unfair dismissal or minimum wage protections, also depend upon employment status. These basic and general legal protections from unfair and arbitrary treatment at work are integral to worker empowerment, even though we might not think of them as 'voice' rights in the strict sense.

There has also been fragmentation of the bilateral bond between a single employer and a single worker in a stable and continuing employment relationship. This fragmentation is occurring in a number of ways. Recent litigation against Uber in the United Kingdom and in Canada revealed the organisational complexity of a transnational corporate entity that operated in multiple jurisdictions.[1] This fragmentation of the employing entity, and the allocation of distinct functions across different organisational units, makes it more difficult to identify a single unitary employer (Prassl 2015). Workers themselves may even have different apps open simultaneously in order to maximise the opportunities for paid work, which could mean that they have many employers at a single point in time.[2] This presents significant challenges to regulators in allocating employer responsibilities fairly across different entities. It also magnifies the challenges of effective enforcement of labour standards, which depend upon the clear ascription of responsibilities that correlate with specific employment rights.

Searching for new foundations: The theoretical turn to republican theories and fundamental rights

As already noted, the regulatory challenges presented by the growth in new forms of precarious employment have been accompanied by a greater interest in the philosophical foundations of labour rights. Whereas post-war political philosophy was focused on general questions of justice, and the legitimacy of basic political institutions, there has been a recent turn towards work and labour as a vital area of independent philosophical concern. In turn, labour lawyers have increasingly drawn upon political philosophy and democratic theory to elucidate the justifications for labour regulation. This may be understood as a reaction to the fundamental repudiation of labour laws as illegitimate interferences in 'free' markets in the 1980s and 1990s. Once regulatory interventions are no longer supported by political consensus, as with the political rise of neoliberalism in the 1980s, there is a more urgent need for theoretical interrogation of foundations of labour law.

This new theoretical landscape of labour law's foundations has been dominated by two general approaches: neo-republican theories and theories of rights. Both approaches speak powerfully to the contemporary challenges of realising worker voice in the gig economy. Neo-republican theories develop a systematic analysis of power, and the policies and institutions needed to counteract arbitrary domination by public and private actors. The growth in new forms of private power in the gig economy, facilitated through technologies of surveillance, means that neo-republican theories are particularly appealing as an analytical schema and for justifying regulatory interventions. Theories of rights examine the foundations of labour rights, identifying which rights count as fundamental, and which values or interests those rights are grounded upon (Collins 1997). Freedom of association is usually identified as a fundamental right in many theoretical accounts. This rights-based approach provides a neat theoretical counterpart to the rise of strategic litigation in the gig economy context.

As 'self-employed' gig workers are treated as excluded from statutory labour protections restricted to those working under employment contracts, workers and their unions have increasingly turned towards human rights to secure universal entitlements through constitutional litigation. This idea of 'labour rights as human rights' has had a particular resonance for gig workers, and for other legally marginalised groups such as domestic workers and migrant workers. Human rights have provided a way of securing legal inclusion in an era when the employment contract has operated as an exclusionary barrier for the most disadvantaged workers in the labour market. Each of these general theoretical approaches is promising in justifying voice in the gig economy. We nevertheless recognise that each represents a complex tradition of thought rather than a single idea or argument, and it is important to be attentive to that complexity in the context of gig work.

There is a basic distinction in the republican tradition between interpersonal and structural accounts of non-domination, with non-domination understood as an equal civic status that insulates citizens from arbitrary exercises of private and public power. For example, Frank Lovett defends an interpersonal account of domination which locates it within unequal social relationships involving dependence, so that a stronger agent wields arbitrary power over a weaker agent (Lovett 2010). On this approach many kinds of private relationship involving agents (employment, family) will involve relations of domination. This focus on interpersonal domination has been reflected in the prominence of republican proposals for enhancing exit rights for dominated agents. Where exit is properly resourced, dependence is reduced, and this provides an ameliorative response to domination in unequal relationships. By contrast, Alex Gourevitch adopts a structural approach to domination. This is constituted by deep inequalities of property and wealth which mean that, for most workers at least, there is no choice but to be dominated by some agency or another (Gourevitch 2014, 178–79). In these circumstances, exit is not sufficient because it does not address the structural conditions of private domination. These differences are not simply of theoretical significance. They also matter at the level of specific legal proposals for regulating labour markets. For example, interpersonal accounts of non-domination often identify unions and collectivised worker power as an object of republican concern: private domination is always troubling regardless of its source. Whereas on a structural approach to domination, the dominating presence of labour unions under existing economic conditions would hardly register as a priority for republican policies. We suggest that there are three approaches in the literature that are relevant to the foundations of worker voice in the gig economy. We describe these as the 'exit' approach, the 'constitutional rights' approach, and the 'radical' approach.

'Exit' as a response to private domination

The 'exit' approach has been developed most fully in the neo-republican work of Lovett and Robert S. Taylor. They provide a range of policy proposals to ensure that workers enjoy effective opportunities for exiting employment. For example, Taylor proposes the provision of 'capitalist demogrants' to enable workers to become self-employed entrepreneurs (Taylor 2017, 62).[3] Lovett proposes other measures to ensure that worker exit is effectively resourced, such as generous unemployment benefits and legal proscription of employer blacklisting (Lovett 2010, 54). Support for a 'universal basic income' among republican theorists can also be understood as an element in this empowered exit strategy (Pettit 2007). This republican focus on exit rights, and the legal contours of affirmative support such as limitations on restrictive covenants or financial grants for employment training, provides important ideas for legal reforms to support gig workers. The provision of affirmative support for exit would make a significant positive difference to the lives of many gig workers. It is more problematic when 'exit' strategies are linked to a wider deregulatory argument that labour standards and public administrative enforcement are sources of public domination (of employers). This 'exit is enough' position, which comes through most strongly in the republican work of Taylor, fails to account for freedom of association (including the rights to bargain collectively and strike) as fundamental labour rights (Bogg and Estlund, 2018).

'Constitutional rights' as a response to private domination

The 'constitutional rights' approach finds its most powerful republican articulation in the work of Pettit. Pettit criticises a 'strategy of reciprocal power' for securing non-domination, under which 'each achieves non-domination through having resources sufficient to ensure that every act of interference by another can be effectively resisted' (Pettit 1999, 239). The problem with this 'reciprocal power' approach is that self-protection may lead to all citizens being worse off. It would be better for non-domination to be secured through constitutional mechanisms. While there is sometimes a degree of ambivalence about strike action in Pettit's republicanism (Bogg 2017), perhaps reflecting deeper reservations about 'reciprocal power' as a non-domination strategy, autonomous trade union action is framed as a 'reciprocal-power strategy within the framework of a constitutional state' (Pettit 1999, 95). This constitutional vision of the right to strike would certainly be linked to its recognition as a constitutional right, enforceable as a legal right. It would nevertheless depend upon ordered implementation within the legal system, so that the right to strike is rendered compatible with the basic liberties of employers, consumers, and other workers. This could be described as one of the dilemmas of constitutionalisation. The legal recognition of these industrial rights brings with it an inherent limitation of what can be achieved *within* the constitutional limits of the legal system. The legal institutionalisation of industrial conflict channels and constrains it in ways that leave the structural fundamentals of the legal and economic system unchallenged and intact. This includes the existing distribution of private property rights and the enforcement of contracts.

'Radical resistance' as a response to private domination

The 'radical' approach is argued for powerfully by Gourevitch. This 'radical' approach justifies the right to strike as a means for workers to resist oppression in class-divided societies marked by economic and social inequalities. These inequalities are deeply embedded in economic and political structures, and underpinned by legal institutions of property and contract. The right to strike provides a way for workers to resist this legally supported economic oppression, and to achieve a measure of self-determination in the face of it. Since this justificatory argument is sensitive to existing structures of oppression in capitalist societies, its account of the structure of the right to strike is less solicitous of the 'basic liberties' of employers. It would support a wide range of forms of labour unrest and agitation, including sit-downs and mass pickets, and extending to civil disobedience. Since the existing legal framework provides a constitutive underpinning to structural oppression, the moral justification for a radical case for the right to strike will be less concerned with the law's existing allocative pattern. It avoids the common theoretical trap of reasoning about idealised constitutional rights where the society in which they will operate is marked by inequalities, domination, and oppression. This radical approach has evident attractions for gig workers, where the structural rules of the legal order are so evidently stacked against them and in favour of their employers. It provides a moral justification for illegal acts of collective resistance, where legal norms operate as an unjust constraint on collective action. In an era where gig workers and their unions have increasingly turned to legal mobilisation, and human rights litigation in courts, legal officials (such as judges) are less likely to be receptive to arguments predicated on the fundamental illegitimacy of the legal and constitutional order.[4] The judge is an internal participant in the legal order, and this will involve a professional duty to develop legal rights so that they are coherent with the existing laws. In short, the judicial obligation of fidelity to the legal order means that the 'radical' right of resistance is unlikely to be recognised as a constitutional entitlement.

These strategic differences within the republican tradition, which emerge most strongly in the comparison between the 'constitutional rights' and 'radical' approaches, reflects contemporary debates in 'radical politics'. In Chantal Mouffe's work on agonistic democracy, for example, she distinguishes between 'withdrawal from institutions' and 'engagement with institutions' as different approaches to radical politics (Mouffe 2013, chap. 4). The 'withdrawal from institutions' advocates 'desertion and exodus' from the operation of state institutions, which is more radical than specific acts of civil disobedience against individual laws. This total disengagement from the state, and the fostering of self-organised production, represents a radical form of democracy. By contrast, the 'engagement with institutions' advocates 'a combination of parliamentary and extra-parliamentary struggles' leading to 'a profound transformation of those institutions, so as to make them a vehicle for the expression of the manifold of democratic demands which would extend the principle of equality to as many social relations as possible' (Mouffe 2013, 75). This envisages the use of existing institutions, such as courts and constitutional rights, to transform structures of oppression and domination. Of course, these two kinds of radical politics represent ideal-types. Nevertheless, we think that they are valuable in elucidating the diverse industrial strategies of gig workers and unions in the use/rejection of law and legal norms in gig worker activism. In what follows, we see a mixture of different strategies deployed with varying degrees of success.

The 'constitutional rights' strategy in the gig economy

A central strategy for gig workers around the world has been securing employment status through litigation in courts. The importance of employment status is in providing a legal gateway into statutory employment protections. Sometimes this is concerned with basic labour standards like working time protection and the minimum wage, which are only indirectly linked to voice. Sometimes, the focus has been on securing the legal protections associated with freedom of association, which includes important trade union rights. In the UK, there is an intermediate category of 'worker' status. This now encompasses most statutory rights, the significant exception being unfair dismissal protection, which is restricted to employees working under a contract of employment. The two leading employment status cases of recent times are *Uber* and *Deliveroo*. This strategy of seeking legal recognition as workers has had mixed results so far.

Starting with *Uber*, a unanimous seven-member panel of the United Kingdom Supreme Court (UKSC) found in favour of worker status and set out a general interpretive approach to employment status.[5] This was described in the lead judgment, given by Lord Toulson, as a 'purposive' and 'realistic' enquiry. It focused on the economic substance of the work arrangements, to identify whether they displayed the features of subordination, control, and dependence justifying the need for statutory employment protection. This is a highly significant judgment, and one that is widely considered to have reset the boundaries of employment law in a broad and inclusionary way (Bogg and Ford 2021). In this sense, the litigation in *Uber* can be adjudged a success, both instrumentally in terms of securing basic labour rights for Uber drivers and symbolically in galvanising a sense of effective agency among gig workers.

The judgment also had wider effects beyond the specific legal rights claimed in the case itself. Following the judgment, Uber entered into a voluntary recognition agreement with the GMB union (GMB Union 2021). The approach throughout the litigation was to emphasise the collective dimensions of the dispute, and the desirability of collective bargaining. The finding of 'worker' status in *Uber* meant that the company was likely to be presented with a legal recognition claim by one or more of the unions involved in the litigation under the UK collective bargaining machinery. The voluntary recognition agreement with the GMB includes negotiation on 'national earnings principles', discretionary benefits, provision of union representation to challenge account deactivations, and health and safety at work. While this has been widely viewed as a historic turning point, there has also been some scepticism about the deal from smaller grassroots unions such as the Independent Workers' Union of Great Britain (IWGB) and the App Drivers & Couriers Union (ADCU) (Awaad 2021). These reservations have centred on Uber's (non-)compliance with the judgment on the measurement of working time periods for minimum wage rates for 'waiting' time. Given the primacy of voluntary recognition in the UK, the effect of the GMB deal is the pre-emption of competing statutory claims for recognition by other unions. This allows Uber to manage its labour relations policy by excluding unions with a more conflictual approach to its business model. The *Uber* litigation on individual worker rights operated as a springboard for broader collective goals. The success in the Supreme Court led to a reversal of Uber's longstanding refusal of union recognition. It is too early to judge the depth and durability of the collective bargaining arrangements negotiated 'in the shadow' of the individual employment law statutes with its chosen bargaining partner, the GMB. Uber's approach no doubt reflected a strategic calculation of how to retain control over the collective aspirations of its workforce, and to maintain the fundamental features of its business model from disruption.

The experience in the *Deliveroo* litigation tells a very different story. The IWGB made a formal approach to Deliveroo for union recognition in November 2016. It then submitted a formal application under Schedule A1. This is the UK's version of a 'statutory certification' procedure for union bargaining representatives. It is administered by the Central Arbitration Committee (CAC), which operates as an adjudicative agency. The statutory model is based upon single employer bargaining with an independent trade union. The CAC must determine whether the proposed bargaining unit is 'appropriate', and ascertain if the relevant majority support thresholds in the statute have been satisfied by the union. In *Deliveroo*, the CAC issued its decision on the preliminary criteria in November 2017. This preliminary threshold depended upon the Riders being 'workers'. The CAC concluded on the basis of the domestic law on worker status that the Riders were not workers. To date, there has been a Judicial Review in the High Court of the CAC's original decision,[6] which upheld the CAC's determination on worker status, and the Court of Appeal dismissed the IWGB's appeal from the High Court decision in June 2021.[7] At the current time, permission has been sought to appeal to the UKSC. If permission is granted, it may take a further 18 months to 2 years until a final decision is handed down. If it is necessary to seek a ruling from the European Court of Human Rights (ECtHR) in Strasbourg, it may be closer to a decade before a final legal resolution is achieved. These legal delays are likely to have eroded union support and union membership in Deliveroo, because the union's lack of bargaining status undermines its instrumental value to workers.

Shortly before the formal CAC hearing, Deliveroo modified its written contracts and specified a wide contractual power of substitution. The new contract enabled a Rider to designate a substitute to undertake any delivery, and the identity of the substitute was subject only to minimal constraints in the contract. It was possible for a Rider to designate a substitute without prior approval by Deliveroo, and even once a specific delivery job had been accepted on the app. In considering witness evidence, the CAC concluded that these clauses were not a 'sham' but were regarded by the parties as giving rise to genuine contractual rights. According to the CAC, the effect of this wide substitution clause was to negate the undertaking to do the work personally, which is a necessary requirement for a worker contract in UK labour law.[8] Having concluded that the necessary requirement of personal work was not satisfied, the CAC declined to consider any other indicative factors that might have pointed in favour of worker status. The IWGB was granted permission to seek Judicial Review of the CAC decision based upon Article 11 ECHR. The High Court had dismissed the IWGB's case on the ground that since the Riders were not workers under domestic law, they were not in an 'employment relationship' for the purposes of Article 11.[9] The reasoning was problematic because 'employment relationship' under international and European human rights law is an autonomous legal concept. Its scope is not necessarily co-extensive with the legal categories of employment status in national laws and practices.

The Court of Appeal rejected the IWGB's appeal, concluding that even applying the International Labour Organization (ILO) criteria of 'employment relationship' directly to the work arrangements in *Deliveroo*, the presence of the wide substitution clause in *Deliveroo* was fatal to a finding of 'employment relationship'. Accordingly, there was no interference with trade union rights under Article 11 (1) because the Riders were not entitled to them. The operative reasoning on this point is set out rather briefly in paragraph 77 of the Court of Appeal's judgment. Underhill LJ observes that personal work is identified as a relevant indicator in the ILO Recommendation,[10] and that the absence of an undertaking to do the work personally is a 'contra-indicator' of worker status.[11] On that basis, he concluded that the CAC was entitled to treat the absence of personal work as 'decisive', in circumstances where there was no 'sham'.[12]

Any critique of the reasoning in *Deliveroo* must recognise the challenges of applying such international instruments directly to the facts in specific work arrangements. As an international instrument, the ILO Recommendation is addressed to national governments to assist them in the development of national policies and legal tests of employment status. That said, the Recommendation is not lacking in substantive definitional content either. Notwithstanding inevitable flexibility in its application by national courts, the Court of Appeal's application of the ILO Recommendation to the facts in *Deliveroo* is open to legitimate criticism. Paragraph 13 (a) of the Recommendation describes it as a relevant factor that 'the fact that the work…must be carried out personally by the worker'. In contrast to the Court of Appeal's focus on the legal rights and duties in the contract, this is focused on the 'fact' of personal work, with what actually happened in the work arrangement. This concern with factual prevalence of personal work is consistent with the 'primacy of facts', which goes to characterise the general interpretive approach in the Recommendation. It suggests that at any time the worker is undertaking the work herself, she is working personally in line with the Recommendation. It is also inconsistent with the Recommendation to treat personal work as a 'decisive' criterion, which both the CAC and High Court did. Paragraph 11 (a) of the Recommendation specifies 'allowing a broad range of means for determining the existence of an employment relationship'. This is also consistent with the description of specific features in paragraph 13 as 'indicators'. 'Indicators' do not function as decisive factors. They incline the court to a particular conclusion, but they should not be treated as determinative in isolation.

Deliveroo is a powerful lesson in the risks of a 'constitutional rights' strategy of legal mobilisation. Litigation has been time-consuming, expensive, and so far it has yielded nothing substantive for the workers. The IWGB has limited resources to mount an effective legal campaign to secure collective bargaining rights. Both the High Court and the Court of Appeal adopted a narrow and formalistic approach to the ILO's 'employment relationship' category, rather than a more generous and inclusive interpretation characteristic of specialist human rights courts such as the ECtHR. The IWGB has continued to mount vigorous public campaigns against Deliveroo despite losing in the courts. It has worked with media outlets to publicise employment abuses at the company, and this publicity campaign had a damaging impact on Deliveroo's Initial Public Offering on the London Stock Exchange (Ziady 2021). It has also continued to coordinate significant protest and strike action against Deliveroo. While this has not yet led to a collective bargaining relationship, the IWGB has continued to assert its agency and collective power. The engagement with constitutional rights has been one strand in a wider set of economic strategies of resistance.

Overall, it must be recognised that the 'constitutional rights' strategy is necessarily limited in terms of what can be achieved, as *Uber* demonstrates. Perhaps these limitations are endemic to litigation. Even in legal systems where constitutional norms and values are denominated as 'progressive', courts are not generally well-placed to bring about deep structural changes in constitutional democracies. Judges must develop the law incrementally within existing doctrinal parameters and canons of legal reasoning, such as formal or informal respect for precedent. For example, while *Uber* itself was hailed as a landmark legal victory, it represented the gradualist development of the 'sham doctrine' that had been on slow burn for a decade.[13] While unions have been relatively successful in using litigation in the UK, the underlying business models of gig employers have been resilient. There is also a danger that worker status has become fetishised as a kind of emancipatory totem, when in fact establishing worker status is merely the first step in enforcing minimum statutory standards set at a modest level of protection.

Radical resistance in the gig economy

Platform workers are starting to realise that platform companies and existing normative structures impede access to traditional forms of voice such as collective bargaining and strike.[14] Furthermore, the legal models of collective bargaining and striking might themselves operate as obstructions to effective collective agency. For example, the UK system implementing the legal right to strike is highly restrictive, excluding all forms of secondary industrial action from legal protection. Platform workers find difficulties building traditional trust networks between workers (Wilkinson et al. 2010) as the gig economy's business model anonymises and atomises the workforce. In many jurisdictions, platform workers are also under the threat of property, contract, and competition laws when attempting to organise to resist the platforms (Lianos,

Countouris, and De Stefano 2019). This has led platform workers to find ways of organisation and radical resistance against platform companies beyond existing legal structures, recognising some of the limitations that a constitutional rights strategy brings with it. Most of these strategies are based on what Alex Wood termed 'mass self-communication networks' (Wood 2015): virtual places where workers create networks to organise and resist (see ILO 2021, 212). In these virtual places, platform workers discuss strategies of resistance mainly over pay issues.

Against this background, platform workers' strategies of resistance are varied and include social dialogue, wildcat strikes, and walkouts and protests at different levels of the supply chain. For instance, in the UK, food delivery riders called for a national strike that was coordinated to coincide with strikes at McDonald's, TGI Fridays, and Wetherspoons pubs in London, Cambridge, and Brighton (Woodcock and Graham 2020, chap. 4). Other forms of resistance have a more institutional face. For example, in the Republic of Korea, a presidential advisory body facilitated dialogue between platform workers and platforms regardless of collective bargaining not being available for platform workers (ILO 2021, 214).[15]

Perhaps the most visible forms of platform workers' resistance have been strikes. Platform workers meet in a certain hotspot (determined by the algorithm based on consumers' demand) and establish a digital picket line, a form of digital walkout strategy that is breached when a strike-breaker uses the app for work during the strike (ILO 2021, 215). Jamie Woodcock and Mark Graham have reported how platform drivers in Bangalore, India, organised through large WhatsApp groups to strike against Zomato (a food delivery platform) over their falling rates for deliveries. Resistance through a digital picket line was clearer on a similar case in Cape Town, South Africa, against OrderIn (a food delivery platform). When interviewed, one of the strikers declared that if strike-breakers crossed the digital picket line, 'we smashed up their bikes, that's democracy' (Woodcock and Graham 2020, chap. 4). These social norms, subordinating private property rights to acts of democratic resistance, could never be accommodated through a constitutional strategy of resistance through law. There were no leaders of this strategy of resistance in Cape Town, and platform workers interviewed saw no need to join a trade union (Woodcock and Graham 2020). Similar strategies have been reported in London and Buenos Aires, where Deliveroo and PedidosYa workers, respectively, decided to meet in hotspots to resist platform companies' new hourly-rate payment scheme by creating a digital picket line (Woodcock and Graham 2020; ILO 2021, 215).

It is important to note that platform workers' voice was not enabled by local labour laws or platform companies in these examples. It also reveals how the new spatial context of some forms of gig work, where there is no physical workplace that constitutes the employer's proprietary sovereignty, can be harnessed by workers and unions in creative ways. The employer's right to exclude union organisers from its private property has long been one of the central legal issues of the 'right to organise' in many legal systems. These private property rights also augmented the legal capacities of employers to campaign against unionisation using 'captive audience' techniques. It would be naive to suggest that property-based forms of domination have been eclipsed. Rather, they continue to mutate like a virus, for example in the use of proprietary arguments to shield algorithms from effective democratic scrutiny. Yet there is no doubt that the lack of a physical workplace provides new opportunities for worker resistance.

We note similar effects in relation to the casualised nature of gig employment and the 'right to strike'. At common law in England, strikes usually involve a fundamental breach of contract by the individual striker. In organising the strike, the union official or strike organiser has committed an economic tort of inducing breach of contract. This exposes the strike organiser to tort liabilities and remedies. In the UK, the collective legality of the strike depends upon a statutory 'immunity' for the strike organiser. This is conferred in limited circumstances, where there is a 'trade dispute' and where various substantive and procedural requirements have been met, such as a lawful ballot and sufficient notice to the employer. This body of statutory law is highly complex and very restrictive. Paradoxically, the precarious nature of the gig employment model may sometimes provide gig workers with a *wider* freedom to withdraw their labour, both individually and in coordination with others, than 'standard' workers. Where there is no obligation to accept offers of work, as in a casual arrangement, the individual decision to not switch on the App does not constitute a breach of contract. This is because there is no contractual obligation to be available for work. Where there is no breach of contract, there is unlikely to be tort liability for the strike organiser where this has been coordinated as a collective action because a breach of contract has not been 'induced' by a strike organiser. This removes the need for the 'trade dispute' defence and its tight substantive and procedural qualifications it brings with it. The contractual vulnerability can be flipped into a potent weapon of resistance.

Platform workers have also organised to share information and resist individually, as in the case of platform workers 'tricking' apps. Juliet Schor has reported that it is common for platform workers on TaskRabbit (a freelancing services app) to contact their clients through the app and then continue their businesses outside of it. This 'trick' allows both workers and consumers to avoid paying the 20 per cent that TaskRabbit charges to platform workers (Said 2015). Similarly, cloud platform workers paid by the hour have learned to resist platforms' surveillance through screenshots by installing a second screen or by waiting until the screenshot is taken to use their computers for other activities (Wood et al. 2018). Platform workers are also organising and resisting in more proactive ways. This is the case of Turkopticon, a web browser plug-in that enables platform workers to evaluate the platforms they work for and help to build their reputation, mirroring algorithmic management techniques (ILO 2021, chap. 4, S. 4.3) of platform companies over platform workers. Similar cases are The Fair Crowd Work, which enables platform workers to rate the platforms, and Facebook, WhatsApp, and Reddit groups where platform workers share information and evaluate platforms (ILO 2021, 216). Lastly, a promising form of proactive radical resistance is creating platform coop-eratives run and owned by workers to compete against traditional platform companies (Gourevitch 2014).[16] A good example of such initiatives is Stocksy, a platform cooperative in the photography business owned and governed by photographers (Schor 2020, chap. 6).

Law and voice in the gig economy: An agenda for future research

What impact should gig work have on the developing research agenda on law and worker voice? If this question is posed *within* the framework of constitutional rights and legality, the answer may be that the impact should be relatively circumscribed. Gig work is simply the latest instalment in a long process of casualisation and deregulation generating pressures on the 'stand-ard employment relationship'. The task for lawyers and legal scholars is to refine the existing tests of employment status, to ensure that they operate in a broad and inclusive manner in the gig economy. The self-employment in the gig economy is often 'sham' or 'disguised' employment driven by the manipu-lation of contractual documentation. In this respect, legal reform must ensure that gig workers are treated and recognised as working in an 'employment relationship', entitled to the same legal rights and protections as other workers. We should recognise that this represents a conservative methodological response, which is to preserve the existing institutions and doctrinal categories from erosion while ensuring that gig workers are integrated within the existing worker protective edifice.

We acknowledge that there is some value in this conservative exercise, not least in ensuring that some of the most precarious workers in the labour market can access the most basic legal protections already available to employees and workers. For example, strategic litigation has secured fundamental legal rights for gig workers in circumstances of great urgency, as in *Uber*, where those workers did not have the luxury of waiting for a new theoretical paradigm to emerge. There is also scope for important theoretical work on the nature of subordination, the differences between legal and economic mechanisms of control, direct and indirect control, and the changing contours of subordination in an era of AI and technological surveillance. However, this should not distract scholars from the possibility that gig work also provides the moment for a deep theoretical rupture with existing methodological paradigms. We briefly identify three ways in which this might be so. The underlying theme is a growing recognition of the importance of structural over interpersonal accounts of domination and injustice (Mantouvalou 2020).

The first is to question the future of the 'employment contract' or even an 'employment relationship' as the foundational juridical category of labour or employment law. At the practical level, this has been reflected in a growing recognition that the self-employed should be protected from exploitative work arrangements. At the theoretical level, legal scholars are now examining the importance of understanding the role of capitalism in shaping the transactional environment of work (Adams 2020). From this perspective, a fixation on the specific juridical forms of work can obscure the wider structural determinants of exploitation. Exploitative work occurs beyond the employment contract, and emancipation can only be achieved through structural change. Where labour law continues to be fixated on a narrow set of contractual or relational forms, its broader emancipatory goals are undermined. While this disjunction between the employment contract and the structures of capitalism has always been a fault line in labour law, gig work reveals it in a particularly stark form. This presents a methodological opportunity for the discipline.

The second is to explore whether a discipline of labour law, focused on the vindication of individual rights that attach to a specific kind of work relation, must be reassessed in light of the structural critique of labour law as the law of employment contracts. Rights will always remain the basic concern of legal systems as they are central to our understanding of the juridical subject: the primacy of rights is also reflected in the fundamental structure of private law. The gig economy has revealed the importance of competition law, commercial law, and the law of corporations in creating and sustaining the dominance of capital in these new labour markets. It has also demonstrated the resistance of capital to any attempts at democratic control of entrepreneurial freedoms

(Sainato 2021). While rights will continue to have an important role to play in an emancipatory labour law, we must also be vigilant to the ways in which legal norms perform a constitutive role in supporting certain forms of economic organisation (and obstructing others). In this respect, recent work on the 'labour constitution' is important (Dukes 2014). Attempts to reconfigure the discipline as a 'law of the labour market' (Deakin and Wilkinson 2005) also hold promise in understanding how markets are constructed as legal institutions through competition law, corporate law, and other domains that may seem remote from 'labour law'.

The third is to investigate the law of associations as it relates to resistance and empowerment. We have already noted how gig workers are organising in different ways, deploying strategies of resistance that may involve forms of legal disobedience such as the destruction of property. These associations may be more spontaneous and less recognisable as 'trade unions' in the traditional sense. To what extent are these forms of association effective in challenging structural injustices? Can these looser and more unstable forms of organisation precipitate structural changes or are the protests simply episodic flashpoints? Could they undermine existing legal structures that prioritise collective agreements with 'representative' trade unions, and will this disruption operate to the long-term detriment of workers as a class? And to what extent can we expect the law to instantiate a radical right to resist capitalist oppression where that oppression is itself underpinned by the basic categories of private law? The gig economy has placed all of these fundamental issues back at the centre of theoretical debate. In so doing, it may provoke a deep shift in our ways of understanding and framing the discipline of labour law.

Notes

1. [2021] UKSC 5.
2. See the perceptive discussion of multi-apping in a recent Australian gig work case: *Diego Franco v Deliveroo Australia Pty Ltd* [2021] FWC 2818, [117]–[118].
3. This would involve the provision of grants to enable employed workers to transition into self-employed entrepreneurial activities. It would provide a mode of exit not just from an individual employer but from the 'labour market' as a whole (understood as constituted by dependent employment).
4. The radical republican argument for the right to strike is set out fully in Gourevitch 2018.
5. *Uber v Aslam* [2021] UKSC 5.
6. *R (The IWGB) v Central Arbitration Committee* [2018] EWHC 3342 (Admin).
7. [2021] EWCA Civ 952.

8.   Indeed, the personal work requirement is a necessary feature of all employment statuses in UK labour law, workers and employees.
9.   For critical commentary see, e.g., Atkinson and Dhorajiwala 2019; Bogg 2019.
10. See ILO Recommendation 13 (a).
11. *Deliveroo*, [77].
12. Ibid.
13. See *Autoclenz v Belcher* (2011) UKSC 41.
14. Despite some international and local initiatives of dialogue, they remain voluntary, which impedes platform workers' voice. See ILO 2021, 214.
15. A similar case was observed in Costa Rica; see ILO 2021, 216.
16. Recent examples of platform cooperatives include Green Taxi Cooperative, Coopcycle, NursesCan, and Fairmondo; see ILO 2021, 88, Box 2.3.

References

Adams, Zoe. 2020. *Labour and the Wage: A Critical Perspective.* Oxford University Press.

Atkinson, Joe, and Hitesh Dhorajiwala. 2019. 'IWGB v RooFoods: Status, Rights and Substitution'. *Industrial Law Journal* 48 (2): 278–95.

Awaad, Nader. 2021. 'As Drivers, We Know Uber's British Union "Deal" Is Not All It Seems'. *The Guardian*, June 4, 2021. https://www.theguardian.com/commentisfree/2021/jun/04/drivers-uber-british-union-deal-not-all-it-seems-collective-bargaining-on-pay-removal.

Bogg, Alan. 2009. *The Democratic Aspects of Trade Union Recognition.* Hart.

Bogg, Alan. 2017. 'Republican Non-Domination and Labour Law: New Normativity or Trojan Horse?'. *International Journal of Comparative Labour Law and Industrial Relations* 33: 391–417.

Bogg, Alan. 2019. 'Taken for a Ride: Workers in the Gig Economy'. *Law Quarterly Review* 135: 219–26.

Bogg, Alan and Estlund, Cynthia. 2018. 'The Right to Strike and Contestatory Citizenship'. In *The Philosophical Foundations of Labour Law*, edited by Hugh Collins, Gillian Lester, and Virginia Mantouvalou 1st ed., chapter 13, Oxford University Press.

Bogg, Alan, and Michael Ford. 2021. 'The Death of Contract in Determining Employment Status'. *Law Quarterly Review* 137: 392–399.

Collins, Hugh. 1997. *The law of Contract. Law in context.* Butterworths.

Deakin, S.F., and Frank Wilkinson. 2005. *The Law of the Labour Market: Industrialization, Employment, and Legal Evolution.* Oxford University Press.

De Stefano, Valerio. 2016. 'The Rise of the "Just-in-Time Workforce": On-Demand Work, Crowd Work and Labour Protection in the "Gig-Economy"'. *International Labour Office, Inclusive Labour Markets, Labour Relations and Working Conditions* 71.

Dubal, V.B. 2017. 'Winning the Battle, Losing the War?: Assessing the Impact of Misclassification Litigation on Workers in the GIG Economy'. *Wisconsin Law Review* 4: 739–802.

Dukes, Ruth. 2014. *The Labour Constitution: The Enduring Idea of Labour Law.* Oxford University Press.

GMB Union. 2021. 'Uber and GMB Strike Historic Union Deal for 70,000 UK Drivers'. GMB Union. https://www.gmb.org.uk/news/uber-and-gmb-strike-historic-union -deal-70000-uk-drivers.

Gourevitch, Alex. 2014. *From Slavery to the Cooperative Commonwealth: Labor and Republican Liberty in the Nineteenth Century*. Cambridge University Press.

Gourevitch, Alex. 2018. 'The Right to Strike: A Radical View'. *American Political Science Review* 112 (4): 905–17.

International Labour Organization. 2021. 'World Employment and Social Outlook: The Role of Digital Labour Platforms in Transforming the World of Work'.

Lianos, Ioannis, Nicola Countouris, and Valerio De Stefano. 2019. 'Re-Thinking the Competition Law/Labour Law Interaction: Promoting a Fairer Labour Market'. *European Labour Law Journal* 10 (3): 291–333.

Lovett, Frank. 2010. *A General Theory of Domination and Justice*. Oxford University Press.

Mantouvalou, Virginia. 2020. 'Welfare-to-Work, Structural Injustice and Human Rights'. *The Modern Law Review* 83 (5): 929–54.

Mouffe, Chantal. 2013. *Agonistics: Thinking the World Politically*. Verso.

Pettit, Philip. 1999. *Republicanism: A Theory of Freedom and Government*. Oxford University Press.

Pettit, Philip. 2007. 'Republican Right to a Basic Income?'. *Basic Income Studies* 2 (2): 1–8.

Prassl, Jeremias. 2015. 'Autonomous Concepts in Labour Law? The Complexities of the Employing Enterprise Revisited'. In *The Autonomy of Labour Law*, edited by Alan Bogg, Cathryn Costello, A.C.L. Davies, and Jeremias Prassl, 1st ed., 151–68. Hart Publishing.

Prassl, Jeremias. 2018. *Humans as a Service: The Promise and Perils of Work in the Gig Economy*. Oxford University Press.

Said, Carolyn. 2015. 'Could Client Poaching Undercut On-Demand Companies?'. *San Francisco Chronicle*, April 24, 2015. https://www.sfchronicle.com/business/article/ Could-client-poaching-undercut-on-demand-6222919.php#photo-7874032.

Sainato, Michael. 2021. '"I Can't Keep Doing This": Gig Workers Say Pay Has Fallen after California's Prop 22'. *The Guardian*, February 18, 2021. https://www.theguardian .com/us-news/2021/feb/18/uber-lyft-doordash-prop-22-drivers-california.

Schor, Juliet B. 2020. *After the Gig: How the Sharing Economy Got Hijacked and How to Win It Back*. University of California Press.

Taylor, Robert S. 2017. *Exit Left: Markets and Mobility in Republican Thought*. Oxford University Press.

Wilkinson, Adrian, Paul Gollan, Mick Marchington, and David Lewin. 2010. 'Conceptualizing Employee Participation in Organizations'. In *The Oxford Handbook of Participation in Organizations*, 3–26. Oxford University Press.

Wood, Alex J. 2015. 'Networks of Injustice and Worker Mobilisation at Walmart'. *Industrial Relations Journal* 46 (4): 259–74.

Wood, Alex J., Mark Graham, Vili Lehdonvirta, and Isis Hjorth. 2018. 'Good Gig, Bad Gig: Autonomy and Algorithmic Control in the Global Gig Economy'. *Work, Employment and Society* 33 (1): 56–75.

Woodcock, Jamie, and Mark Graham. 2020. *The Gig Economy: A Critical Introduction*. Polity Press.

Ziady, Hanna. 2021. 'London Needed a Win. Instead It Got Its Worst IPO in History'. *CNN Business*, April 2, 2021. https://edition.cnn.com/2021/04/02/investing/london -deliveroo-ipo/index.html.

6

Platform economy and the risk of in-work poverty: A research agenda for social security lawyers

Paul Schoukens[1], Alberto Barrio[2], Eleni De Becker[3]

Introduction

In 2019, almost one worker in ten[4] in Europe was considered at risk of poverty, an increase of 1.4% since 2008 (Ratti, García-Muñoz and Vergnat 2022, 6–7). New trends have also emerged in this domain, with more and more people at work facing a risk of in-work poverty. This is particularly true for workers in atypical employment relationships (e.g., solo self-employment and platform work).

Although in-work poverty is not a new phenomenon (neither in Europe nor elsewhere), the discussion on in-work poverty resurges. In the EU, the fight against poverty and social exclusion has been an important part of EU policymaking for decades. Examples are the Council Recommendation 92/441/EC[5] – also known as the Minimum Income Recommendation – the Lisbon Strategy (2000–2010) and the Europe 2020 Strategy (2010–2020, closely linked to the European Semester; for a discussion of the history of the Lisbon Strategy and the Europe 2020 strategy, see Dawson 2018).[6] The Lisbon and the Europe 2020 strategy were yearly monitoring cycles where EU Member States' policies were reviewed in light of overall goals and indicators. Both strategies have been criticised for not going far enough, and ultimately not being effective enough in achieving its goals as many EU Member States still struggled, and to a large extent failed, to reduce their poverty rates (Aranguiz, Schoukens and De Becker 2021; Schoukens, De Becker and Beke Smets 2015; for a detailed overview on the progress of the EU Member States on the realisation of the Europe 2020 poverty and social exclusion target, see Social Protection Committee of the European Union 2020, 11).

The difficulties for EU Member States to reduce their poverty rates may be caused, at least partly, by the fact that the kind of employment available is increasingly threatening the capacity of individuals to ensure a decent standard of living through employment as a result of technological and institutional changes, such as digitalisation and deregulation (Marx 2019, 1). Nevertheless, EU Member States' activation policies still remain very much focused on valuing and promoting citizens to be active in the labour market. Furthermore, in-work poverty across EU countries particularly increases among unskilled and young workers who are faced with difficulties in finding (suitable) employment (Peña-Casas, Ghailani, Spasova and Vanhercke 2019, 49–51).

At the EU level, the European Pillar of Social Rights (2017)[7] (the EPSR) serves as an effort to strengthen the social dimension of the EU. The EPSR explicitly mentions in its principle 6 that in-work poverty should be combatted by EU Member States as well as the EU. In doing so, the EPSR further develops the right to social assistance and the right to human dignity in the Charter of Fundamental Rights (the CFREU). More recently, the EU's Action Plan to implement the EPSR (2021) sets lifting 15 million people out of poverty among one of its three overarching headline targets to be achieved by 2030.[8]

It is in that perspective that the role of social security systems to protect against the risk of falling into poverty, and the challenges that certain forms of work present for the reduction of in-work poverty, gain particular importance. In this contribution, we will focus on non-standard work (and, especially, platform work) and the challenges it poses for social security schemes. Specifically, we will use the Council Recommendation on access to social protection for workers and the self-employed (hereinafter the Council Recommendation)[9] as a framework to identify a set of challenges that platform work may pose to social security systems' ability to provide effective and adequate, as well as transparent, coverage (and which also jeopardises its capacity to prevent in-work poverty).

Although the Commission launched a proposal for a Directive on improving the working conditions for platform workers in December 2021,[10] the Council Recommendation continues to serve as the main framework for the social security rights of platform workers. The proposal from the Commission contains a rebuttable presumption of an employment relationship, but it does not clarify the social protection rules applicable to platform workers and the difficulties that may arise for this group of workers. Moreover, a large share of platform workers are actually self-employed persons according to the Impact Assessment preceding the proposed Directive (European Commission 2021a, 9; European Commission 2021b, 8–9). Also for this group of workers, the

Council Recommendation continues to serve as the main legal framework in the domain of social security.

First, this contribution discusses the notions of "non-standard forms of work" and "platform work" further in detail, with a particular focus on how non-standard work deviates from a standard employment relationship. Second, the contribution presents a series of challenges for social security lawyers that emanate from the risk of in-work poverty and platform work. This is followed by a presentation of the Council Recommendation and how it may serve as a framework in order to address these challenges. In a final part, this contribution looks ahead at what kind of future (legal) research in the domain of social security could be useful taking into account the challenges arising from in-work poverty and platform work.

From non-standard work to platform work

Labour-related social security schemes have been traditionally designed around the default case of the standard employment relationship, which may be defined as a "stable, open-ended and direct arrangement between dependent, full-time employees and their unitary employer" (Walton 2016, 111–21).[11] This definition not only contains the traditional elements[12] of the employment relationship, but also refers to the outcomes of this traditional labour relationship, being job security and income security. By focusing on the main features of this standard model of work, social security systems generally grant the greatest social security protection to persons who perform work within that type of employment, with those persons in divergent work arrangements receiving lesser protection in correlation to the magnitude of their differences with this model (Dickens 2003, 10).

In recent years, new forms of non-standard work that deviate from other elements of standard work are, however, coming to the fore. Platform work is, arguably, a primary example of this, because of how it combines different features that deviate from the standard employment relationship.

In this regard, this contribution defines platform workers as "persons selected online from a pool of workers through the intermediation of a platform to perform personally[13] on-demand short-term tasks for different persons or companies in exchange for income" (Barrio 2021). It is evident that we restrict ourselves to platform activities that have a (potential) relation to professional work, leaving out platforms that are based exclusively in the non-profit sharing of property or knowledge.

The online character of platforms is one of the major defining features, facilitating access and reducing transaction costs (Valenduc and Vendramin 2017), as it is the platform that acts as an intermediary between the person who receives the service and the person who performs it. In this role as intermediator, the platform typically: (1) possesses essential information about the relationship (e.g., the nature of the tasks performed, remuneration, the identity of the parties); (2) has a monopoly over the contact between the two other parties in the relationship (i.e., the person performing the work and the person receiving it may only contact each other through the platform); (3) provides rules concerning the behaviour of both parties; (4) may monitor the compliance with such rules; and (5) may sanction the lack of compliance with such rules by temporarily or permanently stopping an individual from accessing the platform.

Finally, in the definition of platform work, its on-demand nature is essential as well (Kittur 2013, 2). It means that the performance of a task is offered when and if a person requests it, without any obligation by the platform to ensure that a minimum amount of work is available to the workers registered on it. It goes without saying that significant periods of unremunerated time will often exist, when a worker waits between tasks, for instance. It shows what the fragmentation of work (assignments) can cause with regard to the total working time (all tasks added), the irregularity of work time (tasks can be done at almost any moment of the day, and are thus not confined to a traditional nine-to-five time schedule) and the intermittency of work (tasks do not always fluently follow each other up, meaning that persons often are confronted with non-remunerated waiting periods between assignments).

Challenges for social security law

It is striking that the new forms of work, as described in the previous chapter, increasingly comprise atypical employment elements. In that regard, non-standard work has often evolved into a combination of temporary, part-time and self-employed work, possibly supplemented by other atypical elements including, for instance, the absence of reciprocity, bilateral legal relationships or economic subordination (Schoukens and Barrio 2017).

The European Commission found that it is particularly self-employed and non-standard workers who face obstacles in accessing social protection in specific social protection branches (European Commission 2018b). As noted above, social protection systems were primarily developed for standard workers, implying a long-term, full-time work relationship (Schoukens and Barrio 2017, 327), and thus they are not always tailored to the specific work situations of self-employed and non-standard workers (Schoukens, Barrio and Montebovi 2018, 221–22).

It has been shown in previous studies that persons in non-standard forms of work, including platform work, have a significantly higher risk of in-work poverty (Ratti, García-Muñoz and Vergnat 2022). This observation applies for several EU Member States, although important differences between EU Member States do exist (European Commission 2017, 87–90; European Commission 2018b, 12–13). The reasons behind this vary, but they might be summarised as a combination of both non-standard workers' lower earnings and their partial or full exclusion from certain labour and social security protections.

This risk of in-work poverty for platform work applies to both Bismarckian and Beveredigean social security systems. As benefits are closely related to the contributions paid in Bismarckian systems (e.g., Germany, Belgium), this often leads to low access (and low benefits) for non-standard workers. It is true that universal basic schemes (Beveredigean systems, e.g., Scandinavian countries, the Netherlands or Ireland) offer a greater (in some countries basic) coverage. In those countries, however, such social security schemes are often complemented by occupational and private schemes for which non-standard workers may sometimes not qualify (Keune 2013, 62–63). It should also be noted that, in several systems characterised by universalism, there have been attempts to establish residence requirements or other limits that in practice restrict access to social security benefits for migrant workers, even from the EU (Bruzelius, Chase and Seeleib-Kaiser 2015).

One of the main reasons for the exclusion from social security systems is that such systems have been traditionally designed around the standard employment relationship. As a result, persons in a standard employment relationship are typically fully protected by social security and labour law provisions. In turn, persons in non-standard forms of work often experience a more fragmented protection (Schoukens and Barrio 2017, 330).

In that regard, many non-standard forms of work (such as self-employment and extremely part-time work, even amounting to marginal work) have been primarily considered part of the private "social security" sphere (i.e., commercial relationships, the family or other forms of private income support), and thus they have been largely left uncovered by public labour-related social security schemes (Barrio 2021, 16).

Lack of protection may also result from trying to apply elements of social security and labour law originally designed for standard employment relationships to forms of work with very different features (Schoukens and Barrio 2017, 332). For example, part-time and temporary work have been linked to challenges in fulfilling social security schemes' requirements of minimum insurance periods.

As mentioned above, platform work combines features of different forms of non-standard work, such as its on-demand, temporary and (in some cases) part-time character, as well as adding new features, such as the existence of an (online) intermediary and the algorithmic management. As a result, platform workers experience not only similar challenges as non-standard workers concerning effective and adequate access to social security and labour law, but they also face new challenges. Platform work can result in very irregular work patterns or very marginal work which deviates from the standard employment relationship, but also the role of the algorithm management is difficult to fit in the usual framework on social security law. The amount of work performed at the end of the day can be strongly dependent on the specific algorithm in place, regardless of the hours that a platform worker was waiting for a new task. The relative easiness to take up platform work combined with the algorithm that assigns work to platform workers are two elements that are difficult to accommodate in the current social security legislation of most EU Member States.

This risk of labour instability is particularly clear in the case of thresholds to access certain social insurance schemes, for example, the requirement of having paid contributions during a certain duration within a specific period. As a consequence, persons in atypical forms of work are pushed out of social insurance schemes, even though they may accumulate in the end a multitude of fixed or part-time work assignments, with each of these assignments too little to be taken into account for social insurance purposes. Labour instability may also hinder the tracking periods of employment as in some cases the persons may perform work for a few hours in a row with one employer, after which long periods of inactivity may follow. Platform work has the potential to increase this instability even more by escaping regular working times (Degryse 2016, 41). Workers may thus come across situations in which they may work a great number of hours in some periods and remain inactive in others, while social security systems are often only equipped to take into account regular working times (Schoukens 2021, 317).

Another challenge that platform workers might face relates to determining the main employer, a key aspect for social security in order to identify who is responsible for paying contributions (financing), deciding on dismissal (unemployment) and granting income replacement (work incapacity) (Schoukens 2021, 316). The features of platform work have led to an ongoing discussion on whether the workers are employed by the users of the platform or the platform itself.[14] A misclassification of false self-employed people prevents them from enjoying rights to which they would be entitled as workers. It should also be noted that platform workers are often active in several platforms simultaneously, while at the same time they may not necessarily be active in all the platforms they are registered on (Valenduc and Vendradmin 2017, 34). This, together with the fact that platforms may be based in different countries, makes it extremely difficult to track employers and the work performed.

Moreover, platform workers also struggle more than other types of workers with the large part of unpaid labour that they need to perform. Platforms provide access to paid work, but they also rely heavily on unpaid work (Pulignano and Mara 2021, 8). Consider for example the lengthy hours spent by workers on platforms, in particular with remote work platforms, to augment one's reputation ratings. Workers may be pushed towards performing those extra hours as they are important for freelancers to develop their portfolios and establish economic transactions and relations with clients in the market more generally (Pulignano and Mara 2021). Workers working within on-location food delivery platforms form another example. This type of worker is also confronted with unpaid labour, irrespective of their professional status or the way in which they are compensated. Even hourly paid workers face a risk of unpaid labour through the shortening of shifts without compensation and squeezed shifts, resulting in work-intensification (Pulignano and Mara 2021, 9). As workers do not receive any wages for unpaid work, those hours will also not be taken into account for social security purposes.

In light of the above, it may be argued that platform work poses several challenges for social security law. These challenges may be summarised as (1) lack of transparency and (2) lack of inclusion (Barrio 2021, 165–66). Lack of transparency stems from the existing uncertainty concerning the professional status of many platform workers, but also from the difficulty in defining the notion of "work" as it regards social security and platform work.[15] Lack of inclusion relates to the following elements, namely lack of formal and effective access to social security schemes and no adequate coverage:

- Formal access: Exclusion from coverage by some or all labour-related social security schemes as it regards platform workers in several EU Member States (e.g., Germany in the case of mini-jobs and Spain in the case of performance of non-regular activities outside an employment relationship, as well as in the case of self-employed persons in many EU Member States).
- Effective access: Difficulties in fulfilling requirements for entitlement to some labour-related social security schemes due to the fragmented character of platform work.
- Adequate coverage: Due to their typically low earnings (because of their low remuneration and/or low work intensity), platform workers may receive low benefits (which may potentially fall under the poverty line).

The Council Recommendation on access to social protection and the questions it poses towards the social protection of platform workers

The Council Recommendation is one of the initiatives stemming from the EPSR. The European Commission launched the EPSR to improve the protection of social rights of EU citizens and to achieve better working and living conditions in the EU, as explained above. The EPSR contains 20 key principles, structured over 3 categories. Under the category "Social protection and inclusion", Principle 12 states that "regardless of the type and duration of their employment relationship, workers and, under comparable conditions, self-employed have the right to adequate social protection".

In order to implement Principle 12, the Council Recommendation was adopted in 2019. A framework for the monitoring of its implementation was later created by the Social Protection Committee in collaboration with the European Commission.

The Council Recommendation seeks to ensure minimum standards in the field of social protection of workers and the self-employed, considering the (limited) competences of the EU in this domain. Specifically, the Council Recommendation aims at ensuring formal, effective, adequate and transparent access to social protection for all workers – regardless of whether they are working in a standard or non-standard manner – as well as for all self-employed persons.

Essential in the Council Recommendation is the neutral character of the labour status: the basic principles shaping social security are equal for all professionally active persons, whatever kind of work they perform.[16] This, however, does not mean that the specific working circumstances should not be considered when applying social security law. States should thus tailor their approach, with particular attention to the different characteristics of the labour performed. This tailor-made approach goes in our opinion beyond the traditional categories of workers and the self-employed, as platform work or other non-standard forms of work will also demand in some cases a tailor-made approach. In that regard, the Council Recommendation even pays particular attention to new non-standard forms of work and the (emerging) atypical workers, especially those groups who risk being left without proper social protection (Schoukens and Bruynseraede 2021, 17–18). The Council Recommendation, in its Article 9, calls upon EU Member States to take account of the specific characteristics of non-standard work and self-employment, as it is often exactly the specific working situation of an atypical worker or self-employed person that leads to an exclusion from social protection (e.g., the restrictive definition of the personal scope or the use of a minimum amount of work or income as thresholds).

Not all traditional aspects of social security are covered by the Council Recommendation, as it only takes into account the traditional labour-related insurance schemes: unemployment benefits, sickness and health care benefits, maternity and equivalent paternity benefits, invalidity benefits, old age benefits, and benefits in respect of accidents at work and occupational diseases. Hence, family benefits, social assistance and minimum income schemes (together with private insurance arrangements) are not included in the material scope. While these exclusions may be due to the Council Recommendation's focus on labour-related schemes, arguments might also be made for the inclusion of these type of schemes, particularly as social security branches in most current social security systems are not isolated but interrelated.

This might be particularly the case concerning family benefits, as key features of certain forms of work (such as those characterised by a large amount of flexibility and uncertainty, as it is the case with platform work) may put greater demands on parents (for example, in order to access childcare). By not paying attention to the composition of the household of a worker or a self-employed person in relation to their need for social protection, the Council Recommendation seems to overlook the importance of this factor.

Moreover, it is questionable whether an analysis that excludes social assistance and minimum income schemes provides an accurate representation of the reality that platform workers face regarding social security, as they are often obliged to resort to these schemes when their formal, effective or adequate access to contributory social security schemes is not ensured. In fact, it seems that the Council Recommendation is aware of the importance of these schemes, as it advocates, when addressing adequacy, for taking into account the whole social protection system of an EU Member State.

The Council Recommendation structures its content primarily around the four aims noted above (which coincide with the challenges identified above), namely formal, effective, adequate and transparent coverage. Below, each of these principles are analysed as to their content and their potential application to platform work.

Formal coverage

EU Member States are encouraged to ensure access to adequate social protection for all workers and self-employed persons (formal coverage) (Art. 7, Sub e Council Recommendation). Formal coverage refers to the elements conditioning the personal scope of (work-related) social insurance. In that regard EU Member States are encouraged to open up their social security schemes wherever possible to all working groups. In the final version of the Council Recommendation, the requirements regarding formal access have been levelled down for the self-employed. Different from employees, formal access is voluntary for the self-employed, unless it is considered appropriate to provide mandatory coverage. This is especially problematic for platform workers, as the issue of legal qualification is still strongly disputed in the majority of EU Member States (Bouget, Ghailani and Vanhercke 2019; Schoukens 2021, 321).[17] The original objective to create level playing field for all workers is thus seriously undercut in the Council Recommendation (Schoukens 2021, 321).[18]

In any case, the requirement of formal coverage, either compulsory or (in the case of self-employed persons, and when appropriate) voluntary, is an important requirement that many EU Member States may not fulfil as it regards self-employed and platform workers. This is not the case because self-employed persons in general are still excluded from social security coverage concerning many contingencies, but also because marginal forms of work are often excluded from social security coverage as well.

Effective coverage

EU Member States are also recommended to ensure effective coverage for all workers, regardless of the type of employment and for the self-employed (effective coverage) (Art. 7, Sub f and Arts 9–10 Council Recommendation).

Effective coverage refers to real protection for employees and the self-employed to build up adequate social security benefits and the ability, in the case of the materialisation of the corresponding risk, to access a given level of benefits. For example, EU Member States are encouraged to cover all employees and self-employed persons in an effective manner by reducing where possible existing thresholds such as minimum work records or insurance periods.

Particularly interesting for platform workers is that the Council Recommendation establishes that rules governing contributions and entitlements should not hinder the possibility of accruing and accessing benefits due to the type of employment relationship or labour market status; and, moreover, that differences in the rules governing the schemes between labour market statuses or types of employment relationship should be proportionate and reflect the specific situation of beneficiaries.

Platform work is (typically) characterised by specific work patterns, leading often to intermittent work periods. Minimum qualifying periods and minimum working periods may prove problematic for this type of worker. However, the Council Recommendation is clear in this regard, and states that such minimum conditions should not impede the effective build-up of social protection for workers with an irregularly built-up insurance record. Such rules should be justified by a clear objective (e.g., financial sustainability, insurance logics such as the respect of equivalence and/or the combat of abuse) and the reasons for their introduction should be unrelated to the labour status of the worker. The difficulties for platform workers to build up social security rights will thus not be solved by merely qualifying them as employees: even if they are qualified as workers, similar problems remain as for other non-standard work and actually acquiring social security rights can remain difficult. Social security schemes should thus provide the necessary safeguards or should be altered in order to provide those safeguards so that platform workers can receive adequate social protection (irrespective of their employment status). Adapting existing thresholds in light of flexible work forms presented by non-standard work can be done by deviating from traditional workday patterns typical to standard work. Conditions can, for example, be rephrased in smaller time units, or use can be made of longer time reference periods within which the thresholds have to be reached. This can even lead to taking non-standard work as a reference framework as to ensure that all existing work forms are included (Schoukens 2021, 322).

Adequate coverage

EU Member States are also encouraged to ensure an adequate level of protection (Art. 11 Council Recommendation), for example by guaranteeing protection levels that keep persons out of poverty and guarantee where possible a living standard in line with the situation previous to the occurrence of a social risk. Although it calls for an adequate level of protection, the Council Recommendation remains rather vague about the level of benefits as it does not include clear figures or references. More information on the notion of adequacy can, however, be found in Recital 17 of the Council Recommendation: "Social protection is considered to be adequate when it allows individuals to uphold a decent standard of living, replace their income loss in a reasonable manner and live with dignity, and prevents them from falling into poverty while contributing where appropriate to activation and facilitating the return to work".

Although the Council Recommendation does not include any figures or references, it makes clear that both employees and the self-employed should be kept out of poverty, meaning that benefit levels should not fall below minimum subsistence levels as applied in social assistance schemes. Social security schemes should, however, go further and provide a reasonable protection against the loss of income. This is in particular a challenge for workers and self-employed persons with a structural low income or with no regular work.

The need for adequate social security benefits also implies that a balance must be struck between the payment of social security contributions and the level of benefits (principle of equivalence). In addition, the principle of proportionality is also important in the design of social security systems. Applying this principle may result in, for example, the need to take into account the length of participation by insured persons in the insurance scheme. Proportionality is particularly important in the case of non-standard work and, especially, platform work. This type of work is often characterised by intermittent work patterns and, therefore, also intermittent insurance periods. The proportionality ratio reflects directly on the benefits level: the longer the period that a worker has paid social security contributions, the more extensive the protection will be and, conversely, the shorter the participation rate, the lower the benefit will be. Proportionality is often translated into a reference insurance record or a minimum work period that needs to be fulfilled in order to enjoy a full benefit or even to open access to benefits. Finding the necessary balance between all these principles is even more essential concerning non-standard workers, as their insurance records and income levels do not always follow a linear pattern (Schoukens 2021, 323).

Transparent coverage

A fourth principle articulated in the Council Recommendation concerns transparent coverage (Art. 7, Sub j Council Recommendation). This entails an obligation for EU Member States to keep the design of the system simple and understandable, so the basic fabric of the system can be easily understood and hence supported by the society at large, and to inform the population of their rights and duties, while also guaranteeing swift access to administration and judiciary.

More specifically, it is recommended that EU Member States ensure transparency in the conditions and rules for entitlement, as well as provide individuals with free access to updated, comprehensive and clearly understandable information about their individual entitlements and obligations. Access to such information is particularly important in the case of platform work as, because of its often short and fragmented character, it may be a challenge for platform workers to know with certainty whether they might fulfil the requirements for access, and even whether they may be considered as performing a professional activity linked to compulsory or voluntary social security insurance.

EU Member States are also recommended to simplify their administrative proceedings, another relevant aspect for platform workers, as platform work, with its capacity to greatly reduce transaction costs, arguably facilitates access to the performance of work to persons who might otherwise not do so (and many of whom might lack knowledge on fulfilling the administrative proceedings related to social security).

The Council Recommendation, however, arguably addressed transparency in a general manner (which might be appropriate for an instrument seeking to cover very different forms of work). Lack of transparency concerning the social security position of platform workers may also stem, however, from their unclear professional status as well as from the opacity of algorithmic management (Barrio 2021, 341–44), aspects that are not addressed explicitly in the Council Recommendation. They are, however, addressed by the proposed Directive on improving working conditions in platform work,[19] which establishes a presumption of employment relationship concerning platform work, as well as obliges online platforms to share information on the functioning of algorithmic management. It is, however, still unclear to which extent the proposed Directive may impact the social security of platform workers, as its material scope only covers working conditions (and not social protection).

Looking forward: Questions for a future research agenda in social security

Our discussion above shows that social security schemes should be redesigned to accommodate new non-standard forms of work and platform work. We have identified several challenges for social security schemes arising from platform work. In particular, the irregularity of work patterns in the case of platform work poses an important challenge, as active periods can be followed by (longer) periods of inactivity or work periods with low income may alternate with high-income work assignments. If social security schemes are not redesigned, they may lose out a large group of work activities that do not coincide with the traditional work organisation, characterised by full-time work assignments with a fixed working time (i.e., nine-to-five jobs).

In general, social security systems face major challenges to ensure, also for future generations, adequate access to social protection in a robust and sustainable manner. In order to address (some) of these challenges, the EU launched the Council Recommendation on access to social protection. Although the Council Recommendation is not without criticism, it does set out a number of standards and principles that should shape EU Member States' social security systems. This instrument may provide a useful tool to further reflect on the future of national social security systems and how non-standard forms of work, such as platform work, should fit in national social security systems (Barrio 2021, 332–49). It also clarifies the underlying principles of the EU social model, something we urged the EU to do in the past (Schoukens 2016).

One way of dealing with the challenges mentioned above could be to adopt a labour-neutral approach to social security. The general principles (such as the personal and material scope of application, the level of benefits, etc.) can be formulated in a more neutral manner so that they can be developed taking into account the specific work situation of each of these groups (e.g., self-employment, part-time work or platform work). In order to make this work, more research is needed on how these principles can or should be formulated, and where differences between different professional groups are necessary or desirable, also taking into account the principle of equality and the prohibition of discrimination. An approach could be to look at specific activities without working with categories of employees and/or self-employed (e.g., in case of disability or unemployment), whereby the nature of the underlying social risk with respect to the different professional groups can be taken into account when developing the specific rules further.

Additionally, it is necessary to think about how social security can deal with work of a very limited nature and this immediately raises the following question: What is work, and from which moment do we consider work to be relevant for the purposes of social security? This also raises the question of how social security systems should deal with platform work that is performed on a very extreme part-time basis, resulting in an income below the poverty line due to the limited number of hours performed. Or, again in other words, at which point is an activity considered as marginal enough as to not provide entitlement to rights traditionally associated with the performance of work.

The case of platform work makes it already very clear that what is considered work and professional income becomes increasingly blurred. If social protection systems will not start to recalibrate their scope of application (and thus the concepts, such as work and income, that are underlying the scope of application) they may lose out on new evolving realities of work. Platform work itself is possibly the exponent of a societal evolution where people's main concern is in the first place to earn sufficient income to earn a living. This can be on the basis of a regular standard job (as this was for many decades the main tool to earn sufficient income), but it can also be through other means, in place of or in combination with a job. Taking into account the latest evolutions in non-standard work (platform work), an increasing emphasis is put upon income protection rather than upon the protection of labour income (Schoukens and Barrio 2017, 328; European Commission 2018b, 32). More than ever before, persons combine a series of activities and/or live from various income sources (from movable and immovable property). Social protection should develop alongside this evolution and incorporate these various income sources both into the financing of social protection and the payment of benefits.

Moreover, particular attention must be given to how social security systems can remain (or become again) financially sound and, at the same time, provide adequate social protection for everyone. From a point of view of sustainability, it is challenging to guarantee adequate (minimum) benefits that are structurally of a higher level than the income upon which contributions were paid in the past. This is rather problematic. Platform work is known to have a strong presence of persons earning a low to very low income. And even though some of these workers have platform work as a second job, the question remains how to take into account these low-income levels for the organisation of labour-related social protection schemes. Low-income work is a challenge for the sustainability of every (labour-related) social insurance scheme, and it will ask in the future for a smart co-existence of social insurance, social assistance and other welfare schemes. It is thus an invitation to have a further look beyond social protection schemes (in the narrow sense) and to see the inter-play with other social schemes, such as social assistance, (health) care, family policies, social housing, etc. Not only the EU Member States have a role to play here, but the EU as well, taking into account their respective competences.

Notes

1. Professor of social security law (comparative, European and international law), KU Leuven and Tilburg University.
2. Postdoctoral researcher, University of Copenhagen.
3. Professor of social security law, Free University of Brussels and substitute lecturer at KU Leuven.
4. The EU-SILC statistics showed an increase from 8.4% in 2008 to 9% in 2019.
5. Council Recommendation 92/441/EEC of 24 June 1992 on common criteria concerning sufficient resources and social assistance in social protection systems, OJ L 245, 26 August 1992, p. 46-48.
6. https://ec.europa.eu/info/business-economy-euro/economic-and-fiscal-policy -coordination/eu-economic-governance-monitoring-prevention-correction/ european-semester/framework/european-semester-explained_en.
7. Interinstitutional Proclamation on the European Pillar of Social Rights, OJ C 428, 13 December 2017, 10–15.
8. The European Pillar of Social Rights action plan, European Commission SWD/46 final 2021.
9. Council Recommendation (EU) of 8 November 2019 on access to social protection for workers and the self-employed, OJ C 387/1, 15 November 2019.
10. European Commission 2021c.
11. For a more detailed definition, see Stone and Arthurs 2013, 1–20; Freedland 2013, 82.
12. Being the presence of personal subordination, the bilateral character of the relationship, and hence mutuality of obligations as a consequence, the wage as (main) source of income, that is provided in return to the offered labour, the economic dependency as the worker depends fully for this income on the employer, and a fixed workplace where the work is done, normally at the premises of the employer.
13. Our focus is thus upon persons who personally deliver the activity and are not in a position to have it done by another person. This means that the platform worker is required to create a personal profile, to which reviews may be linked. While in some cases this feature is expressly mentioned by the platform in its terms of services (see Prassl and Risak 2016), in other cases it might be evident from the personal character of the ratings.
14. Interesting to note was the following statement that among the 28 million people who are estimated to work through digital labour platforms, most people are genuinely self-employed; however, there may be up to 5.5 million people who are "false" self-employed, see European Commission 2021b, 6 and European Commission 2021a.

15. The concept of "transparency" as it regards platform work has been arguably further expanded in the Commission's proposal for a Directive on improving working conditions in platform work; see European Commission 2021c. In that regard, the proposed Directive establishes a presumption of employment relationship concerning platform work, as well as obliges online platforms to ensure transparency as it regards the functioning of algorithmic management. It is, however, unclear yet in which measure the Directive may apply to the field of social security.
16. This is with the exception of those relating to formal access, which should be mandatory in the case of employees and voluntary (unless appropriate otherwise) in the case of self-employed persons, as noted in Article 8(b) of the Recommendation.
17. As noted above, the Commission's proposal for a Directive on improving working conditions in platform work may contribute to clarify this legal qualification.
18. Asking now from Member States to make access to social protection available on a voluntary basis will not change much in this respect as the majority of low income (and high-income) self-employed do in the end not take out social insurance when they are given the freedom to do so: European Commission 2018a.
19. European Commission 2021c.

References

Aranguiz, A., P. Schoukens, and E. De Becker. 2021. "Minimum Income Protection at the EU: What Role to Play for the EU". *EU Law Live* 2021/82: 16–24.

Barrio, A. 2021. *Social Security and Platform Work: Towards a More Transparent and Inclusive Path.* Tilburg: Tilburg University.

Bruzelius, C., E. Chase, and M. Seeleib-Kaiser. 2015. "Social Rights of EU Migrant Citizens: Britain and Germany Compared". *Social Policy and Society* 15(3): 403–16.

Dawson, M. 2018. "New Governance and the Displacement of Social Europe: The Case of the European Semester". *European Constitutional Law Review* 17/3: 191–209.

Degryse, C. 2016. *Digitalisation of the Economy and its Impact on Labour Markets.* Brussels: ETUI.

Dickens, L. 2003. Changing Contours of the Employment Relationship and New Modes of Labour Regulation. Rapporteur Paper, Berlin, International Industrial Relations Association 13th World Congress.

European Commission. 2017. *Working Lives: The Foundation of Prosperity for All Generations.* Employment and Social Developments in Europe in 2017, Brussels: European Commission.

European Commission. 2018a. *Behavioral Study on the Effects of an Extension of Access to Social Protection for People in All Forms of Employment.* Luxembourg: Publications Office for the European Union.

European Commission. 2018b. *Commission Staff Working Document Impact Assessment Accompanying the Document Proposal for a Council Recommendation on Access to Social Protection for Workers and the Self-Employed,* SWD(2018)70 final, Brussels: European Commission.

European Commission. 2021a. *Staff Working Document Impact Assessment Report Accompanying the Document Proposal for a Directive of the European Parliament and of the Council to Improve the Working Conditions in Platform Work in the European Union,* SWD(2021) 396 final. Brussels: European Commission.

European Commission. 2021b. *Communication from the Commission to the European Parliament, the Council, the European Economic and Social Committee and the Committee of the Regions: Better Working Conditions for a Stronger Social Europe: Harnessing the Full Benefits of Digitalisation for the Future of Work*, COM(2021) 761 final. Brussels: European Commission.

European Commission. 2021c. *Proposal for a Directive of the European Parliament and of the Council on Improving Working Conditions in Platform Work*, COM (2021) 762 final, 2021. Brussels: European Commission.

Freedland, M. 2013. "Burying Caesar: What Was the Standard Employment Contract?" in K.V.W. Stone and H.W. Arthurs (eds.), *Rethinking Workplace Regulation: Beyond the Standard Contract of Employment*, 81–94. New York: Russell Sage Foundation.

Keune, M. 2013. "Trade Union Responses to Precarious Work in Seven European Countries". *International Journal of Labour Research* 5(1): 59–78.

Kittur, A. 2013. *The Future of Crowd Work*. https://www.researchgate.net/publication/255969848_The_Future_of_Crowd_Work.

Marx, I. 2019. *Second Structured Dialogue on Minimum Income Implementation*, Brussels: European Commission.

Peña-Casas, R., D. Ghailani, S. Spasova, and B. Vanhercke. 2019. *In-work Poverty in Europe: A Study of National Policies*. Brussels: European Commission.

Prassl, J., and M. Risak. 2016. "Uber, Taskrabbit, & Co: Platforms as Employers? Rethinking the Legal Analysis of Crowdwork". *Comparative Labour Law & Policy Journal* 37(3): 619–52.

Pulignano, V., and C. Mara. 2021. "Working for Nothing in the Platform Economy. Forms and Institutional Contexts of Unpaid Labour". Brussels: Solidar 2021, https://www.solidar.org/en/publications/working-for-nothing-in-the-platform-economy-thematic-publication.

Ratti, L., A. García-Muñoz, and V. Vergnat. 2022. "Chapter 1: Defining, Measuring and Overcoming In-Work Poverty" in L. Ratti (ed.), *In-Work Poverty in Europe*, 1–36. Alphen aan den Rijn: Kluwer Law International.

Schoukens, P. 2016. "The Hidden Social Model". Tilburg Inaugural Speech. https://eiss.be/onewebmedia/oration_Schoukens.pdf%20(final).pdf.

Schoukens, P. 2021. "Building Up and Implementing the European Standards for Platform Workers" in U. Becker and O. Chesalina (eds.), *Social Law 4.0: New Approaches of Ensuring and Financing Social Security in the Digital Age*, 307–34. Baden-Baden: Nomos.

Schoukens, P., and A. Barrio. 2017. "The Changing Concept of Work: When Does Typical Work Become Atypical?". *European Labour Law Journal* 8(4): 306–32.

Schoukens, P., and C. Bruynseraede. 2021. *Access to Social Protection for Self-Employed and Non-Standard Workers: An Analysis Based upon the EU Recommendation on Access to Social Protection*. Leuven: Acco.

Schoukens, P., A. Barrio, and S. Montebovi. 2018. "The EU Social Pillar: An Answer to the Challenge of the Social Protection of Platform Workers?". *European Journal of Social Security* 20(3): 219–41.

Schoukens, P., E. De Becker, and J. Beke Smets. 2015. "Fighting Social Exclusion under the Europe 2020 Strategy: Which Legal Nature for Social Inclusion Recommendations". *International Comparative Jurisprudence* 1(1): 11–23.

Social Protection Committee of the European Union. 2020. *SPC Annual Review of the Social Protection Performance Monitor (SPPM) and Developments in Social Protection Policies Report on Key Social Challenges and Key Messages*. Luxembourg: Publications Office of the European Union.

Spasova, S., D. Bouget, D. Ghailani, and B. Vanhercke. 2019. "Self-Employment and Social Protection: Understanding Variations between Welfare Regimes". *Journal of Poverty and Social Justice* 27(2): 157–75.

Stone, K.V.W., and H.W. Arthurs. 2013. "The Transformation of Employment Regimes: A Worldwide Challenge" in K.V.W. Stone and H. Arthurs (eds.), *Rethinking Workplace Regulation: Beyond the Standard Contract of Employment*, 1–20. New York: Russell Sage Foundation.

Valenduc, G., and P. Vendramin. 2017. *Work in the Digital Economy: Sorting the Old from the New.* Brussels: ETUI.

Walton, M.J. 2016. "The Shifting Nature of Work and Its Implications". *Industrial Law Journal* 45(2): 111–30.

7 Platform work and precariousness: Low earnings and limited control of work

Iain Campbell

Platform work, understood in this chapter as 'paid labour intermediated by online labour platforms' (Kilhoffer 2021, 2), has become a significant topic in social science. Research into platform work has mushroomed to include overviews, theoretical reflections and, most important, an increasing abundance of empirical studies, built up from secondary data analysis, dedicated surveys, administrative data and case-study analysis (Joyce et al. 2020; Kilhoffer et al. 2019).

Research into platforms and platform work proceeds in different ways. Many empirical studies draw on the conceptual framework of precariousness (or precarity), widely used in employment research to analyse labour restructuring in contemporary societies (e.g., Kalleberg 2011; 2018). Application of the 'precarity lens' (Mallett 2020) tackles the widespread concern that the growth of platform work signals deteriorating job quality and a redistribution of costs and risks of employment to workers (Berg 2019). Subsequent studies generally conclude that precariousness, though varying in composition and incidence, is indeed pervasive and that all or most platform work can be regarded as precarious (e.g., Hauben, Lenaerts and Wayaert 2020; Huws, Spencer and Syrdal 2018; Tucker 2020; Woodcock and Graham 2020).

Research findings on platform work and precariousness challenge *inter alia* efforts to treat platform work research as an isolated research silo, which can safely disregard the overlaps and connections with other forms of work. The precariousness framework establishes a bridge to broader labour market changes, pointing towards similarities with the highly precarious forms of work that are found elsewhere in the employment structure (Berg 2019; Huws, Spencer and Coates 2019; Joyce et al. 2020). Much platform work can be compared, in particular, to *casualised work*, in which labour processes are disaggregated and re-structured in terms of short-term and occasional tasks and workers are mobilised as a just-in-time workforce to undertake these tasks on a pay-as-you-go basis (De Stefano 2016; Eurofound 2019).[1] Casualised work, characterised by fragmented and variable work schedules together with intermittency and low earnings, dominated labour markets in industrialised societies before the consolidation of labour movements and national systems of labour regulation and social protection (Stanford 2017). It remains significant in the present, not only in low-income societies but also in high-income industrialised societies, where varied forms of on-demand work such as zero-hours work arrangements have proliferated in recent years within 'gaps' or 'grey zones' in the established systems of regulatory protection (Eurofound 2015; ILO 2016; Jaehrling and Kalina 2020; O'Sullivan et al. 2019; Rubery et al. 2018).

This chapter dips into the rich research findings on platform work and precariousness. It is organised into four sections. The first section sets the scene for the later discussion by outlining three axes of division for labour platforms: (a) the type of platform; (b) national geography; and (c) firm strategies. The second section presents the evolution of the precariousness approach in employment research, noting its recent extension beyond job characteristics to social relations outside the workplace. The third section then turns to platform work and precariousness, critically reviewing selected findings concerning low average earnings and limited control of work, especially working-time schedules. The fourth section suggests areas for future research.

Labour platforms

Divisions amongst labour platforms are sometimes downplayed, but they are important for understanding work and work experiences, including precariousness. To set the scene for subsequent discussion, this section outlines three major axes of division: (a) platform type; (b) national geography; and (c) firm strategies.

Platform type

Labour platforms can be divided into types, largely in terms of material features of the labour process. Most typologies of platform work start with a division according to where the work is performed, whether online or location-based (ILO 2021). Each category can be further sub-divided according to the content of the constituent tasks. Thus, online web-based work can be split between lower-skilled work on microtask platforms, often called 'crowdwork', and higher-skilled work on freelance platforms in areas such as professional services, graphic design, creative and multi-media work, writing and translating. Location-based work, where the labour service is mediated by software applications ('apps') but physically undertaken in a local area, can be differentiated into assorted services, predominantly lower-skilled, such as personal transport ('ride hail'), delivery of food and other goods, and household services such as (domestic) cleaning (ILO 2021, 40; see also Kilhoffer 2021; Forde et al. 2017). These differences in platform types overlap with differences in the scale of the tasks, ranging from highly disaggregated microtasks, such as photo tagging, through more lumpy services, as in ride hail and food delivery, to more protracted project work, as in graphic design.

National geography

Platform work is distributed widely in both the Global North and Global South. Geography matters in at least two respects. First, the distribution of different types of platform work varies geographically. Online web-based work, primarily commissioned by business clients in high-income countries, can in principle be undertaken anywhere, but it is commonly performed by workers in low-income countries with low wage costs, reliable IT infrastructure and English-language skills (Graham, Hjorth and Leydonvirta 2017; ILO 2021, 43–47). Location-based work such as food delivery and ride hail is present in cities of both the Global North and Global South, but other forms of location-based work such as house maintenance and care are concentrated in cities of the Global North (ILO 2021). Second, beyond differences in the types of platform work, geographical location implies differences in the local labour market context, national regulatory system and patterns of integration into global relations, all of which are likely to affect work and worker experiences (Berg and Rani 2021).

Firm strategies

Different firm strategies are another axis of division, even when the type of platform work and the geographic location are much the same. This dimension is crucial, though often neglected. Almost all firms involved in this space have a capitalist character, with business models and labour-use strategies dominated by imperatives of surplus labour extraction (Tucker 2020). But how surplus extraction plays out in practice is variable. One complicating factor, familiar from mainstream employment research on outsourcing and the fissured workplace, is the triangular structure of labour platforms (worker, platform and client), which re-distributes and obscures management functions such as recruitment of workers, allocation of tasks, performance monitoring, evaluation and remuneration (Weil 2014). The triangular structure is especially challenging when, as in many online web-based platforms, the client firm is itself a large business and may play a leading role in regulating wages and conditions (Tucker 2020, 185–86).

One pivot for firm labour-use strategies concerns the determination of employment status. Most platform workers, in accordance with the preferences of platform firms, are designated as self-employed ('independent contractors') and paid by the task. Nevertheless, empirical research shows that some platforms may substitute or accede to an alternative employment status, when influenced by litigation, new regulations and union or worker pressure (De Stefano et al., Chapter 2, this volume; Ilsøe and Larsen 2021), or when they need to attract a large pool of workers during start up (ILO 2021, 90–91) or to differentiate themselves from competitors (Ilsøe and Jesnes 2020; Schreyer 2021, 75). Irrespective of the selected employment status, platform firms may adopt different labour-management practices (Ravenelle 2019; Griesbach et al. 2019). Case studies in food delivery, for example, document the different working-time and pay systems used by competing firms within the one country or one city (Heiland 2022; Ivanova et al. 2018). Even within a single firm, one employment model may be applied to one workforce group, while a different model is applied to another group (Liu and Friedman 2021; ILO 2021, 165). Many case studies describe a process of constant experimentation and frequent alterations, imposed on workers without consultation or notice and generally aimed at reducing labour costs at the expense of workers (Ivanova et al. 2018). Firms may initially offer good payment systems as part of a set-up process but then tighten conditions when they have secured a large-enough pool of committed workers (van Doorn and Chen 2021). As a result, employment strategies are rarely stable but instead shift in varied ways, ranging from fine-tuning of one or more elements of the system to complete overhauls, sparked by takeovers and mergers and sometimes ending in sudden exit from the market, as in the case of Deliveroo from Germany (van Doorn 2020) or Foodora from Ontario (Lee 2021).

Diversity within labour platforms

These three axes help to explain the diversity within labour platforms (Kilhoffer et al. 2019; Kuhn and Maleki 2017), and they point to potential differences in the nature and degree of precariousness. Freelance platforms, for example, rely on workers with relatively high and in-demand skills, who have more individual bargaining power and are likely to achieve better payments and conditions (Vandaele 2021; ILO 2021; Berg et al. 2018). Workers on freelance platforms may be better able to sidestep other precariousness risks, e.g., by finding functional equivalents to state-supported social protection and by stabilising their employment by rolling one project over into another (Sutherland et al. 2020). Thus freelance platforms might be expected to involve less precariousness for workers. Geographic location is also significant for precariousness, starting with the apparent disadvantage of workers in the Global South in terms of temporal demands and hourly payments (Berg and Rani 2021; Berg et al. 2018; ILO 2021). Finally, strategic choices of firms concerning self-employment status and adjustment to payment systems directly affect labour costs and shape the degree of precariousness in platform work.

The precariousness approach: A brief history

Precariousness (or 'precarity') first appeared in employment research as an underlying principle for a new, multi-dimensional framework for analysing jobs, built around typologies of objective job characteristics related to labour (in)security. Common schemas of employment precariousness include that sketched out by Gerry Rodgers, which encompasses low certainty of continuing work, low income, low levels of regulatory protection and limited control over work (1989; see also Vosko, MacDonald and Campbell 2009). Another influential schema was developed in research at the International Labour Organization (ILO) and is widely disseminated in Guy Standing's writings (Standing 2011; see ILO 2016). Also starting from objective characteristics is a four-part framework, based on dimensions of security, opportunity, fair treatment and life beyond work (Rubery et al. 2018). Schemas of precariousness in employment have been developed in parallel to similar schemas couched in terms of (poor) job quality (Kilhoffer et al. 2019, 50–54). Such schemas are widely used for analysing the multiple forms of non-standard and casualised work in industrialised societies, but they can in principle be applied to all forms of work, including so-called standard work (Rubery et al. 2018; Vosko, MacDonald and Campbell 2009).

Contemporary employment research continues to use multi-dimensional precariousness schemas focused on job characteristics. These schemas have proven to be useful in highlighting dimensions of work such as working time, which are pivotal in contemporary labour restructuring and the resurgence of casualised work arrangements (Rubery, Ward and Grimshaw 2006). In recent years, however, the precariousness approach has been extended well beyond the workplace to other domains of life that constitute sources of insecurity, such as household relations, citizenship, social welfare/protection, caring for others, housing, personal healthcare, debt, and access to savings or wealth (Kalleberg 2018; Motakef 2019). In this perspective, precarious lives (Clement et al. 2009) or precarious life arrangements (Motakef 2019) need to be analysed in terms of what can be called 'social location', which acknowledges the ways in which individuals are *embedded* in interconnected social processes and social relations both inside and outside the workplace. Trends in the different domains may overlap and converge, producing cumulative effects on individuals, but they may sometimes proceed in tension, e.g., when increased precariousness at the workplace is counter-balanced by social assistance programs provided to the household (Harris and Scully 2015).

Platform work and precariousness

The precariousness approach figures prominently within platform work research, primarily in the form of job schemas. Surveys or mixed-method approaches have been used to assess a range of job characteristics, often starting with lack of labour and social protection (Eurofound 2018; Forde et al. 2017; Ilsøe and Larsen 2020). Other dimensions, such as employment insecurity, low earnings, lack of control of wages and working time, work intensity, physical environment, social environment, lack of training and career progression and lack of voice, are also covered (Eurofound 2018; Hauben, Lenaerts and Wayaert 2020; ILO 2021). Individual case studies are more scattered, but some similarly uncover significant problems of precariousness and poor job quality (e.g., Goods, Veen and Barratt 2019; Kahancová, Meszmann and Sedláková 2020; Qi and Li 2020).

This section focuses on two themes that have been intensively discussed in platform work research: (a) low earnings; and (b) limited control of work. Both represent important dimensions in standard schemas for analysing job characteristic (e.g., Rodgers 1989), but both also invite an extended perspective that would look beyond work to workers and worker experiences.

Low earnings

Earnings are a crucial dimension of job schemas. The way in which workers are remunerated for platform work, i.e., the pricing models, are primarily determined by the platform firms themselves, specified in their terms and conditions. The most common payment method, consistent with the framing of platform workers as self-employed, is via some sort of task-based or piece-rate mechanism, but payment systems can also include elaborate incentives (bonuses, multipliers and discretionary payments) and even regular hourly payments, whether in conjunction with piece rates or separately (Eurofound

2018; Tucker 2020, 191–92; van Doorn and Chen 2021). A common result is unstable as well as low earnings (Hauben, Lenaerts and Wayaert 2020, 30–34).

Survey evidence indicates that earnings accrued by workers from labour platforms are varied but are generally 'scarce', falling away in some cases to almost nothing (ILO 2021; Ilsøe and Larsen 2020; Piasna and Drahokoupil 2019).[2] Findings on estimated *hourly rates* suggest a meagre overall average. On crowdwork platforms, for example, average hourly earnings were estimated at US$4.43 when considering only paid work or US$3.29 when taking into account unpaid hours. Effective hourly rates were generally well below the minimum wage in the local area (Berg et al. 2018, 49, 50). At the same time, *lack of sufficient work* is a common complaint of platform workers (ILO 2021, 149–54, 166; see Berg et al. 2018, 62–67), and this component is often more powerful than low hourly rates in constituting low earnings and generating income insecurity and precariousness. Insufficient availability of paid work, whether occasional or persistent, is bound up with irregularity of hours and earnings. Insufficiency may have the perverse effect of encouraging long hours, as workers devote more unpaid time to the search for extra or better-paying orders (Berg and Rani 2021, 104). Insufficient paid work is generally an incidental by-product of loose labour markets, but it is sometimes a deliberate outcome of 'overstaffing' at the level of individual platforms, intended to dampen workplace bargaining power and encourage greater commitment from workers (Vandaele 2022).

The findings on earnings draw attention to patterns of worker engagement in platform work. Low average earnings suggest first that much participation is likely to be transitory or sporadic, linked to high levels of turnover and churn in platform labour markets (Huws, Spencer and Coates 2019; Piasna and Drahokoupil 2019; Urzì Brancati, Pesole and Fernández-Macías 2020). They suggest second that only a minority of platform workers, even of those with a more enduring attachment, will be able to secure an adequate income from platform work, leaving the majority to combine such work with other activities and other sources of income (Huws, Spencer and Coates 2019; ILO 2021; Ilsøe, Larsen and Bach 2021; Piasna and Drahokoupil 2019).

Both points have been elaborated in current platform research. I return below to the issue of high turnover and exit. With respect to the second point, survey questions on the relationship of platform earnings to other sources of income suggest a differentiated pattern, whereby only a minority of platform workers cite platform work as their sole source of income ('main' platform workers), while most ('sporadic', 'marginal' and 'secondary' platform workers) state that they combine it with other sources of income (Urzì Brancati, Pesole and

Fernández-Macías 2020, 14–17). The combination is often complex, and the pattern varies somewhat according to platform type and geographic location. Thus, reliance on platform earnings appears stronger in freelance platforms and in low-income countries (ILO 2021, 154; Berg and Rani 2021), while it appears more muted in other cases, especially in location-based platform work in high-income countries in Europe (Huws, Spencer and Coates 2019; Piasna and Drahokoupil 2019; Urzì Brancati, Pesole and Fernández-Macías 2020; for similar US estimates see Schor et al. 2020; for Australia see McDonald et al. 2019).

These results are generally treated as an indicator of *economic dependence* on platform earnings. Thus, only a minority of platform workers is categorised as highly dependent, while the majority, using platform work for 'supplementary earnings', is categorised as relatively less dependent. The measure of dependence is somewhat opaque, and it would be best to add other measures such as level of earnings and perceptions of financial precariousness at the household level (Berg et al. 2018, 41–42, 57–59) and perhaps duration of working hours (Urzì Brancati, Pesole and Fernández-Macías 2020). Nevertheless, the evidence is suggestive of significant workforce diversity, based on different ways in which individual workers are embedded in extra-workplace relations.

An emerging debate in platform work research has begun to grapple with the implications of this differentiated pattern. It is clearly wrong to suggest, as some platform firms do, that workers who are less dependent are not really workers (Woodcock and Graham 2020, 115). But neither is it adequate to assume that alternative sources of income necessarily act to soften or even eliminate precariousness in platform work. At first glance, this assumption appears plausible (Schor et al. 2020, 847, 850–2; see also Kuhn and Maleki 2017; Vallas and Schor 2020).[3] But, as other scholars note, it skates over important differences in the significance of the alternative sources of income. The three main alternative sources are: (a) social security payments, including unemployment benefits and pensions; (b) household transfers; and (c) other paid job(s) (Berg et al. 2018, 58–59).[4] The example of *social security* payments fits the notion of a cushion for precariousness at work. A Danish national population survey revealed that many platform workers relied on unemployment benefits and social assistance for their main source of income. In this context, the alternative source of income not only played a positive role in 'buffering' the precariousness associated with scarce earnings from platform work but also had broader positive effects in putting a floor on wages in the platform sector (Ilsøe and Larsen 2020, 18–19). The second alternative source, *household transfers*, is more internally varied and more complex in its implications. It can involve parental support for tertiary students, who, in several

European countries, combine platform work such as food delivery with their studies (Eurofound 2018, 23; Timko and van Melik, 2021). Alternatively, it can involve a traditional household division of labour, in which the earnings of one household member support a dependent spouse who takes up sporadic platform work, sometimes undertaken in the home itself, in conjunction with unpaid work such as care for dependents. In the latter case, household relations can themselves be sources of precariousness, linked to deep-seated forms of economic, social and psychological dependence on a [male] breadwinning partner. *Other paid job(s)*, i.e., multiple job holding, is the most frequently cited example of an alternative source of income (Ilsøe and Larsen 2021, 210) and the one that appears to make the most substantial contribution to total earnings for less dependent platform workers (Berg et al. 2018, 58). It too is internally varied and somewhat indeterminate in its implications, given that the job in question could be a regular waged job, traditional freelance work, a casualised job or another form of marginal self-employment (Berg et al. 2018, 42; Huws, Spencer and Coates 2019; Piasna and Drahokoupil 2019, 37–39, 44).

These reflections suggest that the implications of alternative sources of income for precariousness are not straightforward. Workers who are judged to be less economically dependent on platform work may nevertheless still be in a precarious labour market and social position. For workers combining platform work with other paid work, for example, the implications for precariousness will largely depend on the nature of the non-platform job(s). A regular waged job, perhaps with all the rights and entitlements of the standard employment relation, including rights to social protection, could be expected to cushion any precariousness from platform work. A casualised job or marginal self-employment, by contrast, could amplify precariousness, as the worker tries to juggle the competing imperatives of multiple jobs characterised by low pay rates, insufficient work and fluctuating schedules and earnings.

One consequence of low earnings is exit from the job in pursuit of better opportunities elsewhere. We know that turnover in platform work is high, generally due to voluntary quits, but little is known of the characteristics of those who exit and those who remain (Piasna and Drahokoupil 2019, 43, 32). It is not clear whether those who remain should be regarded as less vulnerable or more vulnerable workers, e.g., migrant workers who lack alternative job options and access to social security benefits.

The authors of a recent European study use the data on occasional participation and supplementary earnings in order to argue that many platform workers are best seen as part of a growing group of vulnerable workers engaged in 'patchwork livelihoods' within casualised low-wage urban labour markets

(Huws, Spencer and Coates 2019; see also Huws, Spencer and Syrdal 2018). In this perspective, singling out platform workers as a special kind of worker, or indeed platform work as a special kind of work, risks being misleading (Huws, Spencer and Coates 2019, 14).

In short, the research indicates that low average earnings are a strong feature of platform work. They represent a major dimension of precariousness, presenting risks of financial distress. Experiences of low earnings may, however, vary, not only as a result of any variation in the level of earnings but also as a result of extra-workplace social relations that act to cushion or amplify the degree of precariousness.

Limited control of work

Limited control is a slippery topic, which can refer to different aspects of work and employment (Kilhoffer et al. 2019). It is a topic that, unsurprisingly, is tackled more often and more successfully in case studies than in survey research. This section focuses just on food delivery and just on findings with respect to *working-time schedules*. Food delivery has distinctive features, but it is a fertile field for examination because of the abundant number of studies, the centrality of temporal structures and the evidence of strong though diverse management controls (Vandaele 2022). Working-time schedules concern the choice of when to work and how much to work, and they are commonly discussed in terms of *flexibility* either for firms or for workers. 'Flexible schedules' have been presented as a leading motive for worker engagement in platform work (Piasna and Drahokoupil 2021, 1405–6; see ILO 2021, 143–46) and as a key area of autonomy for platform workers (e.g., Schor 2021, 4, 6).

The question of *when to work* concerns the timing of work over the day or week. Individual workers have preferences, in response to their labour market situation and their commitments outside the workplace, but case studies confirm the powerful interest of platforms in organising worker schedules. The co-ordination of a complex, on-demand process depends on the availability of an adequate supply of labour, especially during peak periods such as weekends (Richardson 2020; Heiland 2022). Management methods to secure worker availability vary, but, under common conditions of piece-rate payments and self-employment, co-ordination generally requires having enough couriers logged on and ready (in the right zone) to respond to delivery orders and then having a system of order allocation that encourages acceptance rather than rejection by the worker (Griesbach et al. 2019; Heiland 2022; Ivanova et al. 2018). These are challenging requirements, but the platforms control the payment system, and they can freely use monetary incentives and disincentives. A higher delivery rate for peak periods is one option, but by itself this rarely provides enough predictability and flexibility, and it has been increasingly supplanted or supplemented by other techniques. An alternative is to organise workers to report their availability (or non-availability) and then to design and allocate one-hour or more 'shifts' to suit the times desired by the platform firm. The allocation of such shifts can proceed in different ways, and workers may retain greater or lesser rights to choose, but allocation is generally directed by the platform and accompanied by behavioural prompts. The latter include not only monetary incentives but also ranking systems, which introduce competition amongst workers using the copious data on worker performance that is generated by the app. An often-elaborate system of grades or badges provides a solid framework both for rewards, including priority access to more and better shifts, and for sanctions, including deactivation, in order to promote worker acquiescence to platform requirements of when to work (Griesbach et al. 2019; Ivanova et al. 2018; Richardson 2020; Shapiro 2018).

The question of *how much to work* concerns the duration of working time. Many couriers, like other platform workers, describe a lack of sufficient work and complain that this functions to displace their own preferences (Drahokoupil and Piasna 2019). Insufficient work has a dual face; it is partly to do with constraints on the total daily or weekly hours logged on, e.g., as a result of sparse shift allocation, and partly to do with a poor balance of paid and unpaid work within the logged-on hours. For both platform firms and workers, the latter aspect is important and often fiercely contested. Food delivery workers have a rough idea of how long they wish to work in order to obtain a target income, and they may seek to log-on for those hours, but earnings will be affected both by the delivery rates and by the amount of unpaid time spent waiting for orders. Couriers seek to minimise unpaid or poorly paid working time, while maximising the time spent on higher-paying deliveries, using varied tricks and artifices, including exercising their nominal right to reject orders. Platforms aim to restrict this ability, again by using a shifting mix of monetary incentives, rewards and sanctions for performance, and information asymmetries in the allocation process, e.g., by withholding information on the destination of the allocated delivery until after the worker has accepted (Griesbach et al. 2019; ILO 2021; Richardson 2020; Shapiro 2018).

Flexible schedules figure in two intriguing episodes described in the case-study literature. In Barcelona, Deliveroo initiated a change from its previous, rather elaborate shift allocation and payment system to a new 'free login' system, which promised registered couriers that they could work whenever, wherever and as much as they liked. Though the change was initially welcomed by couriers, their attitude changed when they realised that incomes had dropped, as a result of decisions by management to reduce the minimum payment per delivery and increase the size of the workforce (Cano, Espelt and Morell 2021). Similarly, in Brussels Deliveroo ended its agreement with the intermediary (SMart), which had given couriers the option of employee status, with benefits such as shifts and minimum shift payments, replacing it with a per delivery remuneration system within a self-employment framework. The firm promised increased flexibility for the worker, but the change was judged by surviving couriers to be advantageous for the firm and a blow to worker flexibility. From the worker perspective, it was the structure of institutional support provided for employees by protective labour regulation that had secured worker-oriented flexibility, enabling them to achieve a degree of predictability and control over working time and earnings (Drahokoupil and Piasna, 2019; see also Piasna and Drahokoupil 2021). The two episodes are revealing in several ways. They confirm the basic 'decision-making power' of the platform firms, which allows them to unilaterally modify the terms and conditions of work, including working-time schedules (Shanahan and Smith 2021). At the same time, the episodes point to the ideological dimension of management control and the ongoing uncertainty surrounding promises of flexible schedules (Shanahan and Smith 2021). In both cases, the inflated rhetoric that promoted self-employment as a vehicle for worker-oriented flexibility was pierced by evidence of unilateral payment reductions. But in the Barcelona case this rhetoric was initially accepted by many workers, and in the Brussels case, though it was more quickly rejected, awareness of its deceptive quality dissipated as experienced couriers left and new recruits entered the workforce.

The food delivery case studies challenge prevalent notions that platform workers can control their own working-time schedules. They suggest that management controls, based on a mix of direct and indirect methods, constrain worker behaviour in order to ensure conformity with platform needs and preferences. The result is that flexibility for the platform tends to override flexibility for the workers (Richardson 2020, 629). Nevertheless, it would be wrong to conclude that all worker autonomy and flexibility has been eliminated. An architecture of choice remains in place, e.g., in the decision on whether or not to log-on and whether or not to decline specific orders. Similarly, valued elements of schedule flexibility may survive, such as an ability to swap shifts or to cancel them with adequate notice (Griesbach et al. 2019). Also important is the uneven distribution of experiences of constraints, as a result of the fact that some individual workers have working-time preferences that more easily 'fit' platform needs (Goods, Veen and Barratt 2019; Heiland 2022).

Conclusion: Further research

Low earnings and limited control are just two elements in the rich empirical research on platform work and precariousness. The investigation of these and other dimensions of platform work is far from finished. There are at least three broad areas where research should be further developed.

First is a closer examination of the nature of the workforce in the different forms of platform work. The notion of a heterogeneous workforce is stressed in much platform work research, but more could be done to unpack 'heterogeneity' and to uncover the underlying social relations and their implications for worker experiences of precariousness. The current platform work literature includes useful commentary on unequal gender relations (e.g., Piasna and Drahokoupil 2017; Kaine, Flanagan and Ravenswood 2020) and more attention is starting to be given to young workers (Laursen, Nielsen and Dyreborg 2021) and migration processes (van Doorn and Vijay 2021). But insights in these areas, which are well developed in mainstream employment research, could be further taken up and applied to platform work research.

Second is a reorientation of the discussion of worker agency, especially in case studies. Much of the existing case-study literature is preoccupied with *management* agency, often in an overly narrow sense that focuses on algorithmic control (Joyce and Stuart 2021; Wood 2021). Worker agency tends to be framed in terms of worker responses at the workplace to management controls, primarily in the form of *resistance* (Joyce and Stuart 2021). Case studies in food delivery, which is a sector that has hosted several episodes of collective action, incorporate valuable reflections on individual and collective resistance at the workplace (e.g., Liu and Friedman 2021; Tassanari and Maccarrone 2020; van Doorn 2020; Vandaele 2021). Both management control and worker resistance are important topics, but discussion of worker agency could benefit from a wider scope. A first step would be more attention to individualised expressions of agency such as 'resilience' and 'coping' (Shanahan and Smith 2021; Barratt, Goods and Veen 2020). A further step would examine forms of worker agency that span the workplace and domains of life outside the workplace, such as entry into and exit from platform jobs and longer-term practices of 'household livelihood'.

Third is a more intensive consideration of the links to casualised work arrangements outside platform work. Similarities with these work arrangements are especially strong in the case of lower-skilled location-based platform work, where work seems dominated by fragmented and variable schedules, insufficiency, unpaid hours and low and irregular earnings (Eurofound 2018; Kilhoffer et al. 2019). These are classic features of casualised work within the non-platform economy, apparent in forms of casualised work that have flourished either within the framework of 'bogus self-employment' (Moore and Newsome 2018) or within the framework of wage labour (Eurofound 2019; ILO 2016). As analysis of low-wage labour markets and worker engagement with platform work indicates, these similarities are more than mere parallels. They reflect real overlaps in practice both at the level of the lives of vulnerable workers and at the level of labour market dynamics (Huws, Spencer and Coates 2019). The appropriate path forward is to integrate research on casualised work arrangements, both platform and non-platform, within a broader program of research on contemporary labour restructuring.

Notes

1. The concept of casualised work arrangements refers to varied forms of on-demand work, which can be terminated at very short notice and/or do not guarantee specific working-time schedules. An alternative concept of 'gig work' is widely used to refer to on-demand work, but I prefer not to use the term here since its scope is uncertain and unstable – sometimes used to refer to all forms of casualised work, sometimes just to platform work, and sometimes just to one component of platform work.
2. Survey results can be weakened by problems of sampling, definition and measurement (Kilhoffer 2021), as well as difficulties faced by respondents in accounting accurately for platform fees, costs of equipment or resources, taxation obligations, non-payment and cancellation or return of orders, and unpaid work time spent searching for and waiting around for commissions (ILO 2021, 147–48, 157–58).
3. Some US researchers leap from this assumption to a conclusion that the precariousness approach is therefore inapplicable to platform workers (Schor et al. 2020, 833, 835, 837; see Vallas and Schor 2020). As well as being too hasty in its interpretation of 'supplementary earnings', this conclusion seems predicated on a misunderstanding of the precariousness approach.
4. This does not exhaust all possibilities. Other sources of income for working-class households, particularly in the past, include petty trade, informal activities such as laundry and cleaning and renting out rooms (Huws, Spencer and Coates 2019).

References

Barratt, Tom, Caleb Goods, and Alex Veen. 2020. "'I'm my own boss...': Active Intermediation and 'Entrepreneurial' Worker Agency in the Australian Gig-economy". *EPA: Economy and Space* 52(8): 1643–61.

Berg, Janine. 2019. "Protecting Workers in the Digital Age: Technology, Outsourcing, and the Growing Precariousness of Work". *Comparative Labor Law and Policy Journal* 41(1): 69–93.

Berg, Janine, and Uma Rani. 2021. "Working Conditions, Geography and Gender in Global Cloudwork". In *Work and Labour Relations in Global Platform Capitalism*, edited by Julieta Haidar and Maarten Keune, 93–110. Cheltenham, UK and Northampton, MA, USA: Edward Elgar Publishing.

Berg, Janine, Marianne Furrer, Ellie Harmon, Uma Rani, and M. Six Silverman. 2018. *Digital Labour Platforms and the Future of Work: Towards Decent Work in the Online World.* Geneva: International Labour Office.

Cano, Melissa Renau, Ricard Espelt, and Mayo Fuster Morell. 2021. "Flexibility and Freedom for Whom? Precarity, Freedom and Flexibility in On-Demand Food Delivery". *Work Organisation, Labour and Globalisation* 15(1): 46–68.

Clement, Wallace, Sophie Mathieu, Steven Prus, and Emre Uckardesler. 2009. "Precarious Lives in the New Economy: Comparative Intersectional Analysis". In *Gender and the Contours of Precarious Employment*, edited by Leah Vosko, Martha MacDonald and Iain Campbell, 240–255. London: Routledge.

De Stefano, Valerio. 2016. "The Rise of the 'Just-in-Time Workforce': On-Demand Work, Crowdwork, and Labor Protection in the 'Gig-Economy'". *Comparative Labor Law and Policy Journal* 37: 471–503.

Drahokoupil, Jan, and Agnieszka Piasna. 2019. "Work in the Platform Economy: Deliveroo Riders in Belgium and the SMart Arrangement". ETUI Working Paper 2019.01. Brussels: European Trade Union Institute.

Eurofound. 2015. *New Forms of Employment.* Luxembourg: Publications Office of the European Union.

Eurofound. 2018. *Employment and Working Conditions of Selected Types of Platform Work.* Luxembourg: Publications Office of the European Union.

Eurofound. 2019. *Casual Work: Characteristics and Implications.* New Forms of Employment Series. Luxembourg: Publications Office of the European Union.

Forde, Chris, Mark Stuart, Simon Joyce, Liz Oliver, Danat Valizade, Gabriella Alberti, Kate Hardy, Vera Trappmann, Charles Umney, and Calum Carson. 2017. *The Social Protection of Workers in the Platform Economy*, European Parliament, available online: http://www.europarl.europa.eu/supporting-analyses.

Goods, Caleb, Alex Veen, and Tom Barratt. 2019. "'Is Your Gig Any Good?' Analysing Job Quality in the Australian Platform-Based Food-Delivery Sector". *Journal of Industrial Relations* 61(4): 502–27.

Graham, Mark, Isis Hjorth, and Vili Lehdonvirta. 2017. "Digital Labour and Development: Impacts of Global Digital Labour Platforms and the Gig Economy on Worker Livelihoods". *Transfer* 23(2): 135–62.

Griesbach, Kathleen, Adam Reich, Luke Elliott-Negri, and Ruth Milkman. 2019. "Algorithmic Control in Platform Food Delivery Work". *Socius* 5: 1–14.

Harris, Kevan, and Ben Scully. 2015. "A Hidden Counter-Movement? Precarity, Politics, and Social Protection Before and Beyond the Neoliberal Era". *Theory and Society* 44(5): 415–44.

Hauben, Harald, Karolien Lenaerts, and Willem Wayaert. 2020. *The Platform Economy and Precarious Work.* Policy Department for Economic, Scientific and Quality of Life Policies. Luxembourg: European Parliament.

Heiland, Heiner. 2022. "Neither Timeless nor Placeless: Control of Food Delivery Gig Work via Place-Based Working Time Regimes". *Human Relations* 75(9): 1824–48.

Huws, Ursula, Neil Spencer, and Matt Coates. 2019. *The Platformisation of Work in Europe: Highlights from Research in 13 European Countries*. Brussels: Foundation for European Progressive Studies.

Huws, Ursula, Neil Spencer, and Dag Syrdal. 2018. "Online, on Call: The Spread of Digitally Organised Just-in-Time Working and Its Implications for Standard Employment Models". *New Technology, Work and Employment* 33(2): 113–29.

ILO (International Labour Organization). 2016. *Non-Standard Employment Around the World: Understanding Challenges, Shaping Prospects*. Geneva: International Labour Office.

ILO (International Labour Organization). 2021. *World Employment and Social Outlook 2021: The Role of Digital Labour Platforms in Transforming the World of Work*. Geneva: International Labour Office.

Ilsøe, Anna, and Kristin Jesnes. 2020. "Collective Agreements for Platforms and Workers – Two Cases from the Nordic Countries". In *Platform Work in the Nordic Models: Issues, Cases and Responses*, edited by Kristin Jesnes and Sigurd Oppegaard, 53–67. Oslo: Nordic Council of Ministers.

Ilsøe, Anna, and Trine Larsen. 2020. "Digital Platforms at Work. Champagne or Cocktail of Risks?". In *The Impact of the Sharing Economy on Business and Society*, edited by Abbas Strømmen-Bakhtiar and Evgueni Vinogradov, 1–20. London: Routledge.

Ilsøe, Anna, and Trine Larsen. 2021. "Why Do Labour Platforms Negotiate? Platform Strategies in Tax-Based Welfare States". Forthcoming *Economic and Industrial Democracy*.

Ilsøe, Anna, Trine Larsen, and Emma Bach. 2021. "Multiple Jobholding in the Digital Platform Economy: Signs of Segmentation". *Transfer* 27(2): 201–18.

Ivanova, Mirela, Joanna Bronowicka, Eva Kocher, and Anne Degner. 2018. "Foodora and Deliveroo: The App as a Boss? Control and Autonomy in App-Based Management – the Case of Food Delivery Riders". Working Paper Forschungsförderung no. 107. Düsseldorf: Hans-Böckler-Stiftung.

Jaehrling, Karin, and Thorsten Kalina. 2020. "'Grey Zones' within Dependent Employment: Formal and Informal Forms of on-Call Work in Germany". *Transfer* 26(4): 447–63.

Joyce, Simon, and Mark Stuart. 2021. "Digitalised Management, Control and Resistance in Platform Work: A Labour Process Analysis". In *Work and Labour Relations in Global Platform Capitalism*, edited by Julieta Haidar and Maarten Keune, 158–84. Cheltenham, UK and Northampton MA, USA: Edward Elgar Publishing.

Joyce, Simon, Mark Stuart, Chris Forde, and Danat Valizade. 2020. "Work and Social Protection in the Platform Economy in Europe". *Advances in Industrial and Labor Relations* 25: 153–84.

Kahancová, Marta, Tibor Meszmann, and Mária Sedláková. 2020. "Precarization via Digitalization? Work Arrangements in the On-Demand Platform Economy in Hungary and Slovakia". *Frontiers in Sociology* 5(3), 1–11.

Kaine, Sarah, Frances Flanagan, and Katherine Ravenswood. 2020. "Future of Work (FoW) and Gender". In *The Future of Work and Employment*, edited by Adrian Wilkinson and Michael Barry, 119–38. Cheltenham, UK and Northampton, MA, USA: Edward Elgar Publishing.

Kalleberg, Arne. 2011. *Good Jobs, Bad Jobs: The Rise of Polarized and Precarious Employment Systems in the United States, 1970s to 2000s*. New York: Russell Sage Foundation.

Kalleberg, Arne. 2018. *Precarious Lives: Job Insecurity and Well-Being in Rich Democracies*. Cambridge: Polity Press.

Kilhoffer, Zachary. 2021. *State-of-the-Art. Data on the Platform Economy*. Deliverable no. 12.3. Leuven: InGRID-2 project 730998-H2020.

Kilhoffer, Zachary, Willem de Groen, Karolien Lenaerts, Ine Smits, Harald Hauben, Willem Wayaert, Elisa Giacumacatos, Jean-Philippe Lhernould, and Sophie Robin-Olivier. 2019. *Study to Gather Evidence on the Working Conditions of Platform Workers*. Final Report. Luxembourg: Publications Office of the European Union.

Kuhn, Kristine, and Amir Maleki. 2017. "Micro-Entrepreneurs, Dependent Contractors, and Instaserfs: Understanding Online Labor Platform Workforces". *Academy of Management Perspectives* 31(3): 183–200.

Laursen, Cæcilie, Mette Nielsen, and Johnny Dyreborg. 2021. "Young Workers on Digital Labor Platforms: Uncovering the Double Autonomy Paradox". *Nordic Journal of Working Life Studies* 11(4): 65–84.

Lee, Youngrong. 2021. "After a Global Platform Leaves: Understanding the Heterogeneity of Gig Workers through Capital Mobility". Forthcoming *Critical Sociology*.

Liu, Chuxuan, and Eli Friedman. 2021. "Resistance under the Radar: Organization of Work and Collective Action in China's Food Delivery Industry". *The China Journal* 86: 68–89.

McDonald, Paula, Penny Williams, Andrew Stewart, Robyn Mayes, and Damian Oliver. 2019. *Digital Platform Work in Australia: Prevalence, Nature and Impact*. Brisbane: QUT.

Mallett, Richard. 2020. "Seeing the 'Changing Nature of Work' through a Precarity Lens". *Global Labour Journal* 11(3): 271–290.

Moore, Sian, and Kirsty Newsome. 2018. "Paying for Free Delivery: Dependent Self-Employment as a Measure of Precarity in Parcel Delivery". *Work, Employment and Society* 32(3): 475–92.

Motakef, Mona. 2019. "Recognition and Precarity of Life Arrangement: Towards an Enlarged Understanding of Precarious Working and Living Conditions". *Distinktion: Journal of Social Theory* 20(2): 156–72.

O'Sullivan, Michelle, Jonathan Lavelle, Juliet McMahon, Lorraine Ryan, Caroline Murphy, Thomas Turner, and Patrick Gunnigle, eds. 2019. *Zero Hours and On-call Work in Anglo-Saxon Countries*. Berlin: Springer.

Piasna, Agnieszka, and Jan Drahokoupil. 2017. "Gender Inequalities in the New World of Work". *Transfer* 23(3): 313–32.

Piasna, Agnieszka, and Jan Drahokoupil. 2019. "Digital Labour in Central and Eastern Europe: Evidence from the ETUI Internet and Platform Work Survey". ETUI Working Paper 2019.12. Brussels: European Trade Union Institute.

Piasna, Agnieszka, and Jan Drahokoupil. 2021. "Flexibility Unbound: Understanding the Heterogeneity of Preferences among Food Delivery Platform Workers". *Socio-Economic Review* 19(4): 1397–419.

Qi, Hao, and Zhongjin Li. 2020. "Putting Precarity Back to Production: A Case Study of Didi Kuaiche Drivers in the City of Nanjing, China". *Review of Radical Political Economics* 52(3): 506–22.

Ravenelle, Alexandrea. 2019. 'We're not Uber': Control, Autonomy and Entrepreneurship in the Gig Economy". *Journal of Managerial Psychology* 34(4): 269–85.

Richardson, Lizzie. 2020. "Platforms, Markets, and Contingent Calculation: The Flexible Arrangement of the Delivered Meal". *Antipode* 52(3): 619–36.

Rodgers, Gerry. 1989. "Precarious Work in Western Europe: The State of the Debate". In *Precarious Jobs in Labour Market Regulation: The Growth of Atypical Employment in Western Europe*, edited by Gerry Rodgers and Janine Rodgers, 1–16. Geneva: International Institute for Labour Studies.

Rubery, Jill, Kevin Ward, and Damian Grimshaw. 2006. "Time, Work and Pay: Understanding the New Relationships". In *Decent Working Time: New Trends, New Issues*, edited by Jean-Yves Boulin, Michel Lallement, Jon Messenger and François Michon, 123–51. Geneva: ILO.

Rubery, Jill, Damian Grimshaw, Arjan Keizer, and Mathew Johnson. 2018. "Challenges and Contradictions in the 'Normalising' of Precarious Work". *Work, Employment and Society* 32(3): 509–27.

Schor, Juliet. 2021. "Dependence and Heterogeneity in the Platform Labor Force". Policy Brief, Berlin, Hertie School.

Schor, Juliet, William Attwood-Charles, Mehmet Cansoy, Isak Ladegaard, and Robert Wengronowitz. 2020. "Dependence and Precarity in the Platform Economy". *Theory and Society* 49: 833–61.

Schreyer, Jasmin. 2021. "Algorithmic Work Co-Ordination and Workers' Voice in the COVID-19 Pandemic: The Case of Foodora/Lieferando". *Work Organisation, Labour and Globalisation* 15(1): 69–84.

Shanahan, Genevieve, and Mark Smith. 2021. "Fair's Fair: Psychological Contracts and Power in Platform Work". *International Journal of Human Resource Management* 32(19): 4078–109.

Shapiro, Aaron. 2018. "Between Autonomy and Control: Strategies of Arbitrage in the 'On-Demand' Economy". *New Media and Society* 20(8): 2954–71.

Standing, Guy. 2011. *The Precariat: The New Dangerous Class*. London: Bloomsbury.

Stanford, Jim. 2017. "The Resurgence of Gig Work: Historical and Theoretical Perspectives". *The Economic and Labour Relations Review* 28(3): 382–401.

Sutherland, Will, Mohammad Hossein Jarrahi, Michael Dunn, and Sarah Nelson. 2020. "Work Precarity and Gig Literacies in Online Freelancing". *Work, Employment and Society* 34(3): 457–75.

Tassanari, Arianna, and Vincenzo Maccarrone. 2020. "Riders on the Storm: Workplace Solidarity among Gig Economy Couriers in Italy and the United Kingdom". *Work, Employment and Society* 34(1): 35–54.

Timko, Peter, and Rianne van Melik. 2021. "Being a Deliveroo Rider: Practices of Platform Labor in Nijmegen and Berlin". *Journal of Contemporary Ethnography* 50(4): 497–523.

Tucker, Eric. 2020. "Towards a Political Economy of Platform-Mediated Work". *Studies in Political Economy* 101 (3): 185–207.

Urzì Brancati, Cesira, Annarosa Pesole, and Enrique Fernández-Macías. 2020. *New Evidence on Platform Workers in Europe. Results from the Second COLLEEM Survey*. Luxembourg: Publications Office of the European Union.

Vallas, Steven, and Juliet Schor. 2020. "What Do Platforms Do? Understanding the Gig Economy". *Annual Review of Sociology* 46: 16.1–22.

Vandaele, Kurt. 2021. "Collective Resistance and Organizational Creativity amongst Europe's Platform Workers: A New Power in the Labour Movement?" In *Work and Labour Relations in Global Platform Capitalism*, edited by J. Haidar and M. Keune, 206–35. Cheltenham, UK and Northampton, MA, USA: Edward Elgar Publishing.

Vandaele, Kurt. 2022. "Vulnerable Food Delivery Platforms under Pressure: Protesting Couriers Seeking 'Algorithmic Justice' and Alternatives". Forthcoming in *Routledge Handbook of the Gig Economy*, edited by I. Ness. New York: Routledge.

van Doorn, Niels. 2020. "At What Price? Labour Politics and Calculative Power Struggles in On-Demand Food Delivery". *Work Organisation, Labour and Globalisation* 14(1): 136–49.

van Doorn, Niels, and Julie Yujie Chen. 2021. "Odds Stacked against Workers: Datafied Gamification on Chinese and American Food Delivery Platforms". *Socio-Economic Review* 19(4): 1345–67.

van Doorn, Niels, and Darsana Vijay. 2021. "Gig Work as Migrant Work: The Platformization of Migration Infrastructure". *Environment and Planning A: Economy and Space*. https://doi.org/10.1177/0308518X211065049.

Vosko, Leah, Martha MacDonald, and Iain Campbell. 2009. "Introduction: Gender and the Concept of Precarious Employment". In *Gender and the Contours of Precarious Employment*, edited by Leah Vosko, Martha MacDonald and Iain Campbell, 1–25. London: Routledge.

Weil, David. 2014. *The Fissured Workplace: Why Work Became So Bad for So Many and What Can be Done to Improve It*. Cambridge: Harvard University Press.

Wood, Alex. 2021. *Algorithmic Management: Consequences for Work Organisation and Working Conditions*. JRC 124874. Seville: European Commission.

Woodcock, Jamie, and Mark Graham. 2020. *The Gig Economy: A Critical Introduction*. Cambridge: Polity Press.

8   On demand work as a legal framework to understand the gig economy

Ruth Dukes[1]

Introduction

The aim of this chapter is to demonstrate the usefulness to scholars, practitioners and policy-makers of characterising gig work as part of a wider category of 'on demand work'.[2] By gig work, I mean both crowd- or cloud-work involving the completion of a series of tasks through online platforms, and 'work on demand via app', meaning the execution of traditional working activities such as transport, cleaning and logistics, through apps managed by firms ('platforms') that also intervene in setting minimum quality standards of service and in the selection and management of the workforce (De Stefano 2016). Here, as elsewhere, I understand 'on demand work' or 'work on demand' broadly, as comprising different forms of contractual and organisational arrangements that are each designed to keep (or have the effect of keeping) the worker hungry for the next shift, and so – in effect – 'on call', ready and willing to work whenever the employer requires it, often at short notice. I use the term 'employer' broadly, too, meaning an organisation that contracts – directly or via a contractual chain – for work in exchange for a wage or a fee.

Categorising gig work as an example of on demand work shines a light on at least three matters of importance when it comes to understanding and regulating gig work. First it highlights the weakness of the platforms' claim to novelty in respect of gig work – the claim that gig work is quite different to work relations of the past. In several important respects, gig work resembles work relations prevalent in early capitalism, before the growth of trade unions and collective bargaining and the creation of modern employment law,[3] and much can be learned from a comparison of the two. Similarly, it demonstrates the weakness of the claim to contemporary uniqueness or difference – the claim that gig work is quite different to other forms of work today and that, therefore, existing employment laws do not apply. Lastly, it suggests a legal framework and lines of legal reasoning that have already been developed by legislatures, courts and scholars, which recognise gig work as wage work, rather than self-employment, and gig workers as the bearers of employment rights.

On demand work

In recent decades, the working relations of increasing numbers of workers have been characterised by impermanence and precarity (Fudge, McCrystal and Sankaran 2012). The once 'standard' employment relationship – full-time employment, on an 'open-ended' rather than 'fixed-term' basis – has tended to become simply one form of work relation among many often less secure and more casual arrangements: for example, agency work, zero-hours contracts and self-employed 'gigging' (Stone and Arthurs 2013). In respect of working relations, and their regulation, there is now much greater variety – and ine- quality – between and within sectors, companies and workplaces.

In this story of fragmentation and precarisation, the weakening of trade unions figures as both cause and effect. Since the 1980s and 1990s, the membership of unions and employers' associations has fallen, in some cases dramatically, and national umbrella organisations have largely lost the positions of authority that they once had within industry and within government (Streeck 2009; Müller, Vandaele and Waddington 2019). The weaker they are, the more difficult the unions find it to resist the kinds of institutional and organisational change that result in precarious work relations. The more precarious work becomes, the more difficult it is to organise workers and to increase union strength. The transformation of previously comprehensive systems of social welfare into a combination of labour market activation devices and, increasingly, only the barest of provision for the otherwise destitute (Glyn 2006) also serves to weaken the ability of workers to refuse low-paid precarious work, since they can't any more rely on an alternative and adequate source of income in the form of unemployment benefits (Adams and Deakin 2014).

As systems of collective industrial relations are dismantled or marginalised, the choice of form of work contract and the drafting of specific terms are increasingly for the employer alone. In some sectors and some organisa- tions, contracts are routinely drafted to take workers outside of the scope of employment rights, including the right to guaranteed hours of work, or to render their situation so precarious that they are ill-placed to enforce any rights that they have. Workers may be designated self-employed within their contracts for work, or hired through an agency, or on a zero-hours contract, or on informal, 'underground' terms, outside of the purview of the authorities and the law. Even where they are hired on contracts of employment, workers may be intentionally underemployed – guaranteed far fewer than the 40 or so hours per week that they would need to earn a full-time wage – and therefore always eager to take on extra shifts should they be offered. As a consequence, work is 'on demand' in the sense that the employer is empowered, in one way or another, to decide when and even if the worker is required. The economic risk of periodic dips in demand – across the course of the day, week or year – is offloaded wholesale onto the worker.

Significant organisational change is a further important part of this story: the shareholder revolution that began in the 1970s and the 'fissuring' of companies and workplaces, to use David Weil's useful term, that has taken place since (Weil 2014). The shareholder revolution was directed at the then dominant idea of the corporation, familiar from Berle and Means (1932), as an organisation much like any other, with professional managers who sought steady growth and who recognised the importance of priorities other than profit-making: 'providing employment, eliminating discrimination [and] avoiding pollution' as Milton Friedman famously put it (1970, 17). According to the new revolutionary creed, managers who pretended to act with 'social responsibility' were in fact pursuing social special interests, namely their own (Friedman 1970). In failing to devote themselves to the maximisation of profit, they stole from their principals, the shareholders, and made the capital entrusted to them less productive than it could have been. Only the market, with its strict principles of ruthless competition on penalty of elimination, kept business honest, and only maximised profits ultimately served a society that depends on a capitalist economy. As eventually facilitated by law reform and, more so, deep-seated cultural change, the shareholder revolution involved a re-privatisation of the corporation, extricating it from its social entanglements and quasi-public status and instituting as supreme the objective of profit-making in the service of capital accumulation. When, in the 1980s and 1990s, globalisation created an unprecedented degree of both capital mobility and competition, the profit constraint on businesses became increasingly tight, and with it the constraints on governments trying to impose social responsibilities on national economies other than the maximisation of profits in increasingly global markets and global value chains (Klare 2002; Bercusson and Estlund 2008; O'Higgins 2004).

As coined by Weil (2014), the term fissuring refers to the variety of means employed by companies to create a legal gap or 'fissure' between themselves and the workers who would otherwise be employed 'in-house', directly by them. Typically, fissuring is achieved through the outsourcing of work to other, smaller firms, or to the workers themselves, who are categorised in that case (in their contracts, and in the eyes of the law) as self-employed. For a lead company, such arrangements involve savings in labour costs as wages are replaced by a price payable for 'labour services', and liability is offloaded for tax and social security contributions and for compensation for workplace accidents and other injuries to the workers' health. For workers, fissuring can mean that jobs that once resided inside lead companies, providing decent earnings and stable employment, now reside with often smaller firms who set wages and other terms under far more competitive conditions. Alternatively, it can mean that jobs disappear entirely to be replaced by offers of contracts for services: offers to perform the work as self-employed workers. In any case, workers are forced into intense competition 'outside' of the lead firms, ensuring that they cannot capture a significant share of those firms' profits, nor rely on the bureaucratic decision-making, disciplinary and grievance procedures typical of larger firms. Union organising and the collective representation of workers' interests become more difficult as decision-making is dispersed along contractual chains, the employer function split between two or more organisations, and workers taken outside of the scope of labour rights. At a societal level, fissuring leads to decreases in tax revenue and social security contributions and to an increase in inequalities as income is transferred from workers to shareholders, company executives and – to a lesser but still significant extent – consumers.

At the same time as globalisation and financialisation have created pressures on businesses and other organisations to shed large parts of their workforces, advances in technology have made it possible both to set quality standards and to monitor compliance without having to take or keep production – and work – in-house. An ever-expanding array of new technologies has been developed including bar codes, electronic data inter-change protocols, product identification, GPS and other methods of tracking products through supply chains and monitoring the provision of services to customers (Weil 2014, 60–72; Rogers 2023). These may make it possible, too, for lead firms or their subcontractors to contract with workers or labour intermediaries in countries of the Global South, likely in a position in which they are forced to accept lower wages or a lower price for the work. Global value chains materialise in the form of global chains of contracts, with the sum that will eventually be paid to the workers squeezed further with each new link (LeBaron 2021; LeBaron and Roberts 2010).

While fissuring may signal the demise of huge organisations as measured by the size of the workforce, it has not entailed the disappearance of firms with huge market shares. Simultaneous to fissuring, an additional contemporary trend has involved, on the contrary, the consolidation of capital and the creation of companies that – if not quite monopolies – exercise sufficient control over essential resources within their sectors to enjoy quasi-monopoly power. Like fissuring, consolidation is facilitated by law – especially weak anti-trust or competition rules and strong intellectual property rights – and by technological advances (Rogers 2023). From a worker's perspective, it results in power disparities of breath-taking proportions between the worker, or the small firm that employs her, and the lead firm; the latter acting either as the employer (and perhaps the only or major employer in a particular locality), or more likely the purchaser of labour services, looking to bring production costs down (Weil 2009).

Something new?

Gig work is an extreme example of fissuring, where the entire labour process is designed to meet the objective of not directly employing *any* workers, bar a tiny core of directors, brand managers and so on. It is central to the business model of platforms such as Uber and TaskRabbit that they should be able to provide services more cheaply than their competitors – at least for as long as it takes for them to achieve monopoly or quasi-monopoly status within a particular market, with winner-takes-all returns (Tucker 2019; Rahman and Thelen 2019). Contracting with self-employed workers not only allows the platform to save on wages, tax and social security, and potentially to avoid liability for accidents at work; it also allows them to offload the costs of machinery and tools (Prassl 2018). Uber drivers must buy or lease their own cars, DoorDash and Deliveroo couriers use their own bikes or motorcycles. The only thing that the platform owns is the app.

In order to justify the characterisation of workers as self-employed, platforms describe themselves as mere third parties, facilitating contracts of sale between customers and drivers, couriers and domestic workers, and providing clever algorithms and sophisticated ratings and other technology to keep transaction costs low to negligible. Workers are actively encouraged to think of themselves as 'entrepreneurs', enjoying freedom, flexibility and autonomy (Ravenelle 2017, 286–8). Innovation is an important part of the platforms' branding and they present themselves accordingly as doing something truly novel – not taxi provision but 'ride-sharing'; not cleaning and ironing but 'neighbours helping neighbours' – something, importantly, to which existing laws and regulations do not apply (Prassl 2018). Indeed, to insist upon the application of burdensome rules and regulations to these activities, so the narrative goes, would stifle innovation in a way that was damaging not only to the platforms but also to customers and 'entrepreneurs' alike (Tucker 2019).

When the most prominent platforms launched around a decade ago,[4] commentators in business schools willingly parroted the platforms' lines, hailing the arrival of a truly novel form of institution (Sundararajan 2016, 69). Sociologists and scholars of employment law, in contrast, were quick to call the platforms out on the purported novelty of gig work (De Stefano 2016; Huws, Spencer and Syrdal 2018). As empirical analysis soon revealed, it was categorically *not* the case that platforms had invented a modus operandi which obviated the need for the kind of top-down control of the labour process under managerial prerogative, typical of vertically integrated employing organisations (De Stefano 2016; Dubal 2017). For Uber, TaskRabbit and the like to function as intended, they require at a minimum that a sufficient number of drivers, couriers or taskers make themselves available for work at the right times of day and, second, that those workers readily agree to undertake whatever gigs are assigned to them. In some cases, platforms also require that the gigs be completed in a particular way, for example, with a particular level of customer service.

While they have not done away with the need for control and direction, however, the platforms have succeeded in minimising or obviating their reliance on contractual obligations to ensure that workers perform as required. In part this is achieved through technological innovation, including close monitoring and the embedding within the app of a ratings system (which transfers arbitrary power over workers from managers to consumers). Technology of this kind can depersonalise managerial control making it appear impartial and 'objective', in the sense of a natural condition of the material world. At a time when weakened employment rights and rights to social welfare have significantly lessened the attractiveness of exit options for gig workers, the constant threat of 'deactivation' – summary dismissal, by any other name – or lesser forms of punishment, such as the withholding by the platform of better (more lucrative) gigs, also contribute significantly to ensuring good behaviour (Ravenelle 2019). To orchestrate a supply of labour that is always sufficient to meet demand for services, meanwhile, platforms wield the promise of the award to a worker not only of a better rate of pay – 'surge-pricing' – but of a higher rating and, consequently, better gigs; the threat of a lower rating and poorer gigs (Cant 2020). There is nothing transparent about these ratings systems, however, and of course no right of appeal for workers when they don't function as promised or expected (Prassl 2019).

In his 2018 book, *Humans as a Service*, Jeremias Prassl argued that it was precisely on the question of the nature of work and working relations in the gig economy that the platforms' claims to innovation could most resolutely be refuted. Gig work had been said to herald a 'revolution' in economic activity; an 'interesting hybrid of a market and a hierarchy', involving, in particular, a reversal of previous trends to ever greater specialisation in work organisation and a previously unknown immediacy of labour supply (Sundararajan 2016, 69; Prassl 2018, 73). With reference to two examples from the nineteenth century – outwork (or 'homework') and dock work – Prassl demonstrated convincingly that these aspects of gig work were anything but new. Like gig workers, outworkers relied on middlemen to bring them orders from buyers. As such they could find their earnings squeezed by the middlemen taking their cut and, yet further, by the obligations imposed upon them to buy and maintain their own equipment and machinery. If orders dried up, they received no income at all. At the docks, where there was a perennial oversupply of labour, workers were made to stand – literally in 'crowds' – hoping to be one of the chosen few to be offered work that day. Even when work was offered, there was no guarantee of a full day's employment and pay. Both kinds of work were characterised, then, by extreme precarity, vulnerability and low pay.

If neoliberalism implies a desired return to the political economy of the nineteenth century – the stateless, globally integrated world economy of the gold standard (Streeck 2019) – then there is indeed a logic to scrutinising the labour and service markets of that era for precursors of gig work: markets that were characterised by gross inequalities of wealth, by only minimal public services and by the fragmented, non-universal, provision of social welfare, or charity in lieu of welfare. A prominent but frequently underacknowledged feature of those markets was the magnitude of the percentage of the workforce that was employed in domestic service. At its height, at the end of the nineteenth century, 40% of women workers in the UK were domestic workers and in 1902, over 200,000 men were also employed in that sector, mostly in gardening, the care of horses or as drivers (Delap 2011, 12, 14). Moreover, the employment of domestic servants was very widespread, and not at all confined to the upper classes: middle and even working-class families also frequently employed 'help' (Delap 2011, 63–97). If we define domestic service broadly to include stable hands, chauffeurs and governesses as well as maids, cooks and manservants, then we might conclude that, in time, domestic workers were replaced by motor cars and kitchen appliances, and by the improved provision of public services: schools, nurseries and transport. Domestic work did not, however, disappear and, since the 1980s, has been on the increase again in the UK and other developed economies (Delap 2011, 3). Today it might take a similar form to the domestic service of the nineteenth century, albeit with an updated nomenclature – 'personal assistants', 'cleaners', 'housekeepers', 'nannies' – or it might be arranged via online platforms: TaskRabbit, Uber or Deliveroo.

That domestic service is so often overlooked in discussions of gig work is regrettable since there is much to learn from a comparison of the two. In addition to functional continuities between domestic service in the nineteenth and twentieth centuries and many kinds of platform work today, for example, the manner of their management and regulation is comparable by reason of the key role played, in each case, by employer or customer ratings. In the nineteenth and early twentieth centuries, the reference that a domestic worker might request of her employer was known as a 'character', emphasising that this would be testament, first and foremost, to the servant's moral qualities rather than her experience or qualifications (Flanagan 2019). Although the worker's ability to find new employment might rest to a very great extent on the possession of a good reference, the current or former employer was under no legal obligation to provide one. The ability to withhold or to threaten to withhold a reference was thus an extremely powerful tool of management or control of the servant, and went some way towards giving the working relationship the form of something more like servitude than service or (arm's length contractual) employment (Delap 2011, 51–52, 74–75). In the gig economy today, customer ratings are amalgamated and displayed to future users as an aid to their decision whether or not to choose the worker in question (Prassl 2018, 53–55). They are also used by the platform itself as a tool of management, as data fed into the algorithms that determine such critical matters as the distribution of gigs – who will be offered which work. As a result, workers can feel pressured to undertake a good deal of additional, unpaid labour, including emotional labour, aimed at 'optimising the customer experience', or, more simply, making the customer like them. Moreover, the higher the rating they achieve, the more tightly they become bound to a particular platform, since leaving that platform for another will mean leaving the rating behind too (Prassl 2018, 111–13).

Like gig work, domestic work poses particular challenges when it comes to the collective organisation of the workforce. In the late nineteenth and early twentieth centuries, several attempts were made to unionise domestic servants but faltered, in part, at least, because of the workers' isolation from one another, and their singularly long hours of work (Delap 2011, 89–93; Schwartz 2014). It was also the case that the major trade unions were reluctant to include domestic workers as members, Ernest Bevin declaring in 1931 that he would not seek to recruit (the mostly female) servants in private employment to the Transport and General Union, but only the (mostly male) gardeners, chauffeurs and other servants employed in public institutions (Delap 2011,

89–90). Where efforts at organisation were partially or temporarily successful, it is interesting to note that – contra the purportedly 'voluntarist' tradition in British industrial relations – the demands made on behalf of the membership were formulated in terms of decidedly legal rights and obligations (Delap 2011, 50, 87). The primary desire was to transform domestic service from a status to a contractual relationship (Streeck 1992). Given the imbalance of power in the anticipated relationship, however, not only the emancipatory but also the potentially exploitative elements of this move were recognised by the workers. Consequently, their desiderata included not only the contract but also a series of statutory rights that would function to limit the parties' contractual freedom (in practice, the employer's freedom to exploit): both those rights already accorded to other types of worker – maximum hours, holiday pay, health and safety inspections – and additional rights tailored to the particularities of domestic service, such as to decent accommodation and to a fair reference (Schwartz 2014, 187–88).

Without either significant membership or the support of the stronger, better established trade unions, domestic workers' unions found their demands for decent work easily neglected by the British state. In contrast to other sectors in which unions remained weak and wages low, no trades board or wages council was ever created in respect of domestic service, and no legislation ever passed to extend the statutory rights of industrial workers to that sector. At the end of the First World War, when women's enforced redundancy from wartime factory and agricultural jobs inflated the numbers of unemployed workers registering at Employment Exchanges, and as eligible for state unemployment benefits, a policy decision was taken to encourage women workers, very actively, into domestic service (Aiken 2002). In 1922, for example, new regulations required the Exchanges to offer female claimants domestic work. This placed a woman in a double bind: if she rejected the job, she would be ineligible for unemployment benefit on the basis that she had refused work that she was capable of doing. If she accepted it, she left the unemployment scheme completely, since domestic service was not among the specified 'insured trades' (Whiteside 2015).

The experience of these workers in the 1920s raises important questions regarding the role of the state in the emergence and growing prevalence today of gig and other forms of precarious, low-paid work. As Noel Whiteside has carefully illustrated with detailed historical and comparative accounts, governments can construct different definitions of 'the unemployed' – meaning quite specifically those to whom unemployment benefits of one kind or another may be paid – in accordance with the policy aims of the day: 'The category of "unemployed" can never be a given fact…but is largely a socio-political product derived from prevalent assumptions about how labour markets should work and the role (if any) public authorities are expected to play in this operation' (Whiteside 2015, 152).

If a government is so minded, legal definitions of unemployment, and the provision of welfare payments consequent upon them, may be fashioned so as to contribute to the creation of a 'floor' of minimum wages and other terms and conditions below which workers needn't accept work. If they refuse lower paid or more insecure work, they will not lose their entitlement to benefits.

At the beginning of the twentieth century in the UK, a system of government funded and administered social security was introduced with the primary aim of addressing poverty and pauperism consequent on a 'want of work' (Whiteside 2015, 154). The terms of the new legislation were shaped by a rationale which sought to concentrate available work in the hands of the most productive workmen so as to promote industrial efficiency and, at the same time, decasualisation. As the then young William Beveridge put it in 1907:

> Irregular work and earnings make for irregular habits; conditions of employment in which a man stands to gain or lose so little by his good or bad behaviour make for irresponsibility, laziness, insubordination [...] The line between independence and dependence, between the efficient and the unemployable, must be made clearer. Every place in 'free' industry, carrying with it the rights of citizenship – civil liberty, fatherhood, conduct of one's own life and government of a family – should be a 'whole' place involving full employment and earnings up to a definite minimum. (Beveridge 1907, 326–27, cited Whiteside 2015, 155)

In the National Insurance Act of 1911, an unemployed worker was defined as he who was capable of work but unable to find a 'suitable' position. Importantly, 'suitable' was here interpreted to mean suitable for the particular worker in question – his particular trade, skills and experience – and this, in turn, was understood to mean that a worker should not be expected to work for less than the going (i.e., collectively agreed) rate (Deakin and Wilkinson 2005, 166–67). In line with the aim of combatting casualisation, in other words, the Act was used to support rather than to undermine the collective negotiation of decent wages by trade unions and employers' associations.

By reason of the exclusion of domestic service from this system of social welfare, as we have seen, a gap in the floor was created through which domestic workers were allowed to fall. And they were allowed to fall, moreover, quite deliberately, and not at all by accident, so as to ensure an adequate supply of domestic workers (solving the 'servant problem' that was so much discussed in the media of the day) and, at the same time, to limit the costs to the public purse of the new National Insurance (Aiken 2002). Today, in this post-financial crisis age of austerity, can we assume that cuts to welfare benefits are partly to blame for the emergence and growth of gig work? What of welfare systems that actively incentivise workers to accept low-paid and 'low hour' work through the provision of tax credits (Adams and Deakin 2014); or through the institution of a universal minimum income of the type advocated for – and this should come as no surprise – by Silicon Valley insiders (Sadowski 2016)? To what extent are governments complicit, in other words, in the prevalence of 'indecent' work, perhaps actively encouraging people into insecure and poorly paid jobs with the aim of keeping unemployment figures low?

Further clues as to government complicity or hesitancy in respect of the regulation of gig work can be found in the growing literature on the political economy of 'platform capitalism' (Srnicek 2017; Rahman and Thelen 2019). Here we learn the secrets of the platforms' ability to provide services at such very low prices; lower even than routine tax and social security avoidance would otherwise allow. A first point to note is the extent to which platforms' business models can rest on the capacity to extract ('harvest') immense amounts of data from all those who interact with the platform: workers, customers, producers and advertisers. That data is then either harnessed by the platforms themselves in their interactions with platform users, and/or sold on to third parties. As Nick Srnicek has shown, data can serve a number of 'key capitalist functions': educating and giving competitive advantage to algorithms; enabling the coordination of workers; allowing for the optimisation and flexibility of productive processes; and making possible the transformation of low-margin goods into high-margin services (Srnicek 2017, 41–42). That the 'visible' element of platforms' activities – taxi provision, food delivery, odd jobs – is often quite secondary to such data harvesting goes some way to explaining why platforms are able to undercut competitor service providers (Srnicek 2017, 60). Amazon, for example, regularly makes losses on its sale and delivery of consumer goods, but cross-subsidises these from other branches of its empire (Srnicek 2017, 60–61).

A second explanation for the capacity of platforms to sustain losses lies with their easy access to 'patient capital' (Rahman and Thelen 2019). Since the financial crisis of 2008, a cash glut has arisen in the global economy by reason of the monetary policy interventions of national governments, combined with increases in corporate savings and the expansion of tax havens (Srnicek 2017). Tech start-ups have been among the main beneficiaries of investors who are in no great hurry to turn a profit. As Rahman and Thelen explain, however, this patient capital is quite different to the patient capital characteristic of coordinated market economies in the twentieth century: patience is no longer exercised in the interests of all stakeholders, including labour, but rather to facilitate the concentration of control in the interests of powerful managers and investors pursuing monopoly or near-monopoly status in service markets and – eventually – winner-take-all returns (Rahman and Thelen 2019).

In addition to user-friendly apps and clever marketing, platforms' ability to provide services at very low and even loss-making prices explains, in turn, their great popularity with consumers (Rahman and Thelen 2019). As wages fall or stagnate across the board, and public services are cut and cut again, consumers can become reliant on cheap services; platforms can come to form part of the infrastructure of their lives – as domestic servants did 100 years ago. Capitalising on this, platforms portray themselves as the champions of consumer interests and enlist the captive consumers as political allies. Here then is a further explanation of the apparent reluctance of government in some jurisdictions to enforce laws, including employment laws, against the platforms. Politicians face the risk that regulation might alienate their constituents, denying them access to the cheap goods and services upon which they have come to depend (Culpepper and Thelen 2019).

Something different?

With political will lacking, in many jurisdictions, to protect the rights of gig workers by means of legislation, workers and trade unions have increasingly turned to the courts. Time and again, judges have rejected the platforms' claims that the terms of their contracts with workers and specifically, the lack of contractual obligations on the part of workers to turn up for work, mean that the workers are self-employed (De Stefano et al. 2021). Instead, courts have tended to focus on the powers that the platform has *in reality* to direct the worker and control the manner of work, finding variously that workers are employees or dependent contractors with employment rights, rather than independent self-employed workers (De Stefano et al. 2021). In doing so, they have relied in part on precedent that predates the emergence of platform-mediated gig work and dealt instead with other forms of precarious and on demand work (De Stefano et al. 2021).

However welcome these court decisions may be, they do not constitute a happy ending to the story of gig workers and employment law. In jurisdictions in which employment status is tied to the terms of the contract, any court decision declaring workers to be employees or dependent contractors applies directly only to those workers named in the litigation and, by implication, others employed on *identical contractual terms*. It serves, from the platforms' point of view, as an invitation to redraft their contracts, working around the terms of the new ruling, so as to be able to claim, again, that the workers on the new contracts are self-employed. Even where it seems highly likely that those employed under the new contracts are also employees or dependent contractors, it will take a new decision of the court to confirm that this is so, creating the opportunity for further years-long appeal processes. In many jurisdictions today, moreover, the employment rights accorded to workers as a result of a court victory can be rather meagre. Minimum wages may be set at a level below the cost of living, for example, and other employment rights (including rights to a measure of job security) may not apply for one reason or another. By reason of their precarity, finally, gig workers are likely to face particular difficulties in attempting to enforce those rights that they have.

Looking beyond the question of employment status, there are aspects of platform-mediated work that are – if not, or no longer, unique to such work – genuinely novel, and worthy of consideration by policy-and law-makers. From the perspective of the worker, 'management by algorithm' and the associated lack of easy access to any human representative of the platform can result in extremely time-consuming and highly frustrating efforts to solve work-related problems, such as non-payment or under-payment of wages (Ravenelle 2019; Kantor, Weise and Ashford 2021). When the problem in question involves emotive matters such as perceived unfair treatment, an 'accidental' firing, or work-related illness, frustration may be compounded by feelings of hurt and humiliation at the lack of a human response (Kantor, Weise and Ashford 2021). Management by an algorithm raises questions of the rightful limits of managerial control (Wood et al. 2018; Ravenelle 2019), the dignity and health and safety of the worker, including mental health (Cefaliello and Inversi, this volume), and privacy rights (Rogers 2023). Where customers repeatedly rate female and black workers lower than their white, male counterparts, with significant consequences for the terms and conditions of the workers in question, the possibility arises of breach of equality law (Kullmann 2018).

Conclusion

Court decisions from around the world have tended to confirm the view of legal scholars that gig work is not *sui generis* but rather a further example of highly precarious, casualised work relations, designed by platforms to keep them supplied with work on demand. Platforms propagated the claim to newness as a deliberate strategy of liability avoidance: attempting to characterise the activity as something other than work, and themselves as something other than employers, so as to avoid having to comply with employment laws and to pay taxes and social security contributions (Tucker 2019). Some features of gig work are novel and will require the development of new rules, or the reasoned application of existing rules and principles, by legislatures and courts. The fragility of court decisions regarding employment status points to the desirability of legislation to settle the matter once and for all provided that the necessary political will can be built.

Notes

1. Professor of Labour Law, University of Glasgow. https://orcid.org/0000-0001 -7515-0941
2. The chapter draws on two earlier publications (Dukes 2020; Dukes and Streeck 2022). The project leading to these publications is funded by the European Research Council (ERC) under the European Union's Horizon 2020 research and innovation programme (grant agreement No. 757395).
3. I use 'employment law' widely in this chapter to include what in some jurisdictions is called 'individual' and 'collective' employment law and in others 'employment law' and 'labour law'.
4. TaskRabbit launched in 2008, Uber in 2009, Lyft in 2012, Deliveroo in 2013 and Foodora in 2014.

References

Adams, Zoe and Simon Deakin. 2014. *Reregulating Zero Hours Contracts*. Liverpool: Institute of Employment Rights.
Aiken, Diane. 2002. *The Central Committee on Women's Training and Employment: Tackling the Servant Problem, 1914–1945*. Oxford: Oxford Brookes University.
Bercusson, Brian and Cynthia Estlund. 2008. 'Introduction'. In *Regulating Labour in the Wake of Globalisation: New Challenges, New Institutions*, edited by Brian Bercusson and Cynthia Estlund, 1–18. Oxford: Hart.
Berle, Adolf and Gardiner Means. 1932. *The Modern Corporation and Private Property*. New York: Macmillan.
Beveridge. William H. 1907. 'The Problem of the Unemployed'. *Sociological Papers* 3: 322–29.
Cant, Callum. 2020. *Riding for Deliveroo: Resistance in the New Economy*. Cambridge: Polity.
Culpepper, Pepper D. and Kathleen Thelen. 2019. 'Are we all Amazon Primed? Consumers and the Politics of Platform Power'. *Comparative Political Studies* 53(2): 288–318.
Deakin, Simon and Frank Wilkinson. 2005. *The Law of the Labour Market*. Oxford: Oxford University Press.

Delap, Lucy. 2011. *Knowing Their Place: Domestic Service in Twentieth Century Britain.* Oxford: Oxford University Press.

De Stefano, Valerio. 2016. 'The Rise of the "Just-in-Time Workforce": On-Demand Work, Crowd Work and Labour Protection in the "Gig-Economy"'. *Comparative Labor Law & Policy Journal* 37(3): 471–504.

De Stefano, Valerio, Ilda Durri, Charalampos Stylogiannis and Mathias Wouters. 2021. 'Platform Work and the Employment Relationship'. *ILO Working Paper* 27.

Dubal, Veena B. 2017. 'Winning the Battle, Losing the War: Assessing the Impact of Misclassification Litigation on Workers in the Gig Economy'. *Wisconsin Law Review* 98(1): 739–802.

Dukes, Ruth. 2020. 'Regulating Gigs'. *Modern Law Review* 83(1): 217–28.

Dukes, R. and Wolfgang Streeck. 2022. *Democracy at Work: Contract, Status and Post-Industrial Justice.* Cambridge: Polity.

Flanagan, Frances. 2019. 'Theorising the Gig Economy and Home-based Service Work'. *Journal of Industrial Relations* 61(1): 57–78.

Friedman, Milton. 1970. 'The Social Responsibility of Business is to Increase its Profits'. *The New York Times Magazine*, September 13, 17.

Fudge, Judy, Shae McCrystal and Kamala Sankaran. 2012. *Challenging the Legal Boundaries of Work Regulation.* London: Bloomsbury.

Glyn, Andrew. 2006. *Capitalism Unleashed: Finance Globalization and Welfare.* Oxford: Oxford University Press.

Huws, Ursula, Neil H. Spencer and Dag S. Syrdal. 2018. 'Online, On Call: The Spread of Digitally Organised Just-in-time Working and its Implications for Standard Employment Models'. *New Technology, Work and Employment* 33(2): 113–29.

Kantor, Jodi, Karen Weise and Grace Ashford. 2021. 'The Amazon That Customers Don't See'. *New York Times*, June 15. https:// www .nytimes .com/ 2021/ 06/ 15/ briefing/amazon-warehouse-investigation.html.

Klare, Karl. 2002. 'Horizons of Transformative Labour Law'. In *Labour Law in an Era of Globalisation: Transformative Practices and Possibilities*, edited by Joanne Conaghan, R. Michael Fischl and Karl Klare, 3–30. Oxford: Oxford University Press.

Kullmann, Miriam. 2018. 'Platform Work, Algorithmic Decision-Making, and EU Gender Equality Law'. *International Journal of Comparative Labour Law and Industrial Relations* 34(1): 1–21.

LeBaron, Genevieve. 2021. 'Wages: An Overlooked Dimension of Business and Human Rights in Global Supply Chains'. *Business and Human Rights Journal* 6(1): 1–20.

LeBaron, Genevieve and Adrienne Roberts. 2010. 'Towards a Feminist Political Economy of Capitalism and Carcerality'. *Signs* 36(1): 19–44.

Müller, Torsten, Kurt Vandaele and Jeremy Waddington. 2019. *Collective Bargaining in Europe: Towards an Endgame.* Brussels: European Trade Union Institute.

O'Higgins, Paul. 2004. 'The End of Labour Law as We Have Known It?'. In *The Future of Labour Law; Liber Amicorum Bob Hepple QC*, edited by Catherine Barnard, Simon Deakin and Gillian Morris, 289–302. Oxford: Oxford University Press.

Prassl, Jeremias. 2018. *Humans as a Service: The Promise and Perils of Work in the Gig Economy.* Oxford: Oxford University Press.

Prassl, Jeremias. 2019. 'What if Your Boss Was an Algorithm? Economic Incentives, Legal Challenges, and the Rise of Artificial Intelligence at Work'. *Comparative Labor Law and Policy Journal* 41(1): 123–46.

Rahman, K. Sabeel and Kathleen Thelen. 2019. 'The Rise of the Platform Business Model and the Transformation of Twenty-First Century Capitalism'. *Politics and Society* 47(2): 177–204.

Ravenelle, Alexandrea. 2017. 'Sharing Economy Workers: Selling, Not Sharing'. *Cambridge Journal of Regions, Economy and Society* 10(2): 281–95.

Ravenelle, Alexandrea. 2019. *Hustle and Gig: Struggling and Surviving in the Sharing Economy*. Oakland: University of California Press.

Rogers, Brishen. 2023. *Data and Democracy at Work*. Cambridge: MIT Press, forthcoming.

Sadowski, Jathan. 2016. 'Why Silicon Valley is Embracing Universal Basic Income'. *The Guardian*, June 22.

Schwartz, Laura. 2014. '"What We Think Is Needed Is a Union of Domestics Such As the Miners Have": The Domestic Workers' Union of Great Britain and Ireland 1908–14'. *Twentieth Century British History* 25(2): 173–98.

Srnicek, Nick. 2017. *Platform Capitalism*. Cambridge: Polity.

Stone, Katherine and Harry Arthurs. 2013. *Rethinking Workplace Regulation: Beyond the Standard Contract of Employment*. New York: Russell Sage Foundation.

Streeck, Wolfgang. 1992. 'Revisiting Status and Contract: Pluralism, Corporatism and Flexibility'. In *Social Institutions and Economic Performance* by Wolfgang Streeck, 41–75. Thousand Oaks: Sage.

Streeck, Wolfgang. 2009. *Re-Forming Capitalism: Institutional Change in the German Political Economy*. Oxford: Oxford University Press.

Streeck, Wolfgang. 2019. 'Fighting the State'. *Development and Change* 50(3): 836–47.

Sundararajan, Arun. 2016. *The Sharing Economy: The End of Employment and the Rise of Crowd-Based Capitalism*. Cambridge: MIT Press.

Tucker, Eric. 2019. 'Uber and the Making and Unmaking of Taxi Capitalisms'. In *Law and the 'Sharing Economy': Regulating Online Market Platforms*, edited by Derek McKee, Finn Makela and Teresa Scassa, 357–92. Ottawa: University of Ottawa Press.

Weil, David. 2009. 'Rethinking the Regulation of Vulnerable Work in the USA: A Sector-Based Approach'. *Journal of Industrial Relations* 51(3): 411–30.

Weil, David. 2014. *The Fissured Workplace. Why Work Became So Bad for So Many and What Can Be Done To Improve It*. Harvard: Harvard University Press.

Whiteside, Noel. 2015. 'Who Were the Unemployed? Conventions, Classifications and Social Security Law in Britain (1911–1934)'. *Historical Social Research* 40(1): 150–70.

Wood, Alex, Mark Graham, Vili Lehdonvirta and Isis Hjorth. 2018. 'Good Gig, Bad Gig: Autonomy and Algorithmic Control in the Global Gig Economy'. *Work, Economy and Society* 33(1): 56–75.

9 Domestic work and the gig economy

Natalie Sedacca[1]

Introduction

The gig economy and platform work present a series of challenges for workers' rights, including a lack of security and guaranteed hours, mis-classification of workers as self-employed independent contractors, the absence of basic rights protections, and obstacles to collective bargaining (e.g., De Stefano and Aloisi 2019; Behrendt, Nguyen, and Rani 2019; ILO 2021b). This chapter addresses domestic work in the gig economy: the provision of cleaning, childcare, and other housework through online platforms.[2] This is a growing sector, with figures showing a rise from a total of 28 domestic work platforms worldwide in 2010 to 224 in 2020 (ILO 2021a, xvii) but it has received little attention to date compared to its importance (Mateescu and Ticona 2020, 58; Dukes 2020, 222). As a form of labour primarily performed by women within the 'private sphere' of the home and family, domestic work has long been devalued and is often subject to exclusions from rights protections and/or failures to enforce rights (e.g., Gutiérrez Rodríguez 2010; Mantouvalou 2012; Albin 2012; Mullally and Murphy 2014). The move to provide domestic work through platforms could be expected to increase the sector's visibility and therefore to facilitate increased protection and recognition of domestic workers. However, this chapter argues that the risks in the gig economy model tend to intersect with and exacerbate, rather than offset, longstanding shortcomings in the regulation of domestic work.

The chapter draws on a small number of existing studies of domestic work in the gig economy, which focus on Australia (Flanagan 2019), South Africa (Hunt and Samman 2020), the US (Mateescu and Ticona 2020), Berlin and New York (van Doorn 2021), and Denmark and other Nordic countries (Kilhoffer et al. 2019; Jesnes and Nordli Oppegaard 2020). Given the lack of empirical or detailed studies of domestic work and the gig economy in Britain,[3] it also utilises first-hand analysis of platforms providing cleaning services (cleanzy.com, helpling.co.uk, Handy UK, TaskRabbit UK, eMop and TidyChoice) and childcare (childcare.co.uk, sitters.co.uk, Yoopies and Bubble), which were identified as relevant through references in the limited literature and web searches. Each platform's website was reviewed, including the information this provides about working for them, alongside external articles about the platform and worker reviews on the site indeed.com where available.[4]

The next section addresses key challenges raised by domestic work and the gig economy, considering their interrelations with (a) other forms of domestic work and (b) work in other sectors of the gig economy. It analyses how the denial of employee status and employment rights existing across the gig economy manifests itself in domestic work, creating a precarious situation for workers. It further argues that the increased visibility that comes from working via a platform has not translated to improved rights in and valuation of domestic work, instead exacerbating surveillance and control of workers. Ranking and algorithms amount to a new means for the domination of workers and can undermine the supposed flexibility of work in the gig economy, amplify prejudiced views by service users, and cause unfairness when utilised to determine whether workers can remain on platforms and the work available to them.

Section 3 begins by outlining the longstanding devaluation of domestic work through its association with the 'private sphere' of the home and family and conflation with women's unpaid labour in family homes. It addresses the distinctive manifestation of this phenomenon in the gig economy through a lack of guaranteed hourly rates and unpaid travel time/costs, lower rates for domestic and cleaning work and the segmentation of women into these roles. It argues that these conditions perpetuate devaluation in the sector and undermine attempts to improve conditions. Section 4 considers the difficulties of collective bargaining and organisation in domestic work and the gig economy before presenting two known examples of collective agreements between unions and domestic work platforms. It highlights the significance of these developments and the setbacks the more established agreement has faced, identifying shortcomings in legal protection for gig workers' freedom of association and arguing for the universal protection of collective organisation based on human rights standards. The chapter concludes by outlining an agenda for further research, drawing some preliminary conclusions from the material available to date. Given the continuities it highlights between the exploitation and lack of rights for gig economy domestic workers with those in other types of domestic work as well as elsewhere in the gig economy, it argues for strategies to improve rights to take on board insights from analysis of feminised forms of labour that have traditionally been excluded from labour law protection.

Domestic work and the gig economy – key challenges

Employment rights and status classification

The gig economy is characterised by a lack of employment rights and denial of employment status, allowing platforms to shift risk directly onto workers and leave them outside labour and social rights protections (De Stefano and Aloisi 2019, 366; Hauben, Lenaerts, and Wayaert 2020, 8, 20). In Britain, this plays out against the background of three classifications: employee status, as defined in Employment Rights Act 1996, s230(1) and (2), comes with all statutory employment rights, while s230(3) of the same Act defines 'worker' status ('limb b worker'), which provides for more limited rights, including minimum wage and working time protection, but not remedies for unfair dismissal. Those deemed not to meet either definition are viewed as self-employed independent contractors excluded from even the limited 'limb b worker' set of rights, and many platform websites allude to this third status. The Helpling site, for example, says that 'As a self-employed service provider, you are your own boss… You decide where, when and what cleaning offers you accept and at which hourly rate.' While the opportunity for workers to set their own prices is portrayed as a free choice, this tends to create a 'race to the bottom' (van Doorn 2021, 61). It poses a danger of pay rates that are, at worst, below minimum wage, but in any event not high enough to offset other costs of being self-employed and thus without benefits such as holiday and sick pay. Cleaners placed in direct competition are pushed to minimise the rates they request, while lack of sick pay makes being ill 'a problem that you have to solve' – an especially troubling position to be in during a pandemic (Altenried and Niebler 2021).

The security and protection gaps in the gig economy and other forms of precarious work are often purportedly justified through the concept of 'flexibility' – the idea that workers benefit from choosing when they want to work rather than having to commit to particular hours. While some worker reviews praise flexibility unequivocally (e.g., regarding Tidy Choice), elsewhere this is more tempered. A review of Helpling praises the flexibility of working hours before noting the lack of pension, holiday and sick pay provision give the role's location in the gig economy, exemplifying how flexibility can be a double-edged sword. The situation calls into question why individuals that need some control over their hours should have to pay for this though a lack of basic benefits and security.

Employment security is also a substantial concern. Not only do non-employees fall outside unfair dismissal protections, but also, platform workers often lack access to social protection, which is an especially prevalent problem for those who depend on gig economy work as opposed to those who perform it as a way of generating additional income (Behrendt, Nguyen, and Rani 2019, 20–25). This mirrors the domestic work sector, where lack of social security access has been especially stark in the pandemic context: with 81.2% of domestic workers in informal employment, many lack access to income replacement or support schemes (ILO 2021b, 24, 230). This problem is pronounced in the UK owing to limitations in the coverage of schemes for employed and self-employed persons (Adam, Miller, and Waters 2020; Ewing and Hendy 2020, 519) and the bar on most migrant workers on visas accessing benefits from public funds (Yeo 2019). Even where platforms ostensibly provided sick pay or other benefits during COVID-19, this was hampered by a lack of clarity, overly demanding paperwork requirements and workers' fears of retribution including deactivation if relying on these mechanisms (Mateescu and Ticona 2021). Without a safety net, the consequences of losing platform work are more severe, intensifying pressure to accept poor conditions.

Visibility, surveillance, and control

Domestic work traditionally suffers from a lack of visibility and scrutiny, since it takes place behind closed doors in private households and is not generally subject to the same provisions on inspection as public workplaces (ILO 2016). In the UK, the Health and Safety at Work Act 1974, s51 excludes those employed 'as a domestic servant in a private household' from its scope, leaving workers facing many risks to their health and safety (Rodgers 2016, 181).[5] While individuals working via platforms may be less likely to meet the 'domestic servant' definition, they are conversely more likely to be deemed responsible for their own health and safety protection if classified as fully self-employed. 'Limb b' workers have also received more limited health and safety protection than employees, although a recent challenge to this by the Independent Workers' Union of Great Britain (IWGB)[6] was partially successful (Hobby 2021).

The provision of domestic services through online platforms has the potential to increase the work's visibility, which could be hoped to facilitate improved rights and valuation in the sector. Yet to date there has been little realisation of this potential, with visibility often failing to translate into increased benefits for those performing the work or to subject working conditions to more scrutiny. Instead, the process is often unidirectional, with platforms allowing customers to rate workers while the opposite functionality may either not exist, or have little practical effect for individuals that need to work, leaving them in a disempowered position (Hunt and Machingura 2016, 27; Choudary 2018,

16). Workers often receive little detail about new clients and the amount of time they will be expected to spend (van Doorn 2021, 59) and lack protection against unreasonable demands by service users (Prassl 2018, 57).

At the same time, platforms provide additional mechanisms for surveillance and discipline of workers, who may be under pressure to upload detailed personal information, such as links to social media pages, to attract clients, even if some resist this (Mateescu and Ticona 2020, 63). The increased control and surveillance interacts with pre-existing negative assumptions about domestic workers. This can be traced back to the concentration of racialised women in the sector and the construction of domestic work as dishonourable because of its association with the body and physicality (Anderson 2000, 142), with both 'femininity' and 'raciality' understood as markers of inferiority (Gutiérrez Rodríguez 2010, 110). Accordingly, the new surveillance mechanisms can be understood as 'shaped by centuries of suspicion about the mostly Black and brown women who perform essential reproductive labour' (Ticona 2020). Longstanding distrust can have a particular impact when mediated through a platform. Consider the case of a US parent quoted in a news article on their concerns about using a babysitting app: 'I've tried a few cleaning ones and ended up with crap cleaners. I can cope with an unmopped floor...but can't compromise on my son's safety' – with the platform's response emphasising the screening process and information to be shown about the babysitter's history (Rampton 2019). This demonstrates how such concerns, albeit understandable, can drive an intensification of surveillance, which can be particularly problematic if the impression the platform creates about the worker is shaped by opaque systems of ratings and algorithms.

Discipline and the role of ratings

Domestic work outside the gig economy has been heavily characterised by employer domination, facilitated by legal frameworks that fail to protect workers. In Britain, the historical category of 'menial servant' from the 15th century was a precursor to the 'domestic servant,' with a relationship understood to be based on status rather than contract and a personal, deeply unequal relationship with the 'master' (Albin 2012, 232–38; Dukes, this volume). The current legal framework in Britain recreates the relationship of domination in various ways, including the exclusion of workers classed as 'domestic servants' from normal weekly working hours limits, leaving little time for a private life, and a highly restrictive visa that makes it very difficult to change employer or challenge poor conditions (Mantouvalou 2015; Gower 2016; Sedacca 2021b, 144–47).

In the gig economy, direct domination by a single employer is superseded by the discipline and control of workers through the platforms' systems of ratings/rankings and algorithms (Prassl 2018, 54). As platform labour substitutes for more direct and casual ways of obtaining domestic services, a transition takes place 'from *servant labour* to *capitalist service labour*' with workers 'brought directly within the disciplinary scope of transnational corporations: closely monitored, expected to be available at short notice' but lacking the 'job security or collective voice' expected in a unionised workplace (Huws 2019, 19–20). This can be conceptualised as a shift from 'dyadic domination,' marked by the need to fulfil the whims of an individual employer, to 'structural domination,' where the market becomes the primary method of disciplining workers via rules that lack transparency and are not open to workers' contestation (Flanagan 2019, 71). Therefore, even where workers are nominally free to move jobs, this does not necessarily amount to a substantive liberty because alternatives fail to offer 'sufficient remuneration or security to facilitate the conditions for a flourishing life' (Flanagan 2019, 71, citing Rahman 2017; see also Bogg and Buendia, this volume).

These systems mean the perceived advantages of working on the platforms are highly contingent, and flexibility may be more apparent than real. Even where work in the gig economy helps working mothers and others with caring responsibilities, the emphasis on adaptable schedules alone fails to address societal structures that lead to the expectation on women to perform the bulk of this unpaid labour (Hunt and Samman 2019, 23). In any event, since the ratings systems tend to favour those with wider availability, those seeking hours that are more limited are often disadvantaged. Cancellation tends to have a negative impact on ratings (van Doorn 2021, 62), with Handy workers in the US reporting severe penalties for missing jobs and needing to keep extremely high ratings to earn competitive wages (Griswold 2015). Such practices clearly stand to disadvantage those with caring responsibilities who may become unavailable at short notice or have more restricted schedules. In a claim against Deliveroo in Italy, the algorithm's failure to consider whether cancellations were caused by legitimate grounds such as childcare needs was held to contribute to its discriminatory nature (Gramano and Kullmann, this volume).

Ratings are also susceptible to be influenced by prejudice related to factors such as ethnicity, gender, and age (Hunt and Machingura 2016, 27; Prassl 2018, 62), such that the need to protect workers against the adverse effect of algorithms is increasingly recognised (European Commission 2021, 7). For example, a worker review of handy.com in the UK refers to racism among customers, leading to bad feedback even after being told they had completed jobs well. Despite the opaque processes behind ratings, they often have a very significant impact, including on whether a worker can continue getting work through the platform at all, and the quality of jobs available to them (Prassl 2018, 61–62). Across the gig economy, there is significant variation in the way platforms terminate or suspend workers' contracts, which often happens without a review process or even an explanation, fuelling exploitation and precariousness (Hauben, Lenaerts, and Wayaert 2020, 27–28). For example, a worker's comment on TaskRabbit refers to carrying out almost 500 tasks over two years with an excellent rating followed by a sudden removal from the platform without reason. The lack of recourse to challenge decisions made on the platform is compounded by exclusion from unfair dismissal remedies for those who are not employees.

Additionally, the ratings-driven system tends to increase competition, exerting downward pressure on hourly rates (van Doorn 2021, 60–61) and compelling workers to self-brand and market themselves online. A US study shows care workers' view of platforms as obscuring differences between roles and longevity in the sector, undermining a view of their work as a long-term vocation and making it difficult to 'stand out in the crowd,' compelling many to use extra payable features (Mateescu and Ticona 2020, 69–74). While some workers have a positive experience of using platforms to build client networks that can translate into reputation and sustained income (Mateescu and Ticona 2020, 74–75), this depends on being comfortable with self-branding and technology, which not all are. The result is increased stratification, leaving those who do not 'make it' with inadequate hours and earnings. In South Africa, a 2018 analysis of platform-based domestic work shows around a quarter of available working hours being taken by the 'top' 10% of workers, who were successful based on their ratings, availability, and length of time on the platform, again suggesting pressure on workers to have widespread availability (Hunt and Samman 2020, 111–12). The stringent management of domestic workers through technology can therefore be viewed as a new mechanism and distribution for a longstanding dynamic of domination. While the varied form of employer control creates new challenges, its intensity is not novel but mirrors historical forms of control, such as the central role of employer references in 19th century Britain, which made the relationship 'more like vassalage' than a contractual relationship (Dukes 2020, 222–23). This has parallels in the ongoing devaluation of domestic labour and the understanding of domestic workers as being 'like a member of the family.'

Devaluation of domestic work and gendered bifurcation of roles

The devaluation of domestic work is a longstanding phenomenon, which is related to its association with the 'private sphere' of women, the home, and the family, as opposed to the 'public sphere' of law, work, and rationality (e.g., Duffy 2007; Fredman and Fudge 2016). The divide between public and private spheres obscures the work and requirements of women through the assumption that only paid work in the public sphere contributes to the economy or properly counts as work (Charlesworth, Chinkin, and Wright 1991, 626, 640; Okin 1998, 116). As industrialisation brought an end to the subsistence economy and led to monetary relations dominating economic life, domestic labour increasingly came to be viewed as inferior (Boyd 1997, 8; Federici 2014, 63–74; Fredman and Fudge 2016, 232; Davis 2019, 505). There are many examples of devaluation of work in the private sphere that play out in the treatment of paid domestic workers. These include their frequent conceptualisation as akin to members of the employing family (Albin and Mantouvalou 2012, 68) based on conflating their labour with work women would otherwise perform for free for their own families (Cox 2012, 45–46).

In Britain today, devaluation is manifested in the exclusion of workers classed as 'domestic servants' from normal weekly limits on working hours (Working Time Regulations – SI 1998/1833, Reg 19). Furthermore, s57(3) of the National Minimum Wage Regulations 2015/621 allows for an exemption for minimum wage for live-in domestic workers where they are 'treated as a member of the family' as regards accommodation, meals and the sharing of tasks and leisure activities. After a judgment[7] holding the application of this exemption to a former domestic worker to be unlawful and indirectly discriminatory, its repeal has now been recommended (Low Pay Commission 2021), but the fact it has existed for so long starkly demonstrates the devaluation of domestic work (Sedacca 2021a).

Domestic work based on an employment relationship with a single employer therefore tends to be marked by working very long hours for low pay. The position in the gig economy raises distinct issues, including a lack of guaranteed hours and the expectation on workers to bear waiting time, unpaid travel time and travel costs (Flanagan 2019, 74). A negative Handy review refers to the rate of £8 per hour and a lack of work in the local area making it difficult to make money, highlighting the lack of guaranteed hours as well as low pay for workers, with a high proportion of fees going to the platforms. Even more positive or mixed workers' feedback can demonstrate analogous issues. For example, a reference to the lack of payment towards travel expenses from Helpling underscores how otherwise acceptable hourly rates can be undermined by additional exclusions. Furthermore, the dominance of ratings systems can push workers to carry out work beyond what they are paid for to gain the service user's approval (Dukes 2020, 223), which dovetails with the extensive and 'boundless' set of tasks that domestic workers have often been expected to perform (ILO 2010, 7).

Furthermore, rates of pay for domestic workers on platforms are often low compared with other roles. Of the UK platforms analysed, the Handy website is most emphatic about providing low-cost labour, with its website referring to 'cheap cleaning services' and 'the best cleaner…at a price that doesn't break the bank.' While stating that it is 'not an employer, but simply connects independent service professionals with customers,' it shows a maximum hourly rate for a cleaner as £9, a little above the minimum wage for employed people (£8.72 for those age 25-plus) and well below the real living wage as calculated by the Living Wage Foundation (currently £9.90 UK-wide and £11.05 in London). Its hourly rates for a 'handyman' or lawn care pro, which are less stereotypically associated with women, are significantly higher at £30 and £44 respectively. The differences are not as pronounced on other platforms reviewed, such as TaskRabbit, but the existence of any distinction reflects the gendered devaluation of domestic work, based on viewing the role as 'women's work' and its association with unpaid work in the family home.

Gendered devaluation is also reflected in the 'high degree of occupational segregation' seen on gig economy platforms: 86.5% of cleaners on the Hassle platform in the UK are women, reflecting the trend that while women are less likely than men to work in the gig economy overall, where they do, they are more concentrated in cleaning and domestic work than in other sectors such as taxi driving (Hunt and Samman 2019, 12–13). Although some platforms have tried to push back against the idea of cleaning being a women's role, the demand for male cleaners remains lower (Altenried and Niebler 2021), demonstrating the pervasiveness of the idea that domestic work is women's work. There is a lack of intersectional analysis specific to domestic work in the gig economy, but workers marginalised on a class and/or ethnic basis are often concentrated in the lowest paid gig work (Hunt and Samman 2019, 14), and there is a high degree of recent migrants working on platforms (Altenried and Niebler 2021). Taken together with broader trends, this indicates that domestic workers in the gig economy are likely to be disproportionately low income, ethnic minority and/or migrant women. Just as working via a platform does not address the lack of scrutiny on employers, instead making workers hyper-visible, it also appears to perpetuate the devaluation of domestic labour.

On demand domestic work has therefore been aptly denoted 'as largely "more of the same"', exploiting 'the undervalued labour of marginalised women workers' and risking undermining longstanding efforts to improve conditions in the sector by reproducing poor working conditions (Hunt and Samman 2020, 116–21). For example, if the 'family worker' exemption discussed above is finally repealed in the UK, the new requirement to pay minimum wage to all domestic workers could still remain ineffective for those who are classified as fully self-employed rather than workers or employees.

Collective bargaining and organisation

Challenges in the domestic work sector and the gig economy

Across both the domestic work sector and the gig economy, collective bargaining and organisation pose serious challenges. A key obstacle is the isolated nature of domestic labour, with many in a workplace of one, while further issues include a lack of awareness of unions among the most vulnerable, often migrant, workers, fears over migration status, a lack of time for union activities because of long working hours, and difficulty paying membership fees on low wages (Albin and Mantouvalou 2016, 327–31; Jiang and Korczynski 2016, 815–21; ILO 2021a, 223; Sedacca 2021b, 133, 171). Historically, the domestic work sector received a lack of support from the union movement (Dukes 2020, 224), as did other types of insecure, precarious and low-paid work (Stylogiannis 2021, 6). Likewise, in the gig economy, workers tend not to be concentrated in a single workplace, while other factors likely to deter workers from organising include the lack of job security, denial of employment status and dominant effect of ratings (De Stefano and Aloisi 2019, 364–65; Novitz 2021, 654). Given these compounded challenges, collective agreements relating to domestic work platforms are unsurprisingly rare. However, two known exceptions, where unions have made agreements with gig economy platforms in recent years, are discussed below.

Collective agreements: Hilfr Denmark and Handy Pilot US

In 2018, the 3F trade union in Denmark signed an important and innovative agreement with the cleaning platform Hilfr (Kilhoffer et al. 2019, 254; Countouris and De Stefano 2020) ('the Hilfr Agreement'). This introduced a new category of worker, 'Superhilfr,' with employment status, to run alongside the existing freelance arrangement. Each worker chose whether to be classified in this way; after 100 hours of work, they would be classed as such unless they opted out, and otherwise would remain self-employed 'Freelancehilfrs' outside the agreement (Kilhoffer et al. 2019, 254). Once the agreement was in place, some 'Superhilfr' employees set their wages higher than the minimum, demonstrating a positive impact on pay (Jesnes and Nordli Oppegaard 2020, 56). Apart from the competition law challenge discussed below, the agreement faced some practical difficulties. As the government encouraged the parties to enter negotiations, there was an apparent lack of mandate from the workers, who often are not unionised because they view the job as temporary and/ or see union fees as a barrier to entry (Kilhoffer et al. 2019, 255; Jesnes and Nordli Oppegaard 2020, 58), reflecting broader issues in the domestic work sector. Relatedly, the numbers of workers benefitting from the agreement was very small, with just 36 employed 'Superhilfrs' as at January 2020, possibly stemming from a competitive disadvantage as compared with other companies that have lower costs based on less favourable conditions (Jesnes and Nordli Oppegaard 2020, 57). This demonstrates the limitations of regulation only through agreements with individual companies and points to the need for sector-wide protection.

That said, there is a further recent encouraging example of collective bargaining from the US. In June 2021, the Handy cleaning platform made an agreement with the NDWA Gig Worker Advocates, an independent entity linked to the National Domestic Workers Alliance (NDWA), which negotiates with gig economy companies (Poo and Gearhart 2021). Currently a pilot scheme in three states, the agreement makes important provisions for workers' rights, including for negotiation, paid time off, a guaranteed wage of $15 per hour (higher than federal and relevant state minimums) and health/disability insurance for occupational accidents, setting a floor rather than a ceiling so that it does not lock workers into second-class employment status (Andrias and Sachs 2021). Albeit not a full collective bargaining structure, it is a notable advance for domestic workers who have been excluded from coverage of the National Labor Relations Act, and includes mechanisms built in for workers to make their voices heard via a committee, a Facebook group and/or an online suggestions box (Andrias and Sachs 2021). While still at an early stage, the agreement appears to contain promising avenues to overcome difficulties in engaging workers.

The need for effective legal protection based on human rights standards

The limited examples of collective agreements and the difficulties faced by the Hilfr Agreement underscore how it is 'particularly urgent to reinforce the collective protection of non-standard workers' (De Stefano and Aloisi

2019, 371). However, far from consistent protective measures being taken, gig workers' rights to collective bargaining have been threatened, primarily by virtue of their 'self-employed' status. A notable example is the reaction to the Hilfr Agreement. Despite its limitation to some workers and scope for opt out, the relevant Danish authority attacked the agreement, holding that both forms of 'Hilfr's were enterprises and that the minimum hourly fee could limit competition between 'Freelancehilfrs' by creating a 'price floor' (Danish Competition and Consumer Authority 2020). In response, Hilfr committed to ensure Superhilfrs were employees and to remove the minimum fee for Freelancehilfrs (Danish Competition and Consumer Authority 2020). The authority's decision was rightly criticised as unrealistically applying 'competition law to self-employed to domestic workers as if they were undertakings' (Countouris and De Stefano 2020). In EU law, even those who fall outside 'worker' status and are self-employed persons are not necessarily 'undertakings' to whom competition law applies unless, for example, they are professionally licensed or create a partnership or company with others (McGaughey 2021, 3). To date the Court of Justice of the European Union has only made it clear that those 'falsely' classed as self-employed are entitled to bargain collectively, which is overly constrictive and falls short of the expansive way the right should be understood (De Stefano and Aloisi 2019, 373–8). However, the European Commission is now consulting on new guidelines to allow collective bargaining by a wider range of self-employed people who rely on their own labour.

Crucially, allowing the supposedly 'self-employed' status of workers in the gig economy to create a bar to collective agreements is also likely to be incompatible with international/regional human rights law, which determines these rights on a more universalist basis (Stylogiannis 2021). Of particular relevance is Article 11 of the European Convention on Human Rights (ECHR), the right to freedom of association. Although not mentioned explicitly in Article 11, case law such as *Demir & Baykara v Turkey*[8] has indicated that it encompasses the right to collective bargaining. Unfortunately, in the recent *Deliveroo* case the English Court of Appeal rejected an argument on this basis by the IWGB union, holding that riders did not have the right to bargain collectively because the trade union freedom aspect of Article 11 is contingent on the existence of an employment relationship.[9] The decision relied on ILO Recommendation 198 including a requirement that work be performed personally for an employment relationship to exist (paras 42–57). While acknowledging other ILO statements that individuals outside an employment relationship should have the right to organise collectively, Underhill LJ held that this did not apply to the specific right to organise *as a trade union* (86).

The Deliveroo decision may be subject to further appeal and can be criticised for an overly narrow application of the relevant ILO Recommendation and its factual acceptance of Deliveroo's account of the terms of work (Bogg and Buendia, this volume) as well as its failure to take a universalist approach to Article 11 ECHR. Furthermore, the European Committee on Social Rights has confirmed that Article 6 of the European Social Charter covers self-employed individuals, while ILO Convention 98 on the right to organise does not exclude the self-employed (Countouris and De Stefano 2020). There is a compelling argument that competition law concerns should not be given primacy over labour and human rights standards – especially as limiting application of trade union rights to domestic and other workers in the gig economy denies protection to some of those sectors most in need of it. Another parallel can be drawn here to domestic work, for which the universality of human rights law is important for counteracting traditional exclusion from the protection of labour law based on factors such as migration status and the gendered public/private sphere divide (Sedacca 2021b, 269).

Research agenda and preliminary conclusions

Given the increasing prevalence of domestic work in the gig economy alongside the relative lack of existing studies, an in-depth investigation of this sector in Britain would be a valuable topic for future empirical research. This could take the form of an online survey and/or semi-structured interviews with gig economy platform workers, having regard to factors such as ethnicity, gender, and migration status, and covering areas including working hours, rates of pay, social security access, and the extent to which flexibility is experienced as a benefit. It would also be illuminating to study workers' experience of the rating system and other forms of surveillance, including whether this is perceived as fair and non-discriminatory, as well as examining prospects for and barriers to collective organisation. This study would require a carefully thought-out strategy on how to make contact with workers given their low level of organisation.

Pending further investigation, it is possible to draw some preliminary conclusions from the material analysed above. The challenges domestic workers face in the gig economy overlap in some respects and diverge in others from domestic workers in standard employment relationships, and from workers in other sectors of the gig economy. Compared to the extremely long hours and employer domination that often characterise traditional domestic labour, work in the gig economy is frequently marked by a lack of security, guaranteed hours, or minimum pay rates, with systems of ratings, reviews, and algorithms serving to discipline workers, create competition between them, and potentially put their continued work on the platform at risk. Constraints on collective bargaining exist across both sectors, as demonstrated by the rarity of collective agreements and the challenges faced where these have been made. These obstacles demonstrate the importance of legal protection for platform workers' freedom of association, in contrast to the current position that makes this contingent on worker or even employee status, and point to the need for a broader regulatory framework setting standards across the gig economy.

A common theme in domestic work both in and outside the gig economy is the gendered bifurcation of roles and the concentration of women into feminised household work attracting low pay and poor conditions. A programme for improving conditions on domestic work platforms should therefore draw on insights not only from studies of the gig economy but also from analysis of devalued, feminised forms of labour such as cleaning and domestic work. In addition to setting minimum hourly rates, this is likely to require measures to address shortfalls in payment for ancillary time such as that spent travelling, to counteract the pressure on domestic workers to perform additional labour merely to achieve ratings that give them access to work, and to tackle discrimination based on factors such as gender and ethnicity. Furthermore, regulation should seek to guarantee wider remedies for unfair dismissal so that workers cannot lose their means of livelihood through arbitrary decisions, and a social safety net to mitigate against pressure to accept exploitative and degrading work. Across domestic work and the gig economy, human rights law has an important role to play in insisting that decent work is not contingent on a particular employment status, sector type or migration status, but applies to everyone by virtue of their humanity.

Notes

1.   Assistant Professor in Employment Law, Durham University [natalie.m.sedacca@durham.ac.uk]. ORCID ID 0000-0003-1694-528X. I am very grateful to Valerio De Stefano, Ilda Durri, Charalampos Stylogiannis and Mathias Wouters for written feedback on the first draft chapter, and to participants of the SLS Labour Law section 2021, the online seminar 'A Research Agenda on the Gig Economy,' and the Exeter Human Rights and Democracy Forum for comments on my related presentation. My doctoral research on which this chapter partly draws was funded by the London Arts & Humanities Partnership and UCL Faculty of Laws.
2.   It does not discuss services such as food delivery. Although these contribute to domestic life and social reproduction, their performance outside the home and the

greater attention they have received in the literature on the gig economy puts them outside the chapter's core focus.

3.   The PLUS project (https://project-plus.eu/) addresses four platforms including one cleaning platform across London and six other European cities, but as an ongoing project, limited data is currently available.

4.   This was more common for the cleaning sites than childcare providers, and given the small number of reviews considered for each, they simply provide an initial snapshot and highlight themes for further investigation. Information was initially taken from websites in 2021 and checked in January 2022, at which point the information on company websites was correct, although some indeed.com reviews referred to were no longer freely available to view.

5.   Guidance on the definition is found at https://www.hse.gov.uk/enforce/ enforcementguide/investigation/status-specific.htm#domestic.

6.   *R (IWGB) v Secretary of State for Work and Pensions* [2020] EWHC 2050 (Admin).

7.   *Puthenveettil v Alexander & ors* – Case Number 2361118/2013 – Employment Tribunal judgment of 15 December 2020.

8.   *Demir & Baykara v Turkey* (2009) 48 EHRR 54.

9.   *IWGB v The Central Arbitration Committee v Roofoods Ltd t/a Deliveroo* [2021] EWCA Civ 1746.

References

Adam, Stuart, Helen Miller, and Tom Waters. 2020. "Income Protection for the Self-Employed and Employees during the Coronavirus Crisis". Briefing Note BN277. Institute for Fiscal Studies.

Albin, Einat. 2012. "From 'Domestic Servant' to 'Domestic Worker'". In *Challenging the Legal Boundaries of Work Regulation,* edited by Judy Fudge, Shae McCrystal, and Kamala Sankaran, 231–50. Oxford: Hart.

Albin, Einat, and Virginia Mantouvalou. 2012. "The ILO Convention on Domestic Workers: From the Shadows to the Light". *Industrial Law Journal* 41(1): 67–78.

Albin, Einat, and Virginia Mantouvalou. 2016. "Active Industrial Citizenship of Domestic Workers: Lessons Learned from Unionizing Attempts in Israel and the United Kingdom". *Theoretical Inquiries in Law* 17(1): 321–50.

Altenried, Moritz, and Valentin Niebler. 2021. "Platforms, Social Reproduction, and Migration – the Case of Helpling in Berlin". Presented at the PLUS TALKS, Gender and Platform Labour 2: The Platformisation of Paid Care, Cleaning and Domestic Work, Webinar, February 2021. https:// project -plus .eu/ platformisation -of -paid -care-cleaning-and-domestic-work/.

Anderson, Bridget. 2000. *Doing the Dirty Work?: The Global Politics of Domestic Labour.* London: Zed.

Andrias, Kate, and Benjamin Sachs. 2021. "NDWA-Handy Pilot: Major Gains for Workers Long Excluded from Labor Law's Protections". *OnLabour* (blog), June 17, 2021. https:// onlabor .org/ ndwa -handy -pilot -major -gains -for -workers -long -excluded-from-labor-laws-protections/.

Behrendt, Christina, Quyn Ahn Nguyen, and Uma Rani. 2019. "Social Protection Systems and the Future of Work: Ensuring Social Security for Digital Platform Workers". *International Social Security Review* 72(3): 17–41.

Boyd, Susan B. 1997. "Challenging the Public/Private Divide: An Overview". In *Challenging the Public/Private Divide: Feminism, Law, and Public Policy*, edited by Susan B. Boyd, 3–33. Toronto, London: University of Toronto Press.

Charlesworth, Hilary, Christine Chinkin, and Shelley Wright, 1991. "Feminist Approaches to International Law". *American Journal of International Law* 85(4): 613–45.

Choudary, Sangeet Paul. 2018. "The Architecture of Digital Labour Platforms: Policy Recommendations on Platform Design for Worker Well-Being". The Future of Work Research Paper Series. ILO.

Countouris, Nicola, and Valerio De Stefano. 2020. "Collective-Bargaining Rights for Platform Workers". *Social Europe* (blog), October 6, 2020. https://www.socialeurope.eu/collective-bargaining-rights-for-platform-workers

Cox, Rosie. 2012. "Gendered Work and Migration Regimes". In *Transnational Migration, Gender and Rights*, edited by Liam Leonard, 33–52. Bingley, UK: Emerald.

Danish Competition and Consumer Authority. 2020. "Commitment Decision on the Use of a Minimum Hourly Fee". *Danish Competition and Consumer Authority*, August 26, 2020. https://www.en.kfst.dk/nyheder/kfst/english/decisions/20200826-commitment-decision-on-the-use-of-a-minimum-hourly-fee-hilfr/

Davis, Angela Y. 2019. *Women, Race & Class*. London: Penguin Classics.

De Stefano, Valerio, and Antonio Aloisi. 2019. "Fundamental Labour Rights, Platform Work and Human Rights Protection of Non-Standard Workers". In *Research Handbook on Labour, Business and Human Rights Law*, edited by Janice R. Bellace and Beryl ter Haar, 359–79. Cheltenham, UK and Northampton, MA, USA: Edward Elgar Publishing.

Duffy, Mignon. 2007. "Doing the Dirty Work: Gender, Race, and Reproductive Labour in Historical Perspective". *Gender & Society* 21(3): 313–36.

Dukes, Ruth. 2020. "Regulating Gigs". *Modern Law Review* 83(1): 217–28.

European Commission. 2021. "Better Working Conditions for a Stronger Social Europe: Harnessing the Full Benefits of Digitalisation for the Future of Work". COM (2021) 761 final.

Ewing, K.D., and Lord Hendy. 2020. "Covid-19 and the Failure of Labour Law: Part I". *Industrial Law Journal* 49(4): 497–538.

Federici, Silvia. 2014. *Caliban and the Witch: Women, the Body and Primitive Accumulation*. 2nd ed. New York: Autonomedia.

Flanagan, Frances. 2019. "Theorising the Gig Economy and Home-Based Service Work". *Journal of Industrial Relations* 61(1): 57–78.

Fredman, Sandra, and Judy Fudge. 2016. "The Contract of Employment and Gendered Work.". In *The Contract of Employment,* edited by Mark Freedland, 231–52. Oxford: OUP.

Gower, Melanie. 2016. "Calls to Change Overseas Domestic Worker Visa Conditions". House of Commons Library Briefing Paper 4768.

Griswold, Alison. 2015. "Handy Could Be the Uber of House-Cleaning—if It Can Tidy Its Own Mess." *Slate Magazine*, July 24, 2015. https://slate.com/business/2015/07/handy-a-hot-startup-for-home-cleaning-has-a-big-mess-of-its-own.html.

Gutiérrez Rodríguez, Encarnación. 2010. *Migration, Domestic Work and Affect: A Decolonial Approach on Value and the Feminization of Labor*. New York: Routledge.

Hauben, Harald, Karolien Lenaerts, and William Wayaert. 2020. "The Platform Economy and Precarious Work". PE 652.734. European Parliament.

Hobby, Catherine. 2021. "Workers' Rights: A Public Health Issue: *R (on the application of The Independent Workers' Union of Great Britain) v The Secretary of State for Work and Pensions*". *Industrial Law Journal* 50(3): 467–91.

Hunt, Abigail, and Fortunate Machingura. 2016. "A Good Gig? The Rise of on-Demand Domestic Work." Working Paper 07. ODI.

Hunt, Abigail, and Emma Samman. 2019. "Gender and the Gig Economy – Critical Steps for Evidence-Based Policy". Working Paper 546. ODI.

Hunt, Abigail, and Emma Samman. 2020. "Domestic Work and the Gig Economy in South Africa: Old Wine in New Bottles?". *Anti-Trafficking Review* 15: 102–21.

Huws, Ursula. 2019. "The Hassle of Housework: Digitalisation and the Commodification of Domestic Labour". *Feminist Review* 123(1): 8–23.

ILO. 2010. "Report IV(1) – Decent Work for Domestic Workers – 99th Session of the International Labour Conference".

ILO. 2016. *Labour Inspection and Other Compliance Mechanisms in the Domestic Work Sector: Introductory Guide.*

ILO. 2021a. "Making Decent Work a Reality for Domestic Workers - Progress and Prospects Ten Years After the Adoption of the Domestic Workers Convention, 2011 (No. 189)".

ILO. 2021b. "World Employment and Social Outlook – the Role of Digital Labour Platforms in Transforming the World of Work".

Jesnes, Kristin, and Sigurd M. Nordli Oppegaard. 2020. *Platform Work in the Nordic Models: Issues, Cases and Responses.* Nordic Council of Ministers.

Jiang, Zhe, and Marek Korczynski. 2016. "When the 'Unorganizable' Organize. The Collective Mobilization of Migrant Domestic Workers in London". *Human Relations* 69(3): 813–38.

Kilhoffer, Zachary, Willem Pieter De Groen, Willem Wayaert, Elisa Giacumacatos, Jean-Philippe Lhernould, and Sophie Robin-Olivier. 2019. "Study to Gather Evidence on the Working Conditions of Platform Workers". VT/2018/032 European Commission.

Low Pay Commission. 2021. "2021 Report – Summary of Findings". https:// assets .publishing.service.gov.uk/ government/ uploads/ system/ uploads/ attachment_data/ file/1028738/LPC_summary_of_findings_2021_A.pdf.

Mantouvalou, Virginia. 2012. "Human Rights for Precarious Workers: The Legislative Precariousness of Domestic Labor". *Comparative Labor Law & Policy Journal* 34(1): 133–64.

Mantouvalou, Virginia. 2015. "'Am I Free Now?' Overseas Domestic Workers in Slavery". *Journal of Law and Society* 42(3): 329–57.

Mateescu, Alexandra, and Julia Ticona. 2020. "Invisible Work, Visible Workers– Visibility Regimes in Online Platforms for Domestic Work". In *Beyond the Algorithm: Qualitative Insights for Gig Work Regulation*, edited by Deepa Das Acevedo, 57–81. Cambridge: CUP.

Mateescu, Alexandra, and Julia Ticona. 2021. "US Domestic Work Platforms in the Covid Crisis – Workers, Platforms and the State". Presented at the PLUS TALKS, Gender and Platform Labour 2: The Platformisation of Paid Care, Cleaning and Domestic Work, Webinar, February 2021. https://project-plus.eu/platformisation-of -paid-care-cleaning-and-domestic-work/.

McGaughey, Ewan. 2021. "Competition and Labour Law in the United Kingdom: History, Theory and Practice". SSRN Scholarly Paper ID 3926801. Rochester: SSRN. https://papers.ssrn.com/abstract=3926801.

Mullally, Siobhán, and Cliodhna Murphy. 2014. "Migrant Domestic Workers in the UK: Enacting Exclusions, Exemptions, and Rights". *Human Rights Quarterly* 36(2): 397–427.

Novitz, Tonia. 2021. "Gig Work as a Manifestation of Short-termism: Crafting a Sustainable Regulatory Agenda". *Industrial Law Journal* 50(4): 636–61.

Okin, Susan Moller. 1998. "Gender, the Public, and the Private". In *Feminism and Politics*, edited by Anne Phillips, 116–41. Oxford: OUP.

Poo, Ai-jen, and Dawn Gearhart. 2021. "Opinion: Domestic Workers Have Long Been Underpaid and Unappreciated. It's Time We Give Them What They Deserve". *CNN*, June 17, 2021. https://edition.cnn.com/2021/06/17/perspectives/domestic-workers-benefits-protections/index.html.

Prassl, Jeremias. 2018. *Humans as a Service: The Promise and Perils of Work in the Gig Economy*. Oxford: OUP.

Rahman, K. Sabeel. 2017. *Democracy against Domination*. New York: OUP.

Rampton, Mike. 2019. "Are Babysitting Apps a Lifesaver or a Worry for Parents?". *HuffPost UK*, February 22, 2019. https:// www .huffingtonpost .co .uk/ entry/ babysitting-apps-for-parents-kids_uk_5c6d4722e4b0e37a1ed35818.

Rodgers, Lisa. 2016. *Labour Law, Vulnerability and the Regulation of Precarious Work*. Cheltenham, UK and Northampton, MA, USA: Edward Elgar Publishing.

Sedacca, Natalie. 2021a. "A Crucial and Long-Needed Step Against the Devaluation of Domestic Work: 'Family Worker' Exemption Dis-Applied in Puthenveettil v Alexander & ors". *UK Labour Law* (blog), March 1, 2021. https://uklabourlawblog .com/ 2021/ 03/ 01/ a -crucial -and -long -needed -step -against -the -devaluation -of -domestic -work -family -worker -exemption -dis -applied -in -puthenveettil -v -alexander-ors-by-natalie-sedecca/.

Sedacca, Natalie. 2021b. "Domestic Labour and Human Rights: Challenging the Exclusion of Domestic Workers". PhD Thesis. University College London.

Stylogiannis, Charalampos. 2021. "Freedom of Association and Collective Bargaining in the Platform Economy: A Human Rights-Based Approach and an Over Increasing Mobilization of Workers". *International Labour Review*. https://onlinelibrary.wiley .com/doi/10.1111/ilr.12340.

Ticona, Julia. 2020. "Essential and Untrusted". *Dissent Magazine* (blog), Fall 2020. https://www.dissentmagazine.org/article/essential-and-untrusted.

van Doorn, Niels. 2021. "Stepping Stone or Dead End? The Ambiguities of Platform-Mediated Domestic Work under Conditions of Austerity. Comparative Landscapes of Austerity and the Gig Economy: New York and Berlin". In *Working in the Context of Austerity: Challenges and Struggles*, edited by Donna Baines and Ian Cunningham, 49–69. Bristol, UK: Bristol University Press.

Yeo, Colin. 2019. "What Is the No Recourse to Public Funds Condition?". *Free Movement* (blog), August 5, 2019. https:// www .freemovement.org.uk/ what -is -the -no-recourse-to-public-funds-condition/.

10 Is flexibility and autonomy a myth or reality on taxi platforms? Comparison between traditional and app-based taxi drivers in developing countries

Uma Rani, Nora Gobel, Rishabh Kumar Dhir

Introduction

The growth in internet connectivity has led to an enhanced use of mobile devices in many developing countries; however, there still remains a digital divide as many people and businesses in rural areas[1] do not have access to the internet. Despite the digital divide, digital labour platforms[2] have proliferated in many of these countries and are transforming the world of work. Platforms providing taxi or delivery services, in particular have gained prominence due to the availability of venture capital funds (ILO 2021). This has also led to the emergence of several players in developing countries, such as DiDi in China or Ola in India or Gojek in Southeast Asia. Moreover, some international taxi platform companies such as Uber or Bolt have also aggressively entered developing country markets, with an attempt to capture and expand their markets and also to provide services where traditional taxis are viewed to be inconvenient and inefficient to customers.[3] They have been contributing to changing consumer behaviour by providing customers access to services on-demand through a click on an app (Panse et al. 2019; Teo, Mustaffa and Rozi 2018; Dhawan and Yadav 2018).

Developing countries continue to have a huge informal economy and struggle to create employment opportunities. Work opportunities generated through taxi and delivery platforms have been posited to be a way to create employment opportunities, and provide flexibility and autonomy to workers (Mastercard 2020; Tandem Research 2019). This has led governments in many developing countries to promote such platforms, expand digital infrastructure, and even provide loans to workers to purchase vehicles (also see KPMG 2020; Prabhat, Nanavati and Rangaswamy 2019; Graham, Hjorth and Lehdonvirta 2017). However, it is important to emphasise that digital platforms are not creating *new* employment opportunities as the work performed on such platforms has existed in the past, and continues to be performed in the offline labour markets including taxi or domestic services. Platforms are using technology in the existing labour markets to mediate workers and connect them with businesses and clients.

It has been argued that being a platform worker, for instance a driver on a taxi platform, "is a step up from the traditional informal worker", given the "independence, agency, and most importantly guaranteed-payments by the clients upon completion of service" (Ramachandran and Raman 2021, 11; also see Lakemann and Lay 2019) and a move towards formalisation. However, the development of a platform-based business model does not necessarily alleviate the concerns of the high degree of informality, precarity or exploitation often observed among informal workers in a number of sectors (Hunt and Samman 2020) but further precaritises them through the algorithmic management practices. The workers on these platforms are often categorised as self-employed or independent contractors or driver-partners, and as they do not have an employment relationship, they do not enjoy any labour and social protections, thereby creating challenges (ILO 2021; Heeks et al. 2021b).

In this context, this chapter analyses and compares the situation of taxi drivers in both the app-based and traditional segments across eight countries (Chile, Ghana, India, Indonesia, Kenya, Lebanon, Mexico and Morocco), to understand the notions of flexibility and autonomy and the working conditions of the taxi drivers. Taxi platforms particularly serve as a unique area of inquiry, because, in addition to addressing issues of inefficiencies and inconvenience in the taxi sector, such platforms are also considered to provide improved safety for customers and drivers when compared to traditional taxis (Acheampong 2021; Shah 2020).[4] The rapid uptake of such platforms by consumers and the availability of easy venture capital funds has also resulted in a disruptive effect on the sector, in both developing and advanced countries alike (Horan 2019; Bick 2019; Damle 2018). These developments have implications for both traditional and app-based taxi drivers, as well as the consumers who rely on taxi platforms for their affordable services and easy availability. A better understanding of the digital transformations in this sector will shed light on broader implications to the world of work in developing countries.

Flexibility and autonomy on taxi platforms: What does empirical evidence tell us?

In several advanced economies, the perceived flexibility offered by taxi platforms such as Uber has attracted many workers who often already have another job and undertake platform work to supplement their incomes. Many such workers move from different backgrounds and are engaged in sectors other than the taxi sector, as was observed in the United States (Hall and Krueger 2016). In the United Kingdom, about 2 per cent of the Uber drivers were previously unemployed, while a vast majority left permanent part- or full- time jobs to become taxi drivers and about a quarter of the drivers were engaged in other work activities alongside platform work (Berger et al. 2019).

Emerging research from developing countries, however, shows that taxi drivers have been an integral part of the labour force for ride-hailing platforms. For instance, DiDi in China has been specifically targeting taxi drivers to recruit them (Chen 2018a). Similarly, a study in India found that 92 per cent of the drivers were earning an income through driving before joining a taxi platform (Surie and Koduganti 2016). Ola in India also specifically targeted existing auto-rickshaw drivers and added them to their fleet (Muralidhar 2016). The available empirical evidence shows how taxi platforms are attracting traditional taxi drivers and disrupting the traditional mode of transport in developing countries, unlike in the advanced economies where the entire segment has been disrupted impacting the livelihoods of traditional taxi drivers.

The rise of taxi platforms has garnered increasing critical engagement among researchers with the working conditions of drivers on such platforms, how their work is managed, as well as the mechanisms of control, including with regard to algorithmic management practices (ILO 2021; Wu and Li 2019; Mäntymäki, Baiyere and Islam 2019; Chinguno 2019; Rosenblat and Stark 2016). Research undertaken in some developing countries has started to underline some of the challenges faced by workers on taxi platforms. A study in India among taxi drivers using platforms and auto-rickshaw drivers using and not using platforms revealed that, while some new income-generating opportunities are created, platforms push drivers to "work harder for less revenue per kilometer, while distorting a pre-existing market and reducing overall driver autonomy" (Fleitoukh and Toyama 2020, 128). It also finds that platform companies distort the market by providing initial incentives and promotions for recruiting drivers, who later experience difficulties as incentives reduce over time. In addition, platforms also tend to pursue specific marketing techniques that advertise the promise of flexibility to prospective drivers in order to recruit them.[5] Studies in China, Chile and South Africa have however shown that despite the claims of flexibility, many drivers on taxi platforms are faced with long working hours (Fielbaum and Tirachini 2021; Carmody and Fortuin 2019; Chen 2018a).

Further, the algorithmic management practices are closely intertwined with the flexibility and autonomy that workers experience on such platforms. Studies in countries such as China, India and South Africa have shown that work is allocated by the platform's algorithm, monitored through the algorithm with the support of GPS tracking, while also determining rewards and incentives algorithmically (see for example, Verma, Ilavarasan and Kar 2020; Chinguno 2019; Chen 2018a). The platform benefits from "datafication labour" of the drivers, which is used for training the algorithm, while the driver is subjected to more control than the passenger (Chen 2018b, 242). A key aspect through which algorithmic practices exert control over workers is through the ratings and feedback system that provides inputs to the algorithmic system to decide the amount and frequency of work, types of customers, while favouring higher rated drivers for more rides (Verma, Ilavarasan and Kar 2020).

Closely linked to the ratings system is the rewards or incentive pay system offered by platforms that further exerts control over workers. In China for instance, a study found that incomes received from bonuses could be up to 90 per cent of a platform taxi driver's total monthly income (Wu et al. 2019). Such rewards can be linked to sustaining higher ratings, working during peak hours of demand or having completed a certain number of rides (see Wu and Li 2019; Surie and Koduganti 2016).

Reliance on such rewards and bonuses are all the more important to app-based drivers, who have to pay commission fees to the platform, bear the fuel and maintenance cost of the vehicles, and in some instances, also have to repay loans which they have taken to purchase the vehicle (see for example, Prabhat, Nanavati and Rangaswamy 2019). In Chile for instance, app-based drivers who were renting a car were found to work a greater number of hours per week than those who owned the car or borrowed a car for free (Fielbaum and Tirachini 2021). As identified in the literature, the multiple forms of direct and indirect control exerted by the platform through algorithmic management practices underscores the importance of exploring the notion of flexibility and autonomy, and the working conditions of the taxi drivers on platforms in developing countries.

In this regard, a key contribution of this chapter to the existing literature is that it provides a comparative picture of the situation of traditional and app-based taxi drivers across eight developing countries, and in doing so challenges the prevailing notions of greater flexibility and autonomy offered in platform work. While taxi platforms have been able to enhance efficiencies and reduce adverse selection by customers and drivers, "management by algorithm has rendered management processes more opaque to drivers and reduced some of the autonomy over shift patterns and ride acceptance that drivers used to have" (Heeks et al. 2021a, 10). In addition, the research also shows that such platforms have enhanced information-based asymmetry of power between the company and the government, and also created institutional voids by "circumventing the regulatory institutional roles performed by government agencies and driver collective bodies" (Heeks et al. 2021a, 11). In this context, the comparative empirical analysis provided by this chapter contributes towards addressing the need for regulating platform work and promoting decent work opportunities for all.

At a time when many developing countries are looking to address the impacts on labour markets due to the COVID-19 pandemic, and also promote the transition from the informal to the formal economy, it is vital to better situate the current platform-based model in providing work opportunities. By challenging the notions of flexibility and autonomy in taxi platforms through a comparative analysis, this chapter also critically engages with an increasingly prevalent argument that platform work is a "formal job" or provides "better opportunity" for workers in the informal economy, and the belief that an app-based driver "may be better off than his or her taxi driver counterpart" (Lakemann and Lay 2019, 5; also see Ramachandran and Raman 2021).

Research methods and descriptive statistics

The data for this chapter draws on the ILO surveys conducted among the app-based and traditional taxi drivers between 2019 and 2020. The sample comprised 2,539 taxi drivers covering eight developing countries: Chile, Ghana, India, Indonesia, Kenya, Lebanon, Mexico and Morocco (see Table 10.1). The analysis focuses on taxi drivers engaged in both the app-based and traditional segments in order to gain a better understanding of the sector.

The questionnaires captured the respondent's socio-demographic background; work history and information about other jobs; and information related to their working conditions, including working time, income, work-related expenditures, social security coverage, income security, autonomy and control, perceptions of work and workplace solidarities. The questionnaires contained

Table 10.1   Distribution of taxi drivers across countries, 2019 and 2020

| | Taxi sector | |
	App-based	Traditional
Chile	126	147
Ghana	198	196
India	324	328
Indonesia	344	148
Kenya	239	290
Lebanon	200	200
Mexico	200	200
Morocco	194	205
Total	1,825	1,714

Source: ILO country surveys of taxi drivers, 2019 and 2020.

detailed quantitative as well as open-ended qualitative questions and were adapted to the local context and translated into the local language(s) where necessary. The interviews were conducted using computer-assisted personal interviewing (CAPI) with inbuilt validation rules using mobile devices (cell phones, tablets).

Given the lack of official statistics on the number or the characteristics of app-based taxi workers, there was no sampling base for drawing a random sample. In addition, the objective was to understand their working conditions and their experiences on taxi platforms. The target population consisted of workers aged 18 years or older who had been working in the sector for at least three months.

To ensure heterogeneity within the sample, the interviews were conducted in different neighbourhoods, on different days, during different times of the day and with workers who were registered with different platform companies where it was possible. Enumerators located taxi drivers mainly on the street, and other areas such as gas stations, airports, platform company support offices and taxi stands, among others. In addition, snowball sampling was also used in some countries.

Given the small proportion of women workers engaged in this sector, we do not disaggregate the analysis by gender. App-based taxi drivers (36 years) are comparatively younger than traditional drivers (44 years). However, the age range is quite wide, indicating that workers from different age groups engage in this sector, including older workers (see Figure 10.1).

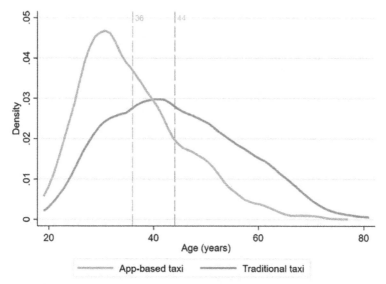

Source: ILO country surveys of taxi drivers, 2019 and 2020.

Figure 10.1   Age distribution of app-based and traditional taxi drivers, developing countries

A sizable proportion of the app-based taxi drivers (22 per cent) have attained a university degree, while these proportions are lower among traditional drivers (9 per cent). A higher proportion of young (aged 18–24 years) app-based taxi drivers are highly educated (19 per cent) compared to traditional taxi drivers (7 per cent).

In most developing countries, driving skills is an important asset for workers, especially those who are not highly educated. An overwhelmingly large proportion of traditional (63 per cent) and app-based taxi drivers (43 per cent) in our sample reported that they started working as taxi drivers due to lack of alternative employment opportunities. Other reasons to work as taxi drivers on platforms included job flexibility (25 per cent), as well as better pay than other available jobs (18 per cent), which were also common among traditional taxi drivers (see Figure 10.2).

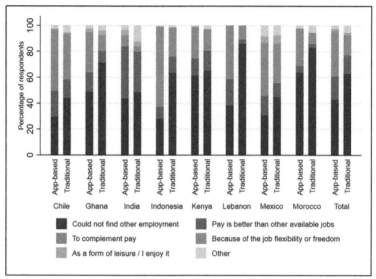

Source: ILO country surveys of taxi drivers, 2019 and 2020.

Figure 10.2   Most important reason for performing work in the taxi
sector, by country

Flexibility and autonomy: A comparison between app-based and traditional taxi drivers

Operating as a taxi driver in the traditional and platform sector

Traditional taxi drivers obtain special licences and permits before they can start operating the vehicle, which is a cost, and can often lead to different entry barriers and unfair competition in the sector. These requirements might vary slightly depending upon the country. Taxi drivers hail their passengers from the streets, taxi stands, airports, railway stations or other locations. The fares or rates for the rides are determined by the local municipality or states, which takes into consideration the waiting time, fuel costs, etc., and there is a basic minimum fare which is charged to the customer. In some instances, fares in the traditional taxi segment are also determined through engagements with taxi unions.[6] Taxi drivers can either own their vehicle and are liable for all costs such as maintenance, gasoline and insurance, or they can rent the vehicles and pay either a rental fee for the vehicle or can be hired on a monthly or weekly basis. They can purchase the car models that are designated for taxis, either new or second hand.

In contrast, app-based taxi drivers have to first register on platforms for which they require formal identification, such as a driving licence, social security or identity card, and vehicle-related information, such as vehicle registration and insurance. The registration process on some platforms in some countries can be rigorous due to regulations that are imposed on them. For example, Uber and DiDi introduced background checks, after incidents of sexual assault of passengers in India and China (Uber 2020a; Yuan 2018). An important difference with the traditional segment is how rides are accessed on platforms and the ride fare is determined. The rides are allocated algorithmically based on ratings and other indicators, and the fares or rates for a ride are determined using an algorithm. The algorithm for pricing takes into consideration distance, time taken to reach the destination, demand, fuel cost, type of vehicle and financial capacity of the customers to spend in a particular geographical area of the city, among others (ILO 2021).

Finally, another key difference relates to their employment status. Workers on taxi platforms are designated as driver-partners, self-employed or independent contractors while in the traditional taxi segment, they can be salaried with a permanent or temporary contract working for a household or company receiving certain benefits or they can be self-employed. If self-employed, they have the flexibility, autonomy and control to decide when to work, which rides to take or not and in which areas to operate in.

How do taxi drivers fare in app-based and traditional settings?

In developing countries where the surveys were conducted, taxi driving is the main source of income for about 95 per cent of the traditional taxi drivers and 84 per cent of app-based taxi drivers, and constitutes an important part of the household income. This is quite contrary to the notion often expressed by the proponents of taxi platforms that workers can earn supplementary income by driving taxis on platforms during their spare time, as this is the main source of their livelihoods. In some developing countries the proportion of workers dependent on app-based taxi driving for their incomes is particularly high, such as in Kenya (91 per cent) and India (94 per cent).

The hourly earnings for taxi drivers include waiting time, as it is unpredictable and difficult to estimate. The hourly earnings of taxi drivers using apps vary between US$1.13 (India) and US$8.22 (Lebanon), and the majority of taxi drivers earn less than the average in all countries. The earnings of the traditional taxi drivers are lower than those using apps and they vary considerably across countries (US$0.62 in India to US$3.74 in Chile and Lebanon) (see Figure 10.3). A statistical analysis controlling for basic characteristics shows

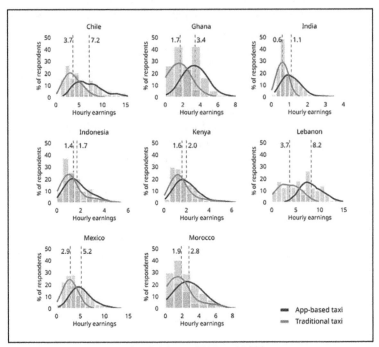

Source: ILO country surveys of taxi drivers, 2019 and 2020.

Figure 10.3   Hourly earnings of app-based and traditional taxi drivers, by country (in US$)

that app-based taxi drivers earn between 26 per cent (Morocco) and 86 per cent (Ghana) more than their traditional counterparts (see Figure 10.4).

There are multiple reasons for higher earnings among app-based drivers compared to traditional taxi drivers, and the findings from the ILO surveys should be interpreted with caution.

First, platforms offer economic incentives or bonuses to attract taxi drivers as well as to motivate and retain them on platforms. More than three-fourths of app-based taxi drivers (77 per cent) reported being offered such bonuses or incentives to stimulate their engagement on platforms. Such bonuses and incentives are offered by all the platforms and the reasons for offering them might vary depending upon the platform. The strategy adopted by a specific platform to attract taxi drivers also differs across countries, as they take into consideration the local demand, cultural context and other competitors in the

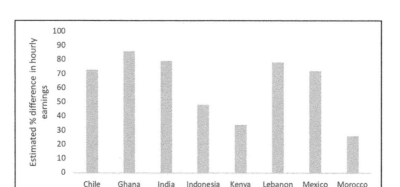

Source: ILO country surveys of taxi drivers, 2019 and 2020.

Figure 10.4   Hourly earnings of app-based taxi drivers compared to their traditional counterparts in the taxi sector, by country (estimated percentage difference)

market (see Table 10.2). The most popular criteria for receiving bonuses or incentives was meeting or exceeding a certain number of rides in almost all countries and platforms. Other factors included working asocial hours, such as at night or on holiday; meeting or exceeding an hourly threshold; or working during high demand or peak hours. These bonuses or incentives often constituted an important part of the taxi drivers' earnings. About 69 per cent of the respondents received such bonuses and almost all these workers (90 per cent) reported that the bonuses were an important part of their incomes.

Second, platforms develop their network effects and customer base by subsidising the cost of rides and keeping them low compared to fares that are charged by traditional taxis. Platforms are able to offer such low prices to consumers largely because of venture capital funding that is made available to them. For instance, one of the major players among the taxi platforms, Uber, has to date received US$25.2 billion and has not made any profits, and it has an accumulated deficit of US$16.4 billion (Uber 2020b). Uber is able to sustain its business and market share largely due to the venture capital funds (Horan 2019).

Such aggressive pricing strategies adopted by platforms have the potential to distort the local labour markets and reduce the demand for traditional taxi services, which eventually has an impact on the taxi drivers' earnings. The survey findings show that about half of the traditional taxi drivers reported a decline in the number of trips made in a single day and also in their earnings since they

Table 10.2   Criteria for receiving bonuses or incentives by platforms, selected countries (percentage of respondents)

		To new drivers	For working asocial hours (night or holiday)	To drivers who meet or exceed an hourly threshold	To drivers who meet or exceed a certain volume of rides	For working hours with high demand (not necessarily inconvenient times)
Uber	Chile	1	25	28	74	28
	Ghana	4	4	27	92	3
	India	0	0	8	98	12
	Kenya	11	27	33	78	0
	Lebanon	3	41	8	58	65
	Mexico	0	4	11	88	38
Bolt	Ghana	4	4	32	98	29
	Kenya	7	7	44	76	7
Careem	Lebanon	0	44	3	81	59
	Morocco	4	8	40	88	8

Source: ILO country surveys of taxi drivers, 2019 and 2020.

started working. For about one-third of the taxi drivers, it remained stable. About 70 per cent of the traditional taxi drivers in Chile, India and Mexico reported that they experienced a decline in the number of trips as well as their earnings since they started working (see Figure 10.5).

These pricing strategies also have the potential for extensive litigations. For instance, traditional taxi drivers and a radio taxi company MERU in India filed a series of complaints before the Competition Commission of India alleging that Ola and Uber were engaging in practices contrary to the prohibition of anti-competitive agreements (Section 3) and abuse of dominant position (Section 4) of the Competition Act 2002. Though the Commission decided in favour of Ola and Uber that *prima facie* there was no evidence of dominance by these platforms, MERU decided to appeal to the Competition Appellate Tribunal where its plea was rejected in July 2021.[7] While the experience of India is not necessarily reflective of other jurisdictions, it clearly brings out the complexity and uncertainty that exists in applying competition law to platform work.

Third, the lack of demand for rides also influenced the waiting time between rides for traditional drivers. On average the waiting time was much lower for app-based taxi drivers (24 minutes) compared to traditional drivers (53 minutes). Such variations were also observed at the country level: for instance,

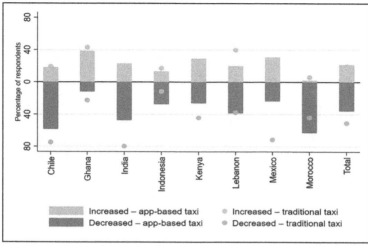

Source: ILO country surveys of taxi drivers, 2019 and 2020.

Figure 10.5   Increase or decrease in demand for rides, app-based and traditional taxi drivers by country (percentage of respondents)

in India traditional taxi drivers waited for about 93 minutes between the two rides, while it was only 16 minutes for app-based taxi drivers. This had implications on the earnings of traditional taxi drivers who ended up working long hours with the hope to receive a ride, and was also a source for their stress (see Figure 10.7).

Challenges faced by app-based taxi drivers to maintain their earnings

While earnings were comparatively higher among app-based drivers they still faced some challenges to maintain their earnings. First, a significant proportion of the earnings of the app-based taxi drivers come from bonuses, which are linked to targets. The taxi drivers in the ILO survey reported that over time the targets were increased and rewards were reduced, which affected their incomes. In most of the countries, except Ghana, Kenya and Lebanon, the proportion of taxi drivers who responded that the bonus amount had declined was quite high compared to those who reported that it had increased (see Figure 10.6). In India and Morocco, almost 80 per cent of the respondents reported that the amount offered as bonus had declined over time. For instance, a taxi driver on Ola in India mentioned, "Initially it was good to join Ola but now the bonuses are reduced, as are the earnings".

About 43 per cent of the app-based drivers reported that it was harder to qualify for bonuses as platforms constantly changed the requirements. They also reported that it became hard to meet the final target and get the bonus, as the algorithm often did not assign drivers enough rides when they were reaching close to their target, which has also been observed by researchers in other countries (Rosenblat and Stark 2016).

Second, the aggressive pricing strategies pursued by the platforms has led to a decline in the demand for the services of traditional taxi drivers. Many of the traditional taxi drivers have had little choice but to join the platforms in order to earn incomes and maintain their livelihoods. A taxi driver on Uber

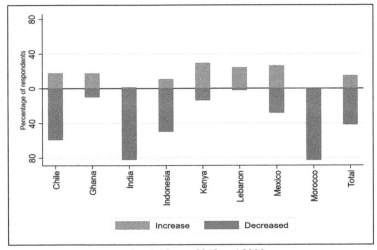

Source: ILO country surveys of taxi drivers, 2019 and 2020.

Figure 10.6   Changes in the amount offered as bonus over time, by country (percentage of respondents)

in Lebanon reported that he "used to work for a traditional taxi company but stopped because demand for traditional companies has dropped". The shift of taxi drivers from traditional to app-based has also increased labour supply on the platforms and increased competition. The oversupply of workers on these platforms has also led to a reduction in fares over a period of time, which was reported by taxi drivers in almost all the countries where the survey was conducted. The intense competition to get rides among these drivers could also be another reason for not being able to meet their targets and to get their bonuses (van Doorn 2017).

Third, the gamification introduced by the platforms to meet the targets to earn bonuses also leads to long working hours for app-based taxi drivers. Workers reported on average working 67 hours per week on platforms, and about half of the workers reported working more than 12 hours per day and about 44 per cent reported working seven days a week so as to be able to qualify for bonuses. This high work intensity not only has an impact on the work and family life balance but also raises concerns about their occupational safety and health, which was reported by 82 per cent of the workers. The safety concerns are largely related to road safety, which was reported by about 72 per cent of the app-based taxi drivers, apart from theft (52 per cent) and physical assault (49 per cent). A taxi driver in Ghana who worked for Bolt reported, "I was hit by another vehicle. I was admitted to the hospital and hence was not able to work for two weeks", and in such instances workers often do not receive any compensation, and as they are unable to work, it adversely impacts their earnings. Apart from safety concerns, a high proportion of app-based taxi drivers (78 per cent) also reported feeling stressed by their working conditions (see Figure 10.7).

Fourth, the earnings of the app-based taxi drivers were also affected by the commission and other fees charged by the platform on the ride, which ranged between 5 to 25 per cent and could go up to 40 per cent on some platforms. Platforms attract drivers by charging lower commission rates when they enter

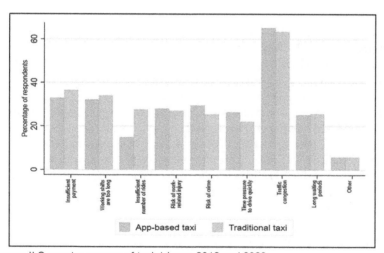

Source: ILO country surveys of taxi drivers, 2019 and 2020.

Figure 10.7   Main reasons for stress among app-based and traditional taxi drivers (percentage of respondents)

a new market, and once they have a sufficient number of taxi drivers on the platform, they increase the rates over time. For instance, in Chile a Uber driver reported that "when I started the commission rate was 15 per cent and now sometimes it reaches up to 30 per cent". Similar experiences were reported in the qualitative responses by taxi drivers in Chile and also in other countries. In India, one of the app-based taxi drivers on Uber explained that the "commission charges increased gradually from 10 to 15 to 20 to 25 and now it is 29 per cent". To address the unpredictability of incomes, Ola in India adopted a standardised commission of 25 per cent nationally for drivers in 2020 and moved away from an incentive-driven model.[8]

Platforms also incentivise drivers to retain them on the platforms by offering them lower commission rates, as was observed in Ghana, where a taxi driver on Uber said that, "a service fee of 25 per cent per week has been scaled down to 3 per cent after completing a specific number of trips". While the practice of charging commission fees was followed by all the platforms, it is contrary to the International Labour Standards such as the ILO Protection of Wages Convention, 1949 (No. 95) and the Private Employment Agencies Convention, 1997 (No. 181), which prohibits agencies, employers and intermediaries from charging fees. Apart from commission fees, taxi drivers also pay a fee for transferring the money to their bank accounts. The traditional self-employed taxi drivers in contrast do not pay any commission charges or fees on the incomes they earn.

Fifth, the earnings of the taxi drivers are also affected by whether they own the vehicle or rent it. ILO surveys show that 67 per cent of the app-based drivers own a vehicle and the hourly earnings of these workers are higher than those who rent the vehicle in all the countries except for Indonesia. The lower earnings could be due to the rental charges they have to pay for the vehicle. The higher earnings for those who own the vehicle are also true in the traditional segment. While many app-based taxi drivers own the vehicle, a sizable proportion of them (70 per cent) have taken loans from platform companies or other sources to purchase them, and are struggling to repay their loans. A taxi driver from India explained, "I took a loan for this car because at the start we used to earn a lot. But then Ola and Uber reduced their rates and now I can't make my monthly loan repayments." This situation has become even more challenging since the COVID-19 pandemic as many drivers could not earn incomes due to lockdowns and were unable to pay their loan instalments. Though platform companies had deferred loan repayments for a short period of time, this was not helpful for taxi drivers who were struggling to earn their incomes. Many taxi drivers who had taken loans from platform companies were locked-in with the company and are facing financial implications.

How do app-based taxi drivers access work and how is their performance managed?

While the proponents of platform work argue that workers have greater auton-omy and control over their work (Mulcahy 2016), questions are being raised as to whether the algorithmic management practices adopted by the platforms lead to new forms of control (Pichault and McKeown 2019; Wood et al. 2019). The algorithmic management practices adopted by the platforms also raise questions around flexibility and the autonomy that the workers enjoy, and can erode job quality and the bargaining power of the worker.

As mentioned earlier, taxi drivers access their rides through the mobile application, which allocates rides to the drivers using an algorithm, based on a number of indicators and the location of the taxi driver. Rating is key to accessing rides on taxi platforms, which was reported by about 70 per cent of the taxi drivers. The rating system adopted by the platforms to evaluate workers allows them to discipline workers. The process of evaluation is trans-ferred to the customers, who after each trip evaluate the taxi drivers based on a five-point star system. The experience of the taxi drivers shows that the ratings had an impact on the number of rides they received and also the type of rides such as long or short distance, the locality they were travelling and earnings (see Figure 10.8). More than half the workers across all countries reported that ratings impacted the number of rides, while the impact on the type of rides they received varied across countries. The ratings were also influ-enced by factors which were beyond the control of the workers, such as traffic congestion or simply the mood of the customer.

In addition, to being disciplined by the algorithm's rating mechanism, taxi platforms also monitor and track worker location and their behaviour on a regular basis and in real time using GPS. Such tracking enables platforms to define the routes that workers take to complete rides and the time spent. It also allows for extensive data collection which is valuable to platforms' pricing, advertising and intermediating strategies (ILO 2021).

Such monitoring and tracking of worker behaviour also leads to self-disciplin-ing on the part of the taxi drivers in order to maintain access to work. In the qualitative responses, the taxi drivers reported that some individual character-istics were key to ensuring access to work, such as providing good customer service; hard work; motivation; having good driving skills; being knowledge-able about the city; good behaviour such as being friendly, polite, cheerful and disciplined; having a good appearance; and providing good customer service (see Figure 10.9). The client reviews capture these characteristics of

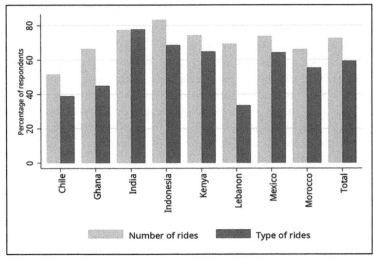

Source: ILO country surveys of taxi drivers, 2019 and 2020.

Figure 10.8   Ratings have an impact on the number of rides and type of rides

the workers, which has a tremendous influence on their continuing access to work. This is because workers whose accounts were deactivated temporarily or permanently often found out that the clients gave a bad review or complained to the platform, which often resulted in not being assigned rides for a period of time or deactivation. What is more, despite the role that customer ratings play in determining the drivers' experience, most platforms do not provide channels for drivers to challenge negative customer ratings. Drivers are often not even aware of the reviews made about them.

Another important aspect of algorithmic management is that it prevents workers from fully benefitting from the freedom and flexibility with regard to time, place and choosing the ride, which self-employed traditional taxi drivers enjoy. App-based taxi drivers have very little time (about 15 to 40 seconds) to decide whether to accept or decline a ride. They are not provided information about the destination, the fare of the ride or the rating of the passengers to take an informed decision about whether to accept the ride. However, even if more information and time were available, cancellation of a ride had repercussions on their work, such as lower ratings, accounts being blocked, fewer rides, lost bonuses, among others, which was reported by about 40 per cent of the taxi drivers (see Figure 10.10). About half of the workers in India, Indonesia and Mexico faced such repercussions for cancelling the rides. As their work sched-

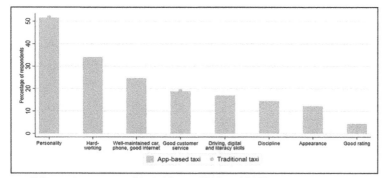

Source: ILO country surveys of taxi drivers, 2019 and 2020.

Figure 10.9   Important characteristics to become a successful app-based taxi driver (percentage of respondents)

ules are determined by the platform's rating mechanism and the incentive and bonus structure, this does not give them any control or autonomy over their work.

In addition, if the ratings are below a particular threshold, it can also lead to deactivation of accounts automatically. Such deactivation of accounts was reported by about one-fifth of the taxi drivers, which basically terminated their access to work through the platform. For about 15 per cent of these workers the deactivation was permanent or lasted for at least one month which had a major impact on their livelihoods (see Figure 10.11). The main reasons for deactivation included complaints from customers (24 per cent), cancellation or not accepting the rides (17 per cent), violation of platform rules (17 per cent) and late payment of service fees (13 per cent). About 64 per cent of app-based drivers who reported deactivation believed that it was unjustified, and a substantial proportion (66 per cent) had appealed against it, with 49 per cent reporting dissatisfaction with the outcome.

Growing worker discontent and regulatory responses in the developing countries

The increasing challenges faced by workers on taxi platforms in a number of developing countries related to their working conditions has led to strikes,

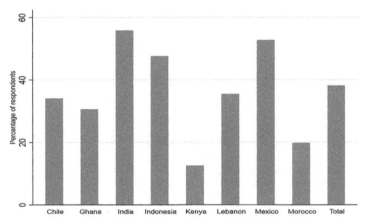

Source: ILO country surveys of taxi drivers, 2019 and 2020.

Figure 10.10   Percentage of respondents who faced repercussions for cancelling rides

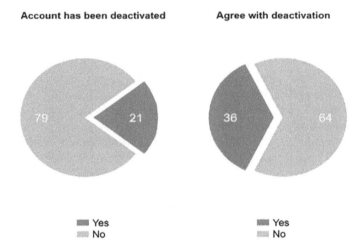

Source: ILO country surveys of taxi drivers, 2019 and 2020.

Figure 10.11   Deactivation of accounts in the app-based taxi sector (percentage of respondents)

demonstrations and litigation. In Kenya for instance, Uber drivers went on strike in 2019 due to low wages and poor working conditions.[9] Similarly in India, app-based taxi drivers have undertaken strike action on several instances.[10] In countries such as Brazil and South Africa, cases have been brought by app-based taxi drivers against Uber (International Lawyers Assisting Workers Network 2021). Since 2015, according to the Leeds Index of Platform Labour Protest, such forms of actions by app-based workers have been growing in developing countries (Bessa et al. 2022; see also Joyce et al. 2020). According to the Leeds index, the reasons for dispute actions prior to the pandemic included issues such as pay (64 per cent), employment status (20 per cent), health and safety (19 per cent) and regulatory aspects (17 per cent). Many of these actions have continued during the COVID-19 pandemic, and since its outbreak, health and safety disputes have constituted more than half the number of disputes, with Latin America being particularly affected. Although strike action has often been associated with pay and working conditions issues, litigation has often focused on employment status and regulatory issues as per the Index.

While such forms of action have been on the rise reflecting a growing discontent, the low level of unionisation on taxi platforms is less than 3 per cent in the eight developing countries surveyed. Some unions have started to engage with and support taxi drivers working on platforms, and platform workers have also formed workers associations to voice their concerns.[11] In Costa Rica, for instance, one such association of platform drivers has been advocating for an independent administrative body for dispute settlement between the companies and drivers, regarding deactivation.[12] To increase their associational power platform workers have sought novel ways to utilise digital means to organise and coordinate their actions via social media (Woodcock and Graham 2020). About 9 per cent of the taxi drivers in the ILO survey reported that they had participated in a coordinated group action such as a protest, or demonstration, or logging out of the app.

Some governments in developing countries have also started to recognise and address concerns regarding working conditions on taxi platforms, and have taken various approaches to extend labour protections to these workers. A number of measures in developing countries relate to social security, work and injury benefits, occupational safety and health and access to data and privacy. For example, in India, the Code on Social Security introduced in 2020 extends protection to all workers, including platform workers, irrespective of the existence of an employment relationship. Meanwhile in Uruguay, app-based taxi drivers can automatically transfer their social security contributions to the relevant authorities through the platform (Behrendt, Nguyen and Rani 2019).

There have also been some measures related to working time and remuneration. India has introduced the Indian Motor Vehicle Aggregators Guidelines[13] of 2020, which regulates fares and also introduces obligations on taxi platforms to ensure that drivers are not logged in for more than 12 hours a day, even if the drivers are engaged with multiple aggregators, as well as have a mandatory break period.

Developing countries have started to engage carefully with data privacy and protection. For instance in Brazil, the Brazilian General Data Protection Law has been in force since 2020; in 2019, Nigeria introduced the Nigerian Data Protection Regulation; and in India, the Personal Data Protection Bill, 2019 is under consideration.[14] Most recently in China, the taxi platform DiDi has faced a probe by the Chinese authorities, just two days after its US$4 billion initial public offering (IPO), with regard to data security, as well as the use and collection of personal information, and the app has also been banned from app stores.[15]

While multiple measures and court decisions have started to shape the regulatory framework in some of the developing countries, these efforts remain disjointed and dispersed and risk maintaining vulnerabilities for workers. In this context, developing a coordinated as well as cohesive policy response at the international level, will be an important point of departure for ensuring decent work for all.

Notes

1. In developing countries, urban access to the internet was found to be 2.3 times as high as rural access (ITU 2020).
2. There are two main types of digital labour platforms: online web-based platforms, where tasks are performed online and remotely by workers and are allocated to a crowd (on microtask and competitive programming platforms) or to individuals (on freelance and contest-based platforms); and location-based platforms, where tasks are performed at a specified physical location by individuals such as taxi drivers and delivery workers (ILO 2021).
3. As expressed by a representative of a taxi platform (Bolt) in an ILO interview in Kenya.
4. Also see regarding safety, for instance, Uber: https://www.uber.com/in/en/safety/ ; Bolt: https://blog.bolt.eu/ke/is-driving-with-bolt-safe-yes-and-here-are-7-things -we-do-to-keep-it-that-way-3/.
5. Uber for example, in its webportal targeting prospective drivers, notes: "Set your own hours" and "You decide when and how often you drive" (for more information see: https://www.uber.com/in/en/drive/). Similarly, Bolt notes: "Work with

your own schedule. No minimum hours and no boss" (for more information see: https://partners.bolt.eu/driver-signup?utm_source=website&utm_medium=header&utm_campaign=bolt-drivers).

6. For instance, see: https://www.businesstoday.in/latest/story/mumbai-taxi-unions-demand-rs-5-hike-in-fares-as-prices-of-cng-go-up-313819-2021-11-29.

7. For more details, see: https://www.businessinsider.in/business/news/merus-plea-against-uber-abusing-its-dominant-status-rejected-by-cci/articleshow/84434982.cms; https://www.cci.gov.in/sites/default/files/96-of-2015.pdf.

8. For more details, see: https://auto.economictimes.indiatimes.com/news/aftermarket/ola-rejigs-commissions-to-retain-drivers/73115178.

9. For more details, see: https://www.bbc.com/news/av/world-africa-49008968.

10. For more details, see: https://mashable.com/article/uber-ola-strike-bangalore-india; https://www.reuters.com/article/us-uber-ola-strike-idUSKCN1MW1WZ; and https://www.dnaindia.com/india/report-ola-uber-drivers-on-strike-march-22-all-you-need-to-know-2882518.

11. For instance, in India, the Indian Federation of App Based Transport Workers is a workers' organisation representing app-based transport and delivery workers; see: https://twitter.com/connect_ifat. In Kenya, app-based drivers, under the Kenya Digital Taxi Association, have undertaken strike action (for more information, see: https://www.kenyans.co.ke/news/22590-online-taxi-drivers-go-strike-nairobi).

12. ILO interview with a representative of ACOPLATEC (Asociación de Conductores de Plataformas Tecnológicas y Afines), Costa Rica, 24 April 2020.

13. For more details, see: https://morth.nic.in/sites/default/files/notifications_document/Motor%20Vehicle%20Aggregators27112020150046.pdf.

14. For more information see, Brazil: https://www.dlapiperdataprotection.com/index.html?t=law&c=BR&c2=; Nigeria: https://www.dlapiperdataprotection.com/index.html?t=law&c=NG&c2=; and India: https://prsindia.org/billtrack/the-personal-data-protection-bill-2019.

15. For more information, see: https://techcrunch.com/2021/07/20/china-roundup-data-security-clampdown/; https://edition.cnn.com/2021/07/04/tech/china-app-store-didi/index.html.

References

Acheampong, Ransford A. 2021. "Societal Impacts of Smart, Digital Platform Mobility Services – an Empirical Study and Policy Implications of Passenger Safety and Security in Ride-Hailing". *Case Studies on Transport Policy* 9 (1): 302–14.

Behrendt, Christina, Quynh Anh Nguyen, and Uma Rani. 2019. "Social Protection Systems and the Future of Work: Ensuring Social Security for Digital Platform Workers". *International Social Security Review* 72 (3): 17–41.

Berger, Thor, Carl Benedikt Frey, Guy Levin, and Santosh Rao Danda. 2019. "Uber Happy? Work and Well-Being in the 'Gig Economy'". *Economic Policy* 34 (99): 429–77.

Bessa, Ioulia, Simon Joyce, Denis Neumann, Mark Stuart, Vera Trappmann, and Charles Umney. 2022. "A Global Analysis of Worker Protest in Digital Labour Platforms". ILO Working Paper 70. Geneva, Switzerland: ILO.

Bick, Geoff. 2019. "Uber SA: Disruption of the Local Taxi Industry?". *Emerald Emerging Markets Case Studies* 9 (2): 1–4.

Carmody, Pádraig, and Alicia Fortuin. 2019. "'Ride-Sharing', Virtual Capital and Impacts on Labor in Cape Town, South Africa". *African Geographical Review* 38 (3): 196–208.

Chen, Julie Yujie. 2018a. "Thrown under the Bus and Outrunning It! The Logic of Didi and Taxi Drivers' Labour and Activism in the On-Demand Economy". *New Media & Society* 20 (8): 2691–711.

Chen, Julie Yujie. 2018b. "Technologies of Control, Communication, and Calculation: Taxi Drivers' Labour in the Platform Economy". In *Humans and Machines at Work: Monitoring, Surveillance and Automation in Contemporary Capitalism*, edited by Phoebe V. Moore, Martin Upchurch, and Xanthe Whittaker, 231–52. Dynamics of Virtual Work. Cham: Springer International Publishing.

Chinguno, Crispen. 2019. "Power Dynamics in the Gig/Share Economy: Uber and Bolt Taxi Platforms in Johannesburg, South Africa". *Labour, Capital and Society* 49 (2): 30–65.

Damle, Vidula. 2018. "Disruptive Innovation: A Case Study of Uber". *International Journal of Advanced Research and Publications* 2 (11): 21–26.

Dhawan, Shivangi, and Priyanka Yadav. 2018. "E-Cab Hailing: A Study of Consumer Behaviour". *ELK Asia Pacific Journal of Marketing and Retail Management* 9 (3): 1–17.

Fielbaum, Andrés, and Alejandro Tirachini. 2021. "The Sharing Economy and the Job Market: The Case of Ride-Hailing Drivers in Chile". *Transportation* 48 (5): 2235–61.

Fleitoukh, Anna, and Kentaro Toyama. 2020. "Are Ride-Sharing Platforms Good for Indian Drivers? An Investigation of Taxi and Auto-Rickshaw Drivers in Delhi". In *The Future of Digital Work: The Challenge of Inequality*, edited by Rajendra K. Bandi, C.R. Ranjini, Stefan Klein, Shirin Madon, and Eric Monteiro, 117–31. IFIP Advances in Information and Communication Technology. Cham: Springer International Publishing.

Graham, Mark, Isis Hjorth, and Vili Lehdonvirta. 2017. "Digital Labour and Development: Impacts of Global Digital Labour Platforms and the Gig Economy on Worker Livelihoods". *Transfer: European Review of Labour and Research* 23 (2): 135–62.

Hall, Jonathan V., and Alan B. Krueger. 2016. "An Analysis of the Labor Market for Uber's Driver-Partners in the United States". NBER Working Paper No. 22843. NBER.

Heeks, Richard, Juan Erasmo Gomez-Morantes, Mark Graham, Kelle Howson, Paul Mungai, Brian Nicholson, and Jean-Paul Van Belle. 2021a. "Digital Platforms and Institutional Voids in Developing Countries: The Case of Ride-Hailing Markets". *World Development* 145: 1–13.

Heeks, Richard, Mark Graham, Paul Mungai, Jean-Paul Van Belle, and Jamie Woodcock. 2021b. "Systematic Evaluation of Gig Work against Decent Work Standards: The Development and Application of the Fairwork Framework". *The Information Society* 37 (5): 267–86.

Horan, Hubert. 2019. "Uber's Path of Destruction". *American Affairs* 3 (2).

Hunt, Abigail, and Emma Samman. 2020. "Domestic Work and the Gig Economy in South Africa: Old Wine in New Bottles?". *Anti-Trafficking Review* 15: 102–21.

International Labour Organization (ILO). 2021. *World Employment and Social Outlook 2021: The Role of Digital Labour Platforms in Transforming the World of Work*. Geneva, Switzerland: ILO.

International Lawyers Assisting Workers Network. 2021. *Taken for a Ride: Litigating the Digital Platform Model.*

International Telecommunication Union (ITU). 2020. *Measuring Digital Development: Facts and Figures 2020.* Geneva, Switzerland: ITU.

Joyce, Simon, Denis Neumann, Vera Trappmann, and Charles Umney. 2020. "A Global Struggle: Worker Protest in the Platform Economy". European Trade Union Institute (ETUI) Policy Brief No. 2.

KPMG. 2020. *Covid-19 as Accelerator for Digital Transformation and the Rise of the Gig Economy.* Saudi Arabia: KPMG.

Lakemann, Tabea, and Jann Lay. 2019. "Digital Platforms in Africa: The 'Uberisation' of Informal Work". *GIGA Focus Afrika* 7.

Mäntymäki, Matti, Abayomi Baiyere, and A.K.M. Najmul Islam. 2019. "Digital Platforms and the Changing Nature of Physical Work: Insights from Ride-Hailing". *International Journal of Information Management* 49: 452–60.

Mastercard. 2020. *The Gig Economy in East Africa: A Gateway to the Financial Mainstream.*

Mulcahy, Diane. 2016. "Who Wins in the Gig Economy, and Who Loses". *Harvard Business Review,* October 27, 2016.

Muralidhar, Srihari Hulikal. 2016. "How Ola Disrupted Taxi Services in India?". *Review of Management* 6 (3–4): 5–17.

Panse, Chetan, Shailesh Rastogi, Arpita Sharma, and Namgay Dorji. 2019. "Understanding Consumer Behaviour Towards Utilization of Online Food Delivery Platforms". *Journal of Theoretical and Applied Information Technology* 97 (16): 4353–65.

Pichault, François, and Tui McKeown. 2019. "Autonomy at Work in the Gig Economy: Analysing Work Status, Work Content and Working Conditions of Independent Professionals". *New Technology, Work and Employment* 34 (1): 59–72.

Prabhat, Shantanu, Sneha Nanavati, and Nimmi Rangaswamy. 2019. "India's 'Uberwallah': Profiling Uber Drivers in the Gig Economy". In *Proceedings of the Tenth International Conference on Information and Communication Technologies and Development,* 1–5. ICTD '19. Ahmedabad, India: Association for Computing Machinery.

Ramachandran, Sreelakshmi, and Aishwarya Raman. 2021. *Unlocking Jobs in the Platform Economy: Propelling India's Post-Covid Recovery.* Ola Mobility Institute.

Rosenblat, Alex, and Luke Stark. 2016. "Algorithmic Labor and Information Asymmetries: A Case Study of Uber's Drivers". *International Journal of Communication* 10: 3758–84.

Shah, Tejas R. 2020. "Service Quality Dimensions of Ride-Sourcing Services in Indian Context". *Benchmarking: An International Journal* 28 (1): 249–66.

Surie, Aditi, and Jyothi Koduganti. 2016. "The Emerging Nature of Work in Platform Economy Companies in Bengaluru, India: The Case of Uber and Ola Cab Drivers". *E-Journal of International and Comparative Labour Studies* 5 (3): 1–30.

Tandem Research. 2019. *Worker Wellbeing on Digital Work Platforms in India: A Study of Ola Cabs & UrbanClap in New Delhi.*

Teo, Boon-Chui, Muhamad Azimulfadli Mustaffa, and Amir Iqbal Mohd Rozi. 2018. "To Grab or Not to Grab? Passenger Ride Intention Towards E-Hailing Services". *Malaysian Journal of Consumer and Family Economics* 21: 153–63.

Uber. 2020a. "What Does the Background Check Look For?" https://help.uber.com/driving-and-delivering/article/what-does-the-background-check-look-for?nodeId=ee210269-89bf-4bd9-87f6-43471300ebf2.

Uber. 2020b. *2019 Annual Report.*

van Doorn, Niels. 2017. "Platform Labor: On the Gendered and Racialized Exploitation of Low-Income Service Work in the 'On-Demand' Economy". *Information, Communication & Society* 20 (6): 898–914.

Verma, Ravinder Kumar, P. Vigneswara Ilavarasan, and Arpan Kumar Kar. 2020. "Inequalities in Ride-Hailing Platforms". In *Platform Capitalism in India*, edited by Adrian Athique and Vibodh Parthasarathi, 177–98. Global Transformations in Media and Communication Research – A Palgrave and IAMCR Series. Cham: Springer International Publishing.

Wood, Alex J., Mark Graham, Vili Lehdonvirta, and Isis Hjorth. 2019. "Good Gig, Bad Gig: Autonomy and Algorithmic Control in the Global Gig Economy". *Work, Employment and Society* 33 (1): 56–75.

Woodcock, Jamie, and Mark Graham. 2020. *The Gig Economy: A Critical Introduction.* New York: Polity Press.

Wu, Qingjun, and Zhen Li. 2019. "Labor Control and Task Autonomy under the Sharing Economy: A Mixed-Method Study of Drivers' Work". *The Journal of Chinese Sociology* 6: 1–21.

Wu, Qingjun, Hao Zhang, Zhen Li, and Kai Liu. 2019. "Labor Control in the Gig Economy: Evidence from Uber in China". *Journal of Industrial Relations* 61 (4): 574–96.

Yuan, Li. 2018. "Customer Died. Will That Be a Wake-up Call for China's Tech Scene?". *The New York Times*, August 29, 2018.

11   The emerging geographies of platform labour: Intensifying trends in global capitalism

Kelle Howson, Alessio Bertolini, Srujana Katta, Funda Ustek-Spilda, Mark Graham[1]

Introduction

Digital labour platforms have rapidly emerged as influential agents in the global organisation of labour and production. To understand the distribution of agency, power, and accumulation in the platform economy, it is important for geographers to trace the ways in which digital labour platforms are interacting with and even transforming the spatial dynamics of labour. We seek to understand where platforms sit within patterns of global economic activity – and to situate the labour and value they mediate in time and space. Where are the platform's shareholders, managers, operational infrastructures, and fixed assets located? Which jurisdictions and regulations are they subject to? How do they interact with and influence urban environments? Where is the value being produced, and where is it being accumulated? And most importantly for labour scholars, what do these shifting economic geographies mean for the millions of workers now subjugated into and dependent on the value networks created by digital labour platforms? This research agenda is crucial in order to account fully for the role of digital labour platforms in global capitalism, and ultimately to develop appropriate policy responses for the harms and inequities they produce. This is a call that has been mounting from labour geographers, and in this chapter we partially respond to it by outlining the uneven geographies created by digital labour platforms and situating them in historical trends in global capitalism, and commodification of labour.

Researchers have demonstrated how platforms exhibit disembedding tendencies which have allowed them to avoid becoming too intertwined with national institutional contexts, and thus obligated to abide by, for example, national labour protections (Graham, 2020; Katta et al., 2020; Tubaro, 2021; Wood et al., 2019a). By aggressively branding themselves as *just* software proprietors or merely digital marketplaces (obfuscating their true role as international labour brokers) they remain slippery and light-footed, avoid costs (Srnicek, 2017), and evade local social responsibilities. However, they still have a profound influence on local working conditions and cityscapes, and extract value from localised service transactions, remaining in another sense 'deeply embedded' (Tubaro, 2021). Viewed in this light, we see how platforms have been designed to operate on different geographical scales (local, regional, and global) in a tactical way. For instance, the digital forms of governance that platforms exert, including algorithmic work allocation, centralised payment systems, the establishment of information asymmetries, and systems to rate, rank, punish, and exclude workers, as well as platforms' social policies (sometimes called 'community guidelines' or 'codes of conduct'), are all deployed from a central point of coordination which is often distant from the worker's local context. However, these instruments of management are often adjusted in order to optimise the value the platform can extract, based on local contingencies (see, for instance, the example of Uber entering into traditional motorcycle taxi markets in East Africa; see Bright, 2018). By strategically occupying different points of geographical embeddedness, platforms can harness and exacerbate existing social and geographical inequalities towards capitalist imperatives – to drive the commodification of labour and to undermine workers' power and agency.

The chapter is organised as follows. The first section of this chapter draws on insights from geographers who have critiqued digital labour platforms, showing that they sit at the forefront of trends which give rise to uneven economic geographies of labour and production. Building on this foundation, the next section argues that these trends have long legacies within global capitalism, which have long been of central concern to labour politics. This context is followed by an empirical section in which we identify countervailing trends of resistance to the harms perpetuated by digital labour platforms. We discuss developments and possibilities in national and supranational regulation, worker resistance, and consumer and third sector campaigns. Our key argument and contribution to the literature is that the platform labour countermovement is increasingly responding to the need to meet platforms at all the geographical scales across which they manifest and attempt to retreat. This includes in local, global, and virtual terrains.

Digital labour platforms at the forefront of the globalisation of labour

The emergence and expansion of digital labour platforms have been facilitated by both technological and economic changes in the last two decades. The global advances in the information and communication technologies entailed that accessing the internet via a smartphone is no longer a privilege of the few. Instead, faster and cheap connectivity through smartphones is taken for granted in many parts of the world. This transformation of the access to technology happened simultaneously with the deregulation of labour; emergence of short-time, zero-hour contracts, erosion of worker power with decreasing unionisation rates and, ultimately, increasing quantification and neo-liberalisation of work. Indeed, the quantification and neo-liberalisation of work goes hand in hand, as the former prepares the medium in which all parts of a work relationship can become commodified, and the parts which cannot be commoditised be discarded.

Seen in this light, both geographically tethered work and cloudwork are subsumed into new complex cross-border assemblages of value, where even the basic cost–profit calculation is re-shaped and re-structured. Many platforms are loss-making companies (Kenney & Zysman, 2020; van Doorn & Badger, 2020). They are loss-making, not because of the high cost of labour or the complexity of sourcing the products or the services on the platforms, but because platforms aim to grow at a speed which would be unimaginable only a few years ago through increased market penetration and aggressive marketing. Even when they are established companies operating in multiple regions and several countries, most platforms identify themselves as 'start-ups' with a small internal operation team, looking for investments to grow their operations across the world. In this setup, platforms and their 'small' head-quarters are usually in a big city which is known to attract large funding from angel and venture capital investors (e.g., Silicon Valley, London, Amsterdam, Bangalore), platform workers are in the cities in which they operate; and their clients can be either in those cities (geographically tethered platforms) or any-where in the world (as in cloudwork). This operational structure entails that the management of platforms, and in some cases even the clients, are spatially distanced from the labour.

In instituting these complex geographical dynamics, platforms create and lead relational global networks of economic exchange in new sectors, or previously highly localised sectors (Grabher & van Tuijl, 2020). They come to dominate (and attempt to establish monopsonies in) sectors like last mile delivery, taxis, and domestic and care work, medical consultation and counselling, sex work, and others, which were not previously the abode of large multinational companies (Kumar, 2020). But platform companies themselves are much leaner than the familiar behemoths who have dominated and directed the international division of labour in the late twentieth and early twenty-first centuries, like Nike and Nestle (Srnicek, 2017). This has led many to point to the fact that as global economic actors, platforms' strategies are reliant on network-effects, or cross-subsidising supply and demand to build a critical mass of users in order to produce value (Langley & Leyshon, 2017; van Doorn & Badger, 2020). Platforms tend to replicate these network strategies across diverse territories, drawing a huge proportion of the world's workforce into cross-border relations of production, where offshore corporations are benefitting from their labour transactions, and influencing the labour process. While they are governed through digital infrastructures, these networks resemble global value chains and production networks in agro-food, clothing and manufactured commodities, which have been established by multinational corporations and have involved high levels of wealth extraction and accumulation to the Global North. They are underpinned by processes of global free market exchange, financialisation, and logics of externalising costs and risks to vulnerable workers, and siphoning surplus value to a lead firm.

We have shown in this section how platforms sit at the forefront of the evolving global division of labour. They interact with and produce highly complex labour geographies with the objective of establishing centralised control and power over locally embedded labour processes which had, to greater or lesser degrees, previously escaped globalising tendencies. The next section historically contextualises the capital–labour relations of the platform economy, and problematises the discourses of innovation and technological change which sit at the heart of platform capitalism.

Historical geographical context of the platform economy

We have shown that digital labour platforms benefit from globalised labour geographies which concentrate power and value at central points of accumulation, while exerting extremely sophisticated forms of control over the behaviour and experiences of workers, as well as influencing local spatialities – like transport systems, and patterns of urban inclusion and exclusion. Through this lens, we can see how platforms' digital infrastructures underpin their multiscalar nature, and they appear highly novel and innovative. However, the trends described in the previous section have historical precedents and, in many ways, deepen pre-existing developments in the globalisation of labour (Peck & Phillips, 2020).

This section advances our argument that digital labour platforms both emerge out of, and extend and deepen, trends in the commodification of labour and production which have been sites of exploitation and resistance at previous points in global capitalism. The following section explores contemporary countermovements to reassert workers' rights and redistribute value more equitably in the platform economy. Having outlined the complex multiscalar dynamics of platform power, we pay particular attention to responses which both re-territorialise labour relations and build international and global solidarities to challenge platform power at a global level.

As we have shown, platform companies utilise new technologies to drive processes of economic globalisation, and to reshape labour geographies. However, many commentators go too far when they claim that the technological infrastructures which underpin digital labour platforms are themselves agents of disruption, which will inevitably radically transform the nature of work independently of the social context they are used in (e.g., Atmore, 2017). In fact, this narrative has been used to justify the harmful outcomes that digital labour platforms have produced – with the implication that they are an unavoidable product of inevitable (and inherently good) progress.

When we situate digital labour platforms in geographies and histories of labour relations, we can identify the ways in which they exploit and reproduce existing dynamics of inequality, as opposed to disrupting and reconstituting work as we know it (Peck & Phillips, 2020). Platforms can be situated in a genealogy of commodification of labour, international outsourcing of work, and managers avoiding responsibilities to workers. Piece-rate payment, or payment based on unit of output (discrete task or service) as opposed to labour time, is a crucial feature of the platform economy, and has lent it its popular name ('gig' economy). This is often presented as an innovative management model; however, the practice has a long and exploitative history within agricultural and factory work. The notorious platform practice of contractually classifying workers as independent contractors too has a contentious history which predates digitalisation, and has been litigated in earlier phases of the labour movement, especially in industrialised countries (Stanford, 2017; Pinsof, 2016).

Digital labour platforms are oriented towards managerial optimisation, using algorithmic management to achieve efficiencies in the labour process, and maximise the amount of value the platform can derive from each transaction. This characteristic drive to increase labour productivity through scientific management was already advocated by Frederick Taylor in the early twentieth century (Taylor, 1911). In the gig economy, this is seen in, for instance, algorithmic price fluctuations responding in real time to conditions of supply and demand, the use of rating and reputational systems to influence how workers work, and 'gamification' features which exploit insights about user behaviour to drive desired outcomes (Scheiber, 2017).

Taking a wider geographical perspective, we can trace how exploitation is distributed and power concentrated on a global scale by digital labour platforms, and how this reproduces uneven historical geographies (Harvey, 2006). Scholars have highlighted the geographic concentration of digital labour platforms within existing centres of wealth and power, most notably California (Kenney & Zysman, 2020). Most cloudwork platforms are theoretically open to users regardless of geographic location. However, many still demonstrate spatial polarisation between labour supply (concentrated in the Global South) and demand (concentrated in the Global North) (Braesemann et al., 2021; Rani et al., 2021). Moreover, research has found that workers based in the Global South are more likely to experience poorer outcomes even under uniform platform systems and policies, owing in part to discrimination stemming from client attitudes and biases about workers from specific locations (Fairwork, 2021). Within these uneven global networks, platforms act as lead firms to extract the surplus value of labour to centres of wealth. In 2019, Upwork generated 62% of its approximately US$300 million revenue through fees charged to workers, compared with 38% from fees charged to clients (Rani et al., 2021, p. 72). Together these empirics demonstrate that platforms exert control over both relational processes of exchange and flows of value, and also over lived experiences of users, and material/concrete spaces. They do so from a central point of power.

However, many Global South policymakers have placed particular emphasis on the potential of digital labour platforms to drive employment, formalisation, and development in spaces which have historically been economically exploited and marginalised. Discourses of 'ICT4D' (ICT for Development) and '4IR' (Fourth Industrial Revolution) have risen to prominence in development policy, based on the hope that deepened inclusion in the digital economy will help to overcome entrenched geographic exploitation and create more equitable outcomes (Heeks, 2008; Unwin, 2009; Ponelis & Holmner, 2015). There is growing acknowledgement, however, that historical extractive and exploitative practices can and are being carried through into digitally mediated networks of labour and production, and equitable outcomes depend not just on inclusion in digital networks, but increased agency and governance for marginalised workers and societies in articulating and shaping outcomes. This was emphasised, for instance, in the report of the Presidential Commission on the Fourth Industrial Revolution in South Africa (Presidential Commission on the Fourth Industrial Revolution, 2020).

It is important to specify that, within the labour geographies created by platforms, territorial unevenness is not the only dimension of inequality which is exacerbated. Economic marginalisation and exploitation across intersecting lines of class (Muntaner, 2018; Standing, 2014), race (McMillan Cottom, 2020), and gender (Barzilay & Ben-David, 2017; Cook et al., 2021) is carried through into the platform economy. Platforms have taken advantage of and benefitted from social inequalities to drive a race-to-the-bottom in labour standards, in turn amplifying dimensions of marginalisation. This is seen clearly in the overrepresentation of already marginalised groups in insecure gig work, including migrants, people of colour, and women (especially in the care and domestic work sectors).

To understand the dynamics of these processes from a global geographical perspective, we can draw on theories of uneven geographical development such as advanced by David Harvey (2006), and global value chains (e.g., Bair, 2005; Gereffi et al., 2005; Humphrey & Schmitz, 2002) and production networks (see Yeung & Coe, 2015; Grabher & van Tuijl, 2020). These perspectives shed light on how platforms commodify labour in international networks through worker misclassification, piece-rate payment, externalisation of costs, and strategies of managerial control, and produce and reproduce spatialities of marginalisation, dependence, and precarity (Schor et al., 2020). By drawing on these traditions from economic geography we remain attuned to the ways in which platforms may simultaneously exploit and attempt to depoliticise historically entrenched global economic inequalities, to commodify (vulnerable) labour, and to concentrate power and value at a global scale.

Multiscalar countermovements

So far platforms have exploited uneven labour geographies to their advantage. It is then important that the countermovement (both workers' resistance and regulation) successfully territorially re-embeds platforms to resist their pull towards disembeddedness and commodification, but equally important that regional and international solidarities and strategies are built to tackle platform power when it manifests at and retreats to the global scale. Hybrid *multiscalar* local–global strategies, which combine local and international resistances into new forms within an overall countermovement, are needed in order to counteract platforms' power where it manifests and operates both in local territories, and in supranational spaces. Put more simply, the harmful outcomes of platformisation of labour are experienced locally, but perpetuated at a global level. As such, they can only be effectively countered by action that takes place at multiple scales. In this section, we present empirical examples of ways in which the platform capitalism countermovement has aimed to re-embed platforms' working models into local contexts and mitigate the impact of de-territorialised practices, but also confront platform power at a global scale.

Worker resistance at the global and local levels

Platform workers' mobilisation and organisation has dialectically accompanied the platform economy's proliferation to evermore sectors and geographical contexts. With each passing week, we hear about a new strike, demonstration, or legal or other protest action that workers and workers' organisations undertake against different aspects of platform work. Laudable initiatives like the China Labour Bulletin (China Labour Bulletin, n.d.), Leeds Index of Platform Labour Protest project (Joyce et al., 2020), and the Collective Action in Tech project (Collective Action in Tech, n.d.) have made ambitious attempts to document or map the worker protest in the platform economy,[2] showing that the geographical scope of platform worker protest – like the platform economy – is global.

Poor (or decreasing) pay, unsafe working conditions, and employment status are the leading causes of platform worker protest (Joyce et al., 2020). In the past year, the financial and health insecurity resulting from the pandemic has become a key locus of workers' mobilisation. The pandemic has had debilitating impacts on platform workers, many of whose earnings dropped drastically, as demand for their services dropped, and as they were forced to compete with the new workers who signed up for platform work due to broader recessionary trends. Moreover, platform workers (particularly ride-hail and delivery workers) face high health risks as they need to traverse busy public spaces in the course of their work, and as they have no access to sick pay and other protections that regular employees are entitled to.

These issues precipitated, for example, a wave of coordinated strikes by food delivery couriers across Brazil, Mexico, Chile, Argentina, and Ecuador between April and August 2020 (Howson et al., 2020). Citing decreasing pay and dangerous working conditions (including the threat of COVID-19, and a lack of PPE), and coordinating via social media platforms, workers registered their protest by logging out of apps like Uber Eats, Rappi, and iFood en masse.

These strikes were accompanied by social media appeals to customers (using hashtags like #BrequeDosApps or #StopTheApps), asking them to support strikers by not ordering anything during the action (Howson et al., 2020). Here, by undertaking large-scale, coordinated, cross-border protest that spans an entire sector, workers confronted platforms at the numerous scales that they occupy.

Such multiscalar workers' protest is also being consolidated in new organisational forms, such as with the formation of bodies such as the Indian Federation of App-based Transport Workers (a pan-Indian federation of unions that coordinates gig workers' actions across Indian cities), the International Alliance of App-based Transport Workers (a global coalition of ride-hail workers' unions and associations from around the world), and the Transnational Federation of Couriers (a coalition of delivery workers' unions from around Europe). Leaders from over 25 gig worker unions from five continents assembled in the UK in January 2020 to found the International Alliance of App-based Transport Workers (IAATW), where they collectively developed a far-reaching manifesto and committed to 'sustain, coordinate, and organize world-wide to stop TNCs from their exploitative and harmful practices, and to improve the lives and professions of drivers all over the world' (IAATW, n.d.). Through organisations like this, workers and their representatives are working to transcend the local scale to tackle platforms at the regional and global scales at which they operate. In so doing, these organisations contain one promising possibility for how workers may confront the slippery platform giants at different geographical scales (Cant & Mogno, 2020).

Rebalancing the asymmetry of information through online tools

One of the key features of labour platforms is the innovative ways through which they perform management functions previously reserved to managers and which enable them to exercise control over work from a distance. Among this is the ability to monitor workers' performance through rating systems (Gandini, 2019). Thanks to ratings, platforms are able to de facto outsource this fundamental management function to customers and clients, and to exercise control over workers located potentially anywhere in the world (Wood et al., 2019b). At the same time, platforms have automated other management functions through algorithms. Algorithms can be used, for instance, to assign tasks, select routes, decide prices and rewards, calculate working times, and match customers with workers, with the platform not needing to be in the same geographical location as the worker (Schor et al., 2020).

These innovative managerial devices create important asymmetries of information between workers and platforms. While a platform can control and monitor potentially all relevant aspects of the labour process from a distance, often in real time, workers are generally left in the dark about important information concerning their work, including how pay is calculated, how tasks are assigned or who the customers are. Issues surrounding the secrecy of algorithms have sparked several platform workers' protests around the world and fostered both court cases and policymakers' initiatives (Aranguiz, 2021a; Lomas, 2021). These asymmetries of information engender an important imbalance of power between an almost 'all-knowing' platform and 'unknowing' workers.

This has prompted several initiatives aimed at reducing these information asymmetries and at mitigating the imbalance of power between platforms and workers. Among these, the most widely known one is Turkopticon. Turkopticon is as a browser extension allowing workers to provide information about their clients on the cloudwork platform Amazon Mechanical Turk (Irani & Silberman, 2013). Amazon Mechanical Turk is one of the largest micro-tasking platforms globally, allowing employers to outsource relatively simple tasks to external workers or 'Turkers' in exchange for a payment. However, while requesters have access to relevant information about workers, especially through the rating system, and are therefore able to sort and select workers based on their previous work performance, workers have very limited knowledge about the requesters, generally no more than their name (Bergvall-Kåreborn & Howcroft, 2014). Workers cannot know whether the requester will pay and on time, whether the task requests are feasible, and whether the requesters are more generally reliable. Given that that platform takes very limited responsibility over disputes between workers and requesters, often the only way for workers to express dissatisfaction is to stop working on the platform (Silberman & Irani, 2016).

Turkopticon was born in order to give workers another way to express dissent and to hold requesters more accountable, by providing workers with the opportunity to rate and write anonymous reviews about requesters they have previously worked with. Ratings and reviews can then be consulted on the Turkopticon webpage (Irani & Silberman, 2013). Turkopticon has been able to increase transparency and accountability on Amazon Mechanical Turk, by providing an important tool to reduce the asymmetry of information inbuilt in the platform. But Turkopticon has done more than that. It has created a tool for mutual aid among Turkers and, by doing so, it has offered the opportunity for Turkers across the world to create social ties and build solidarity, counterbalancing the atomisation and commodification which the platform had engendered (Irani & Silberman, 2013).

Turkopticon is not the only initiative aimed at mitigating the imbalance of power in the platform economy and in increasing transparency and account-ability of platforms. For instance, WeClock is an app which allows platform workers to track several features of their work, including their pay and working time. It was developed by UNI Global Union's Young Workers Lab together with the global collective Guardian Project and the organisation Okthanks (WeClock, n.d.). By providing tracking information to workers, it allows them to contrast the opacity of platforms' algorithms and to hold them accountable. Furthermore, it is a tool to foster workers' solidarity by providing a base for workers' organising and campaigning (WeClock, n.d.).

Social media have also proved to be a fundamental tool for workers to exchange information and build solidarity. With platforms generally purpose-fully designed to avoid direct communication between workers and with the features of platform work making it difficult for workers to meet each other in person (Bergvall-Kåreborn & Howcroft, 2014; Woodcock, 2018), social media play a fundamental if informal role in compensating for this lack of commu-nication. Through social media, workers can ask for information, give advice and more generally provide each other with mutual support (Woodcock & Graham, 2020). Social media have also been found to be a relevant tool for organising and mobilising platform workers (Tassinari and Maccarrone, 2020).

Overall, online tools are important devices to enable at least a partial rebal-ancing in power relations between workers and platforms. Through rating systems and algorithms, platforms have been able to monitor and control almost all-important aspects of the labour process from a distance, while at the same time making management less transparent and accountable to workers. By providing access to previously hidden or opaque information to workers, they allow for a reduction in the asymmetry of information in the relationship between workers and platforms while, at the same time, creating a base upon which workers' solidarity can be built and fostered.

National regulation: Employment status and supply chain responsibility

Some critics have claimed that platforms operate in a regulatory void (Hatzopoulos, 2018). This has given rise to the argument, now also advanced by many platform representatives, that new rules need to be established to account for the specific business and labour models seen in the platform economy. However, it is also clear that platforms have emphasised their historical distinctiveness and exploited their murky and shifting geographical manifestations (Graham, 2020; Katta et al., 2020), in order to claim established legal norms do not apply to them. This strategy has proved largely successful in the short history of digital labour platforms, with geographically tethered and cloudwork platforms managing to avoid accountability to established national employment protections, and tax and competition regimes.

While critics are right to point out that platforms have evaded legal obligations, it is important to challenge the ahistorical claim that this is because they operate within an uncharted regulatory terrain. Calls have also arisen for established labour protection frameworks to be expanded to include gig workers (De Stefano, 2015; Fredman et al., 2020) by better enforcement, by challenging specific instances of worker misclassification, and by expanding the definition of who can be considered a worker or an employee in order to access basic rights. In recent months, digital labour platforms have been called to account to established labour protections by both judicial and legislative bodies (albeit mainly in the Global North). These developments are suggested to have been accelerated by the pressures and contradictions within gig work which have been laid bare by the pandemic (Howson et al., 2021).

For instance, in February 2021 in the culmination of a long legal battle between Uber and drivers' union App Drivers and Couriers Union (ADCU), the UK Supreme Court found that Uber had misclassified drivers as independent contractors, when the relationship of control and dependence in fact meant they were workers entitled to minimum wage and holiday pay. A similar decision was handed down in the case of food delivery platform Glovo by Spain's Supreme Court in September 2020, which preceded legislative action to better protect gig workers under the 'Rider's Law' (Aranguiz, 2021b). The new law forces delivery platforms to recognise their riders as workers with attendant rights and benefits. Importantly, it also establishes the right for trade unions to access information about the algorithmic governance of work. At the time of writing, New York City has just passed sweeping legislation on delivery workers' working conditions, guaranteeing the right to bathroom access, to receiving their tips from platforms, and regulating delivery distances and minimum payment thresholds (Paul, 2021). These examples of progress on the national regulatory front owe much to intense worker activism. However, platforms have resisted in nearly all instances, attempting to undermine litigation and legislative developments (in the case of Proposition 22, which attempted to circumvent rights which had recently been extended to gig workers), threatening to take advantage of their material disembeddedness and ephemerality to relatively cheaply exit markets (as Deliveroo did in response to the Rider's Law), and in some cases refusing to comply with decisions (for instance, Uber still refuses to count waiting time in working hours as mandated by the UK Supreme Court).

Cloudwork platforms, however, have proved much more difficult to bring into the sphere of state level oversight and regulation. Because they make planetary labour markets (Graham & Anwar, 2019) in which clients and workers can transact from anywhere in the world with an internet connection, they establish fluid, shifting networks of production and exchange, in which the labour process is institutionally disembedded (Wood et al., 2019a) and concealed from view (Gray & Suri, 2019; Gruszka & Böhm, 2020). The locations, profiles and conditions of workers on cloudwork platforms remain difficult to ascertain. These features make it extremely difficult for state governments to regulate working conditions in cloudwork. However, a promising recent example has appeared in Germany with a new law obligating multinational companies to protect human rights in their supply chains (Siddique, 2021). The Supply Chain Due Diligence Act may provide a model for enforcing minimum rights and protections for geographically dispersed cloud workforces, through proactive action taken in platforms' – as opposed to workers' – jurisdictions.

International organisations and civil society: Regulating a global workforce

International and supranational organisations can play an important role in re-embedding platforms' working practices. Organisations working on issues of decent work at a regional or international level include institutions like the European Union and the International Labour Organization (ILO), as well as civil society initiatives such as the Fairwork network. While organisations in this category have very different mandates and levels of influence, we have grouped them here due specifically to their multinational or supranational nature and outlook. Given the regulatory limbo in which many platforms operate at the national or local level (Hatzopoulos, 2018), the planetary labour market they often shape and rely on for their operations (Graham & Anwar, 2019), and the multinational nature of a large number of platforms themselves, international organisations can contribute in filling the legal vacuum and clarifying the legal grey areas under which platform work is organised and structured, offering guidelines and highlighting best practices in the regulation of platform work.

Through its Decent Work Agenda, the ILO aims to foster decent and sustainable work at the global level, through its four pillars: employment creation, rights at work, social protection, and social dialogue. Recognising the impact of globalisation and technological change on working conditions, and basing its objectives on several universal human rights declarations and UN resolutions, the Agenda aims to promote job quality and inclusive growth for everyone, regardless of location or employment status (ILO, 2015). Though not specifically focused on the platform economy, the Agenda clearly highlights the characteristics all forms of work should have across the world, providing a comprehensive framework for policy action at the international, national and local level for the regulation of the platform work. In 2015, the Agenda was incorporated into the UN Sustainable Development Goals, making it a priority for all UN member countries until 2030, and it has informed statements and action plans of several multilateral organisations including the G7, G20, and the African Union (ILO, 2015).

Despite highlighting specific policy and regulatory issues in relation to the specific nature of platforms work in several reports and declarations (see, for instance, ILO, 2021), the ILO has so far not proposed a specific convention on platform work. A number of scholars have called for the creation of such a convention, emphasising the importance of setting global standards for decent work in the platform economy. Particularly, they have underlined how an international convention on platform work would contribute in setting binding global labour standards in the platform economy, acknowledging the planetary nature of platform work and the specific vulnerabilities faced by platform workers across the world (Fredman et al., 2021).

In that respect, the European Union probably constitutes the best example of a multilateral organisation attempting to specifically regulate platform work beyond national boundaries. Initially adopting a wait-and-see approach, the European Commission was prompted to intervene in the regulation of platform work following the covid pandemic. The pandemic has in fact spotlighted the vulnerabilities platform workers face across Europe, playing an essential role in delivering goods and services to those self-isolating and at the same time enjoying limited health and safety protection, while at the same time having access to scant income protection in case they are unable to work (Howson et al., 2021). Basing its policy action on the European Pillars of Social Rights, at the beginning of 2021 the Commission announced a regulatory initiative aiming at improving the working conditions of platform workers across the European Union (European Commission, 2021). Later in 2021 the Commission launched an initial consultation with social partners, which was followed by a second consultation with a larger group of stakeholders. With the second consultation now over, the Commission is expected to make a legislative proposal by the end of 2021. Although the exact content of the proposal is still unknown, the legislative initiative is set to cover many of the major issues facing platform workers, including employment status, algorithmic management, legislative enforcement, collective representation and social dialogue, creating a comprehensive regulatory framework for platform work covering 27 countries.

Existing neither in the realm of worker resistance nor formal regulation, initiatives emanating from academia and civil society have also attempted to bring greater accountability and transparency to the platform economy. Drawing on a lineage of corporate social responsibility and voluntary certification in global supply chains, these have tended to be internationally oriented. The World Fair Trade Organization (WFTO), for instance, has recently certified the first fair trade digital platform, a Kenya-based social enterprise called Digital Lions (WFTO, 2021). Our own project, Fairwork, co-produces with workers, industry and experts a series of benchmarks of fair gig and cloudwork and conducts independent research in more than 20 countries to identify whether or not platform companies are meeting these five principles, publishing rankings which can be used by workers, consumers and other stakeholders to hold platforms accountable to minimum standards of fairness. This is a direct response to the twin issues of managerial opacity and regulatory evasion which characterise digital labour platforms. Being voluntary or located in the third sector, such initiatives can never replace the collective power of labour, or responsive national and international regulation, to drive improved outcomes. However, civil society and academic initiatives aimed at improving transparency, reducing information and power asymmetries, and establishing fairer conventions in the platform economy may be more easily able to transcend jurisdictional and geographical constraints, in order to arm and underscore labour and policy responses in specific places.

Conclusion

Labour platforms use sophisticated forms of digital governance to wield power over global value networks. Platformisation serves to accelerate the commodification of labour, erode workers' collective power, and undermine labour standards. It also allows global corporate actors to accumulate rents and surplus value produced by localised labour transactions. Although platform workers are bound to local social and institutional conditions, platforms have been able to escape the costs and risks of local embeddedness (such as regulation) by exerting governance over localities from a social and institutional distance. However, we have argued in this chapter that the labour geographies created and exploited by platforms do not necessarily represent a break or departure, but can be seen as an intensification in certain capitalist trends, especially within globalisation of labour. Likewise, the strategies we point to which have arisen to counter these trends are not necessarily novel strategies, but they have proved successful in previous phases of the labour movement.

In the paper we discussed four multiscalar strategies through which platforms can be re-embedded into local contexts and their ability to transcend geographical boundaries can be counteracted. These are: worker resistance, online tools, national regulations, and international organisations' and civil societies' initiatives. We have shown how each of these strategies have been able to at least partly offset the commodification of labour and to counterbalance the power of platforms. However, the success of these multiscalar local–global strategies depend on understanding how platforms respond to them and to critically evaluate their limitations.

Strikes are usually short-lived responses and the ability to organise and mobilise workers globally faces important institutional, cultural, and organisational barriers. At the same time, online tools can provide important information to workers and build solidarities, but they do little to limit platforms' ability to extract data and control their workforce. If the suggestions by international organisations are not written into law, they are not binding and platforms can easily avoid them. National regulations can be an important tool through which platform geographies can be tied to the local contexts but in the case of cloudwork markets, relying on state government action (in the Global North) to bring rights and protections to a planetary labour market where most precarious labour is located in the Global South will always have important limitations, not least of which is the democratic exclusion of the workers themselves from this process. Likewise, challenging worker misclassification on geographically tethered platforms in hundreds of jurisdictions is an expensive and patchwork approach that does not meet platforms at the scale on which they exert power and control, and struggles to keep up with the pace at which platforms find new ways to circumvent labour protections. These challenges and contradictions bring platforms' scale-switching geographical elusiveness into greater relief, illustrating how they can tap into and commodify labour processes in sectors which were previously more resistant to global corporate concentration – service, knowledge, and creative sectors.

To conclude, our key argument in this chapter and our main contribution to the literature is that the platform countermovement is increasingly responding to the need to meet platforms at all the geographical scales across which they manifest and attempt to retreat. The disembedding tendencies of platforms do not have to be conceived as a necessary outcome of technological progress and the evolution of global capitalism; they are instead the result of tactical ways through which platforms have been able to operate at different geographical scales to their own advantage. The platform countermovement has the potential to reshape the labour geographies created by digital platforms on local, global, and virtual terrains, in a way that re-embeds their practices into the geographical contexts where labour is located and to hold them responsible for the work they create.

Notes

1. All authors are based at the Oxford Internet Institute, University of Oxford.
2. While these ambitious initiatives have created a valuable repository of data on platform work protest, it should be noted that they only provide a partial insight. The task of documenting relevant incidents based on secondary sources is Herculean and leads to unavoidable omissions, particularly as smaller protests and those in the Global South are likely to be under-reported, or at least not reported in the languages that are accessible to researchers' searches. Thus, the actual number of protests in the gig economy is likely to be substantially underestimated.

References

Aranguiz, Ane. 2021a. 'Spain's Platform Workers Win Algorithm Transparency'. *Social Europe*. 18 March 2021. https://socialeurope.eu/spains-platform-workers-win-algorithm-transparency.

Aranguiz, Ane. 2021b. 'Platforms Put a Spoke in the Wheels of Spain's "Riders" Law'. *Social Europe*. 2 September 2021. https://socialeurope.eu/platforms-put-a-spoke-in-the-wheels-of-spains-riders-law.

Atmore, Emily C. 2017. 'Killing the Goose That Laid the Golden Egg: Outdated Employment Laws Are Destroying the Gig Economy'. *Minnesota Law Review* 96: 887–992.

Bair, Jennifer. 2005. 'Global Capitalism and Commodity Chains: Looking Back, Going Forward'. *Competition & Change* 9 (2): 153–80. https:// doi .org/ 10 .1179/ 102452905X45382.

Barzilay, Arianne, and Anat Ben-David. 2017. 'Platform Inequality: Gender in the Gig-Economy'. *Seton Hall Law Review* 47 (2). https:// scholarship .shu .edu/ shlr/ vol47/iss2/2.

Bergvall-Kåreborn, Birgitta, and Debra Howcroft. 2014. 'Amazon Mechanical Turk and the Commodification of Labour'. *New Technology, Work and Employment* 29 (3): 213–23. https://doi.org/10.1111/ntwe.12038.

Braesemann, Fabian, Fabian Stephany, Ole Teutloff, Otto Kässi, Mark Graham, and Vili Lehdonvirta. 2021. 'The Polarisation of Remote Work'. *ArXiv:2108.13356 [Econ, q-Fin]*, August. http://arxiv.org/abs/2108.13356.

Bright, Jake. 2018. 'Uber and Taxify Are Going Head-to-Head to Digitize Africa's Two-Wheeled Taxis'. *Techcrunch*. 30 March 2018. https://techcrunch.com/2018/03/30/uber-and-taxify-are-going-head-to-head-to-digitize-africas-two-wheeled-taxis/.

Cant, Callum, and Clara Mogno. 2020. 'Platform Workers of the World, Unite! The Emergence of the Transnational Federation of Couriers'. *South Atlantic Quarterly* 119 (2): 401–11. https://doi.org/10.1215/00382876-8177971.

China Labour Bulletin. n.d. 'CLB Strikes Map'. *China Labour Bulletin*. Accessed 27 September 2021. https:// maps .clb .org .hk/ ?i18n _language = en _US & map = 1 & startDate = 2021 -03 & endDate = 2021 -09 & eventId = & keyword = & addressId = & parentAddressId = & address = & parentAddress = & industry = & parentIndustry = & industryName=.

Collective Action in Tech. n.d. 'Archive'. *Collective Action in Tech*. Accessed 27 September 2021. https://data.collectiveaction.tech/.

Cook, Cody, Rebecca Diamond, Jonathan V. Hall, John A. List, and Paul Oyer. 2021. 'The Gender Earnings Gap in the Gig Economy: Evidence from over a Million Rideshare Drivers'. *The Review of Economic Studies* 88 (5): 2210–38. https://doi.org/10.1093/restud/rdaa081.

De Stefano, Valerio. 2015. 'The Rise of the "Just-in-Time Workforce": On-Demand Work, Crowd Work and Labour Protection in the "Gig-Economy"'. *Comparative Labour Law and Policy Journal* 37: 471–504. https://doi.org/10.2139/ssrn.2682602.

European Commission. 2021. 'Protecting People Working through Platforms: Commission Launches Second-Stage Consultation of Social Partners'. European Commission. 15 June 2021. https://ec.europa.eu/commission/presscorner/detail/en/IP_21_2944.

Fairwork. 2021. 'Work in the Planetary Labour Market: Fairwork Cloudwork Ratings 2021'. Oxford, United Kingdom.

Fredman, Sandra, Darcy du Toit, Mark Graham, Aradhana Cherupara Vadekkethil, Gautam Bhatia, and Alessio Bertolini. 2021. 'International Regulation of Platform Labor: A Proposal for Action'. *Weizenbaum Journal of the Digital Society* 1 (1). https://doi.org/10.34669/wi.wjds/1.1.4.

Fredman, Sandra, Darcy du Toit, Mark Graham, Kelle Howson, Richard Heeks, Jean-Paul van Belle, Paul Mungai, and Abigail Osiki. 2020. 'Thinking Out of the Box: Fair Work for Platform Workers'. *King's Law Journal* 31 (2): 236–49. https://doi.org/10.1080/09615768.2020.1794196.

Gandini, Alessandro. 2019. 'Labour Process Theory and the Gig Economy'. *Human Relations* 27 (6): 1039–56. https://doi.org/doi.org/10.1177/0018726718790002.

Gereffi, Gary, John Humphrey, and Timothy Sturgeon. 2005. 'The Governance of Global Value Chains'. *Review of International Political Economy* 12 (1): 78–104. https://doi.org/10.1080/09692290500049805.

Grabher, Gernot, and Erwin van Tuijl. 2020. 'Uber-Production: From Global Networks to Digital Platforms'. *Environment and Planning A: Economy and Space* 52 (5): 1005–16. https://doi.org/10.1177/0308518X20916507.

Graham, Mark. 2020. 'Regulate, Replicate, and Resist – the Conjunctural Geographies of Platform Urbanism'. *Urban Geography* 41 (3): 453–57. https://doi.org/10.1080/02723638.2020.1717028.

Graham, Mark, and Mohammad Amir Anwar. 2019. 'The Global Gig Economy: Towards a Planetary Labour Market?'. *First Monday* 24 (4). https://doi.org/10.5210/fm.v24i4.9913.

Gray, Mary L., and Siddharth Suri. 2019. *Ghost Work: How to Stop Silicon Valley from Building a New Global Underclass*. Boston: Eamon Dolan Books.

Gruszka, Katarzyna, and Madeleine Böhm. 2020. 'Out of Sight, Out of Mind? (In)Visibility of/in Platform-Mediated Work'. *New Media & Society*. https://doi.org/10.1177/1461444820977209.

Harvey, David. 2006. *Spaces of Global Capitalism*. London: Verso.

Hatzopoulos, Vassilis. 2018. *The Collaborative Economy and EU Law*. London: Hart Publishing.

Heeks, Richard. 2008. 'ICT4D 2.0: The Next Phase of Applying ICT for International Development'. *Computer* 41 (6): 26–33.

Howson, Kelle, Funda Ustek Spilda, Alessio Bertolini, Richard Heeks, Fabian Ferrari, Srujana Katta, Matthew Cole, et al. 2021. 'Stripping Back the Mask: Working Conditions on Digital Labour Platforms during the COVID-19 Pandemic'. *International Labour Review*. https://doi.org/10.1111/ilr.12222.

Howson, Kelle, Funda Ustek-Spilda, Rafael Grohmann, Nancy Salem, Rodrigo Carelli, Daniel Abs, Julice Salvagni, et al. 2020. '"Just Because You Don't See Your Boss, Doesn't Mean You Don't Have a Boss": Covid-19 and Gig Worker Strikes across Latin America'. *International Union Rights* 27 (3): 20–28.

Humphrey, John, and Hubert Schmitz. 2002. 'How Does Insertion in Global Value Chains Affect Upgrading in Industrial Clusters?'. *Regional Studies* 36 (9): 1017–27. https://doi.org/10.1080/0034340022000022198.

IAATW. n.d. 'Manifesto'. Accessed 27 September 2021. https://iaatw.org/about-us/manifesto/.

ILO. 2015. 'Decent Work'. https://www.ilo.org/global/topics/decent-work/lang--en/index.htm.

ILO. 2021. 'World Employment and Social Outlook – Trends 2021'. https://www.ilo.org/global/research/global-reports/weso/trends2021/lang--en/index.htm.

Irani, Lilly C., and M. Six Silberman. 2013. 'Turkopticon: Interrupting Worker Invisibility in Amazon Mechanical Turk'. In *Proceedings of the SIGCHI Conference on Human Factors in Computing Systems*, 611–20. Paris: ACM. https://doi.org/10.1145/2470654.2470742.

Joyce, Simon, Denis Neumann, Vera Trappmann, and Charles Umney. 2020. 'A Global Struggle: Worker Protest in the Platform Economy'. ETUI Policy Brief 2. European Economic, Employment and Social Policy. ETUI: European Trade Union Institute.

Katta, Srujana, Adam Badger, Mark Graham, Kelle Howson, Funda Ustek-Spilda, and Alessio Bertolini. 2020. '(Dis)Embeddedness and (de)Commodification: COVID-19, Uber, and the Unravelling Logics of the Gig Economy'. *Dialogues in Human Geography* 10 (2): 203–7. https://doi.org/10.1177/2043820620934942.

Kenney, Martin, and John Zysman. 2020. 'The Platform Economy: Restructuring the Space of Capitalist Accumulation'. *Cambridge Journal of Regions, Economy and Society* 13 (1): 55–76. https://doi.org/10.1093/cjres/rsaa001.

Kumar, Ashok. 2020. *Monopsony Capitalism: Power and Production in the Twilight of the Sweatshop Age*. Cambridge: Cambridge University Press.

Langley, Paul, and Andrew Leyshon. 2017. 'Platform Capitalism: The Intermediation and Capitalization of Digital Economic Circulation'. *Finance And Society* 3 (1): 11–31.

Lomas, Natasha. 2021. 'Dutch Court Rejects Uber Drivers' "Robo-Firing" Charge but Tells Ola to Explain Algo-Deductions'. *TechCrunch*. 12 March 2021. https://techcrunch.com/2021/03/12/dutch-court-rejects-uber-drivers-robo-firing-charge-but-tells-ola-to-explain-algo-deductions/.

McMillan Cottom, Tressie. 2020. 'Where Platform Capitalism and Racial Capitalism Meet: The Sociology of Race and Racism in the Digital Society'. *Sociology of Race and Ethnicity* 6 (4): 441–49. https://doi.org/10.1177/2332649220949473.

Muntaner, Carles. 2018. 'Digital Platforms, Gig Economy, Precarious Employment, and the Invisible Hand of Social Class'. *International Journal of Health Services* 48 (4): 597–600. https://doi.org/10.1177/0020731418801413.

Paul, Kari. 2021. 'New York City Delivery Workers Win Rights to Better Tips, Bathrooms and More'. *The Guardian*. 24 September 2021. https://www.theguardian.com/business/2021/sep/23/gig-economy-doordash-grubhub-food-delivery.

Peck, Jamie, and Rachel Phillips. 2020. 'The Platform Conjuncture'. *Sociologica* 14 (3): 73–99. https://doi.org/10.6092/issn.1971-8853/11613.

Pinsof, Jennifer. 2016. 'A New Take on an Old Problem: Employee Misclassification in the Modern Gig-Economy'. *Michigan Telecommunications and Technology Law Review* 22: 341–73. https://repository.law.umich.edu/cgi/viewcontent.cgi?article=1220&context=mttlr.

Ponelis, Shana R., and Marlene A. Holmner. 2015. 'ICT in Africa: Building a Better Life for All'. *Information Technology for Development* 21 (2): 163–77. https://doi.org/10.1080/02681102.2015.1010307.

Presidential Commission on the Fourth Industrial Revolution. 2020. 'Report of the Presidential Commission on the 4th Industrial Revolution'. *Government Gazette* 43834. South Africa. https://www.gov.za/sites/default/files/gcis_document/202010/43834gen591.pdf.

Rani, Uma, Rishabh Kumar Dhir, Marianne Furrer, Nóra Göbel, Angeliki Moraiti, Sean Cooney, and Alberto Coddou Mc Manus. 2021. 'World Employment and Social Outlook: The Role of Digital Labour Platforms in Transforming the World of Work'. *ILO Flagship Report*. Geneva. https://www.ilo.org/wcmsp5/groups/public/---dgreports/---dcomm/---publ/documents/publication/wcms_771749.pdf.

Scheiber, Noam. 2017. 'How Uber Uses Psychological Tricks to Push Its Drivers' Buttons'. *The New York Times*. 2 April 2017. https://www.nytimes.com/interactive/2017/04/02/technology/uber-drivers-psychological-tricks.html.

Schor, Juliet B., William Attwood-Charles, Mehmet Cansoy, Isak Ladegaard, and Robert Wengronowitz. 2020. 'Dependence and Precarity in the Platform Economy'. *Theory and Society* 49 (5): 833–61. https://doi.org/10.1007/s11186-020-09408-y.

Siddique, Haroon. 2021. 'Rights Groups Join Forces to Call for UK Corporate Accountability Laws'. *The Guardian*. 4 July 2021. https://www.theguardian.com/environment/2021/jul/04/rights-groups-join-forces-to-call-for-uk-corporate-accountability-laws.

Silberman, M. Six, and Lilly Irani. 2016. 'Operating an Employer Reputation System: Lessons from Turkopticon, 2008–2015'. *Comparative Labour Law and Policy Journal* 37: 505–41.

Srnicek, Nick. 2017. *Platform Capitalism*. Cambridge: Polity Press.

Standing, Guy. 2014. 'The Precariat'. *Contexts* 13 (4): 10–12. https://doi.org/10.1177/1536504214558209.

Stanford, Jim. 2017. 'The Resurgence of Gig Work: Historical and Theoretical Perspectives'. *The Economic and Labour Relations Review* 28 (3): 382–401. https://doi.org/10.1177/1035304617724303.

Tassinari, Arianna, and Vincenzo Maccarrone. 2020. 'Riders on the Storm: Workplace Solidarity among Gig Economy Couriers in Italy and the UK'. *Work Employment and Society* 34 (3): 35–54. https://doi.org/10.1177/0950017019862954.

Taylor, Frederick Winslow. 1911. *Principles of Scientific Management*. New York: Harpers and Brothers.

Tubaro, Paola. 2021. 'Disembedded or Deeply Embedded? A Multi-Level Network Analysis of Online Labour Platforms'. *Sociology* 55 (5): 927–44. https://doi.org/10.1177/0038038520986082.

Unwin, Tim (Editor). 2009. *ICT4D Information and Communication Technologies for Development*. Cambridge: Cambridge University Press.

van Doorn, Niels, and Adam Badger. 2020. 'Platform Capitalism's Hidden Abode: Producing Data Assets in the Gig Economy'. *Antipode* 52 (5): 1475–95. https://doi.org/10.1111/anti.12641.

WeClock. n.d. 'The Story behind WeClock'. Accessed 27 September 2021. https://weclock.it/about/.

WFTO. 2021. 'Press Release: Digital Goes Fair Trade'. *World Fair Trade Organization*. https://wfto.com/article/press-release-digital-goes-fair-trade.

Wood, Alex J., Mark Graham, Vili Lehdonvirta, and Isis Hjorth. 2019a. 'Networked but Commodified: The (Dis)Embeddedness of Digital Labour in the Gig Economy'. *Sociology* 53 (5): 931–50. https://doi.org/10.1177/0038038519828906.

Wood, Alex, Mark Graham, Vili Lehdonvirta, and Isis Hjorth. 2019b. 'Good Gig, Bad Gig: Autonomy and Algorithmic Control in the Global Gig Economy'. *Work, Employment and Society* 33 (1): 56–75. https://doi.org/doi.org/10.1177%2F0950017018785616.

Woodcock, Jamie. 2018. 'Digital Labour and Workers' Organisation'. In *Global Perspectives on Workers' and Labour Organizations*, edited by Maurizio Atzeni and Immanuel Ness, 157–73. Singapore: Springer.

Woodcock, Jamie, and Mark Graham. 2020. *The Gig Economy: A Critical Introduction*. London: Wiley.

Yeung, Henry Wai-chung, and Neil M. Coe. 2015. 'Toward a Dynamic Theory of Global Production Networks'. *Economic Geography* 91 (1): 29–58.

12 Crowdwork and global supply chains: Regulating digital piecework

Nastazja Potocka-Sionek[1]

Introduction

Crowdwork platforms, i.e., web-based platforms through which work is fragmented and outsourced to an open, geographically dispersed crowd (De Stefano 2016), are sometimes referred to as "the factory of the 21st century" (Degryse 2016, 13) or "the new supply chains" (Choudary 2020). There are indeed compelling similarities between global supply chains (GSCs) and digital labour platforms. Many processes, which have been long present in the supply chain context, such as the commodification of work, fragmentation of international production and managing workflow of remote workers, have now been brought to extremes by digital labour platforms. Yet the parallels between both models of industrial organisation have only recently begun to attract scholarly interest (Howson et al. 2021) and remain greatly under-researched. In particular, the challenges posed by the platform economy and GSCs to the effective governance of global labour markets have been so far studied separately, and the potential linkages between them have not been investigated in detail.

This chapter explores governance options for crowdwork platforms – a topic that has received much less attention than the regulation of location-based platforms such as Uber or Glovo (De Stefano et al. 2021). The analysis focuses on a subcategory of platforms that epitomises the piecework nature of work: microwork platforms whereby routine information processing tasks (e.g., data annotation, image transcription and content moderation) are performed within minutes or seconds. Freelance platforms through which high-skilled work is assigned directly to an individual contractor chosen by a client, as well as location-based platforms, are excluded from the scope of this analysis.

Although, as will be argued, crowdwork companies do not operate in a legal vacuum, the current regulatory framework fails to ensure fair working conditions. The key normative question addressed in the present analysis is, therefore, how to make crowdwork platforms accountable for labour standards in their ecosystem. In many ways, this question is similar to the one that has been crucial in the context of GSCs, namely: how to make lead firms liable for adverse effects of their transnational operations, including at the downstream of their supply chains. The regulatory framework designed for the GSCs provides insights into governance paths for crowdwork platforms, going beyond the question of employment classification.

The remainder of this chapter is structured as follows. Section 2 argues that crowdwork platforms are central actors in their ecosystem and exert a decisive influence on crowdworkers' working conditions. Further, it draws parallels between the power relations, labour rights deficits and governance challenges in the crowdwork and GSCs context. Section 3 maps the current regulatory landscape for crowdwork and GSCs. Section 4 proposes several policy options for regulating crowdwork companies. The chapter concludes with a call for a stronger transnational corporate responsibility for crowdwork platforms.

Power relations, labour standards and governance challenges

The functioning of a crowdwork platform as a "digital assembly line" (Kovács 2017, 84) can be illustrated with an example from the modern automotive industry. In order to develop autonomous vehicles, a massive amount of manually annotated, classified and verified data is needed to train machine learning systems (MLS). Put simply, the production of "self-driving" cars ultimately relies on labour-intensive, human work involving such tasks as identifying objects within a street scene or sorting out blurred pictures. Instead of performing these assignments internally, companies operating in the automotive sector often outsource them to platform companies. The dispersed crowd of anonymous workers performs data tasks at the last mile of automation, which are then delivered by the platform to the client and subsequently used for the MLS (Schmidt 2019; Tubaro and Casilli 2019).

Most microwork platforms, including the prototypic Amazon Mechanical Turk, depict themselves as a non-hierarchical "community" connecting clients ("requestors") with the myriad of "contributors" working as independent contractors. Their structure is, however, not as decentralised as it may seem (Gol, Stein and Avital 2019; Aloisi 2020). Platforms are the centrepiece of the multisided infrastructure, as they set the rules of conduct and manage workers' and clients' interactions. They do so *inter alia* by distributing tasks to a selected group of crowdworkers based on criteria specified by clients; by providing requestors with monitoring tools to track the real-time work progress; or by handling payment and mediating disputes. In some cases, clients use the platform as a "self-service marketplace"; in others, the entire workflow is centralised and governed by platforms to the extent that they resemble a "traditional" firm (Tubaro 2021).

Apart from the coordination of the activities between requestors and workers, a shared characteristic of crowdwork platforms is that the very labour process is controlled through a variety of algorithmic management methods (Gol, Stein and Avital 2019). First, ranking and reputation systems are widely used to "gamify" crowdworkers' behaviour: in order to build a good "digital reputation" (e.g., the status of "master workers" on Amazon Mechanical Turk), crowdworkers are motivated to increase their performance level. Second, some platforms use more direct forms of "automatic output control" by verifying the quality of the results and sanctioning flawed work performance (Krzywdzinski and Gerber 2021). Even if they distribute control over various aspects of the labour process to other actors, they retain centralised power (Vallas and Schor 2020).

Platforms typically do not assume any obligations and costs associated with direct employment, shifting all risks on independent contractors. This leaves crowdworkers outside the scope of the major part of labour and social protection under domestic legal systems. While the lack of employment status is one of the causes of crowdworkers' precarity, it is crucial to analyse their vulnerable situation from a broader perspective. Platforms' design features have a fundamental bearing on crowdworkers' working conditions (Rani and Furrer 2021). For example, the gamification techniques pressurise workers to work intensively, often at the expense of compliance with occupational health and safety regulations (Bérastégui 2021). The massive oversupply of labour power, including from crowdworkers based in developing countries (Graham and Anwar 2019), fuels an extreme race to the bottom in wages. Moreover, challenges to building a collective voice are inherent in the geographically dispersed, "virtual" and individualised nature of crowdwork (Lehdonvirta 2016). The standardisation and commodification of the labour process further decrease crowdworkers' bargaining power *vis-à-vis* platforms, as it renders them easily substitutable (Choudary 2018). Thus, as put bluntly by Fieseler, Bucher and Hoffmann (2019), platforms are "unfair by design."

Platforms' decisive influence on working conditions in their ecosystems, and the evasion of liability therefore, allows us to draw a parallel to the position of lead firms in GSCs. Much as in the case of platform work, coordination and control of the disintegrated production system is fundamental for the effective functioning of GSCs (Gereffi 2001). The lead firm is the "nodal" company responsible for setting the parameters for other firms in the chain (Humphrey and Schmitz 2008). Global buyers "outsource" legal responsibility to suppliers down the production chain (Rühmkorf 2018) and shield themselves from various employment risks, despite their substantial influence on working conditions along their supply chains. Although they do not engage in manufacturing themselves, they exert pressure on their suppliers, *inter alia* through predatory purchasing practices. This, in turn, translates into poor working conditions down the supply chain, since suppliers are forced to intensify the work process and resort to low-cost, precarious forms of work. Thus, the root causes of deteriorating labour conditions at the downstream end of the chains are not limited to the enterprise level but lie in upstream practices of global buyers (Anner, Bair and Blasi 2013).

The second core parallel between crowdwork and GCSs relates to the challenges triggered by the transnational operations of these companies. As observed by Cherry (2019, 12), crowdwork "turns the dependence on national systems for regulation of employment and labour law upside down." Precisely the cross-border dimension of the platform operation is often conceived as one of the main factors contributing to the regulatory gap (Graham and Anwar 2019, 26–27). National regulators in countries from which crowdworkers provide their services have scarce power over foreign-based platform companies due to their extraterritorial operation (Novitz 2020). Crowdworkers whose rights are violated encounter problems with finding the relevant counterparty to the dispute. Seeking justice in courts is further complexified by the jurisdictional maze (Pretelli 2018; Cherry 2019). Hence, the "geographical disembeddedness" of crowdwork platforms (Fairwork 2021, 6) has two salient implications: it enables regulatory evasion and poses obstacles for crowdworkers to claim their rights.

Similarly, challenges related to extraterritorial application of law are pertinent in the context of GSCs. The principle that it is for the host state to ensure compliance with human and labour rights is problematic particularly with regard to states with deficient governance and enforcement structures (Kolben 2011). The risk is that the effective protection of labour rights will be limited to first-tier supplying firms, over which lead firms have leverage. It is, however, in the lower tiers of the supply chain that most decent work deficits occur. Labour inspection of working conditions in the GSCs is severely hindered due to the lack of transparency and traceability of work, as well as the often-informal nature of work in the lower tiers of supply chains (ILO 2011).

Overall, both crowdwork platforms and lead firms in GSCs are a stark manifestation of how powerful multinational companies exert a decisive influence on the working conditions downstream their production chains. The conceptualisation of crowdwork platforms as key actors in the "digital value network" (Howson et al. 2021) justifies regulatory intervention targeting them as actors that should account for labour standards.

Mapping the current regulatory landscape

As emphasised in the previous section, the lack of employment status of crowdworkers is one of the primary causes of their precarity. Hence, the reclassification of crowdworkers as employees has been put forward as a way to make platforms accountable for labour standards (Berg et al. 2018). Such a reclassification became even more viable with the recent proposal for an EU Directive on improving the working conditions in platform work[2] that introduces a rebuttable legal presumption of an employment relationship, provided that the platform exercises control over work performance[3] (Art. 4 (1)). A part of crowdwork platforms is likely to fulfil at least some of these criteria and, thus, be presumed as the crowdworkers' employers (ETUC 2022b). Still, there will be cases where platforms genuinely operate as market intermediaries, and crowdworkers will not fall under the category of an employee. Moreover, it is crucial to bear in mind that a considerable share of crowdworkers is based in the Global South and they, consequently, are not covered by the scope of the proposed Directive, which regulates platforms organising work performed in the EU (Art. 1 (3)).

Without undermining the centrality of the question about the employment status of crowdworkers, the following analysis goes beyond this issue and shows that even when crowdwork platforms are not employers, they do not operate in a legal void. There are a number of public and private governance instruments under which platforms are expected to respect labour and human labour rights.

At the outset, it is often overlooked that platform-based businesses are, just as any other multinational company, covered by several international soft-law instruments in the field of human and labour rights. Under the "Protect, Respect and Remedy" Framework set out in the United Nations Guiding Principles (UNGPs),[4] they shall "respect the human rights of their users and affected parties in all their actions."[5] They should "seek to prevent or mitigate adverse human rights impacts that are directly linked to their operations, products or services by their business relationships, even if they have not contributed to those impacts" (Guiding Principle 13b). This concept of human rights due diligence has been anchored also in other vital international instruments such as the OECD Guidelines for Multinational Enterprises and the Tripartite Declaration of Principles concerning Multinational Enterprises and Social Policy, which are applicable to crowdwork platforms (Berg, Cherry and Rani 2019).

The UNGPs are, however, merely a soft-law instrument that do not create any new obligations for companies and doubts persist as to whether "due diligence alone will effect significant change" (Trebilcock 2015, 107). In view of this intrinsic limitation, the UN Human Rights Council decided in June 2014 to establish an open-ended intergovernmental working group on transnational corporations and other business enterprises with respect to human rights. Its mandate is to "elaborate an international legally binding instrument to regulate, in international human rights law, the activities of transnational corporations and other business enterprises."[6] The draft of this legally binding instrument was first published as a Zero Draft in 2018, and was last revised, for the third time, in August 2021.[7] Its purpose is to clarify and facilitate effective implementation of the states' obligations regarding business-related human rights abuses and the human rights obligations of business enterprises, to prevent human rights abuses by effective mechanisms of monitoring and enforceability, to improve access to justice and remedy for victims of human rights abuses, and to facilitate and strengthen mutual legal assistance and international cooperation to prevent and mitigate human rights abuses (Art. 2). The negotiation process on this politically contentious instrument is moving, albeit slowly, in the right direction of binding regulation. There is still much scope for the clarification and more ambitious approach for combating human rights violations by transnational companies, for example in terms of enhancing access to remedy (López 2021).

Apart from the abovementioned soft-law, some hard-law instruments, namely ILO Conventions, are applicable to certain forms of crowdwork. In particular, crowdworkers in many cases fulfil the criteria to be considered homeworkers under Home Work Convention 1996 (No. 177) (De Stefano and Wouters 2021). Moreover, an array of labour standards rooted in other core ILO instruments and related to occupational safety and health, social security, employment and job creation policy, as well as labour inspection, are relevant in the crowdwork context (ILO 2021). Fundamental principles and rights at work apply to all workers irrespective of their employment status, i.e., also to crowdworkers.[8]

Parallel to public governance instruments, private ordering responses to crowdwork proliferate. First, platforms create their own benchmark of responsible conduct by introducing private codes of conducts. One of the central incentives driving platforms towards the adoption of corporate social responsibility (CSR) mechanisms may be to avoid reputational damage and counter the perception that they are unethical (Woodcock and Graham 2020, 120). These policies tend to be rather vague, presenting only general principles of good practice, although some of them include more firm commitments. For example, Appen's "Crowd Code of Ethics" states that the platform's goal is to pay its crowd above the local minimum wage in the market where crowdworkers operate.[9] Accordingly, the platform algorithmically calculates the minimum payrate applicable to crowdworkers.

Second, transnational multi-stakeholder initiatives (MSIs) are emerging. An example is Fair Crowd Work (2017), a joint project of IG Metall, the Austrian Chamber of Labour, the Austrian Trade Union Confederation, and the Swedish white-collar union Unionen. Fair Crowd Work's mission is to "shed light on the real work of crowd"[10] by collecting information about crowd work from the perspective of workers and unions, and by rating working conditions on different platforms based on surveys with workers. Moreover, it has established a "Crowdsourcing Code of Conduct," signed by eight Germany-based platforms that have agreed to include local wage standards as a factor in setting prices on their platforms. Another important MSI is the Fairwork Foundation, which brings together multiple actors including workers, unions, platforms, academics, governments and third sector organisations. The Foundation has established five core Fairwork Principles with regard to pay, conditions, contracts, management and representation, on the basis of which it evaluates the extent to which platforms are providing decent work for crowdworkers. It incentivises platforms to comply with these principles by producing annual rankings based on the rating scheme (Graham et al. 2020).

These regulatory patterns partly resemble those in the GSCs context. Parallel to the above-discussed international soft-law instruments, the UNGP being the most "authoritative" one (Macchi and Bright 2020), numerous transnational private-sector governance mechanisms have been put in place to improve working conditions in GSCs. Their catalogue is longer than in the case of platforms. Corporate codes of conduct are commonly accompanied by monitoring mechanisms, such as top-down compliance auditing (Bair 2017). In addition, there are incentives to adhere to these standards, either by rewarding the compliant suppliers or by imposing consequences in case of non-compliance (Amengual and Kuruvilla 2020). Another widespread private governance mechanism is MSIs involving a variety of actors such as corporations, business associations, civil society organisations, UN agencies, unions, academics and media. There is a myriad of examples, just a few major initiatives being Fair Wear Foundation (working with 193 member brands in the garment industry) and the Bangladesh Accord on Fire and Building Safety (a legally binding agreement between global union federations and over 200 clothing companies).

There is, however, vast evidence that the roughly twenty-five years of private regulation have resulted in a very limited contribution to protect supply chain workers (Kuruvilla, Li and Jackson 2021; Locke 2013; Barrientos and Smith 2007). Multiple factors account for the failure of private regulation of labour standards in GSCs. Limitations are related to the very nature of private governance mechanisms, that is to their voluntary character, and to the selective choice of labour standards they address. Private regulations are often limited to direct or upper-tier suppliers and usually do not reach the lower tiers of supply chains. Even in cases where the codes of conduct are accompanied by external audit mechanisms and certification schemes, there has been no sustained improvement in enforcing labour standards (LeBaron, Lister and Dauvergne 2017). MSIs, despite their more collaborative approach geared towards capacity building, also fail to yield sustained improvements of corporate behaviour down the supply chain (LeBaron et al. 2021).

Given the limitations of the international soft-law instruments and private governance mechanisms, there has been a noticeable move towards "hard" transnational sustainability laws at the domestic level. States have increasingly enacted corporate disclosure and due diligence laws to regulate GSCs. These domestic laws vary considerably in terms of the definition of supply chains, the coverage, the introduced compliance mechanisms and reporting obligations. Two main regulatory patterns can be distinguished. The first and to date prevalent one takes the form of legislation setting out mere disclosure requirements. Examples include the California Transparency in Supply Chain Act (2010), the UK Modern Slavery Act (2015) and the Australian Modern Slavery Act (2018). In general, this type of regulation requires companies to reveal information regarding their actions undertaken towards their suppliers to prevent human rights abuses. These "soft disclosure" laws do not, however, introduce any substantive, mandatory due diligence standard; neither do they impose penalties for non-compliance. Moreover, their material scope is restricted to a specific issue such as human-trafficking. Deficiencies of these legislative acts are well-documented and widely discussed in literature (LeBaron and Rühmkorf 2019; Nolan and Bott 2018; Fudge 2018).

The second model imposes further-reaching, mandatory human rights due diligence (HRDD) obligations. The prime example is the French Duty of Vigilance Law (2017),[11] which has been heralded as a major breakthrough in the field of business and human rights legislation (Cossart, Chaplier and Beau de Lomenie 2017) and is thus far the most comprehensive public regulatory framework for HRDD. Under this regulation, companies covered by its scope are obliged to draw up a vigilance plan which shall include reasonable measures to identify risks and prevent gross violations stemming from their own or their suppliers' activities. In case of failure to implement the law, interested parties can seek an injunction to order a company to establish, implement and publish a vigilance plan. The law establishes periodic penalties in case of continued non-compliance, as well as a civil liability regime under which interested parties can file proceedings if a company's failure to comply with the duty of vigilance gives rise to damage. The latest examples of national regulations introducing mandatory HRDD are the German Supply Chain Due Diligence Law,[12] adopted in June 2021 and entering into force in 2023, and the Norwegian Transparency Act, also passed in June 2021.[13] While these laws differ substantially in their scope and are not without their weaknesses,[14] they represent significant progress in the development of mandatory due diligence in Europe (Krajewski, Tonstad and Wohltmann 2021).

The overview of measures introducing mandatory HRDD would be incomplete without including the recent EU regulatory developments. On 23 February 2022, the European Commission presented a long-awaited proposal for a Directive on Corporate Sustainability Due Diligence.[15] Under this instrument, Member States shall ensure that companies introduce due diligence procedures concerning impacts of their own operations, the operations of their subsidiaries and value chain operations of entities with whom they have an "established business relationship." Companies will be required to identify, prevent, end or mitigate actual or potential adverse impacts on human rights; put in place a complaints procedure; monitor the effectiveness of their due diligence policy and publicly communicate on it. While this Directive proposal represents an important step forward, it falls short of expectations as it suffers from salient limitations (Human Rights Watch 2022; ETUC 2022a). Regrettably, small, medium and micro enterprises, which account for about 99% of all EU companies, are excluded from its direct scope.[16] Moreover, to name just a few problematic aspects, the civil liability regime is confined to direct suppliers, trade union participation in due diligence procedures is very limited (ETUC 2022a), and there are concerns that the due diligence procedure will become a mere "box-ticking exercise" rather than a principle-based risk assessment (Sjåfjell and Mähönen 2022). It is to be hoped that the Directive proposal will be improved in the course of further discussions by the European Parliament and the Council.

The trend towards mandatory HRDD has not yet been embraced in the context of crowdwork platforms. While replicating the exact same regulatory responses of GSCs in the realm of crowdwork governance would not be "fit for purpose," this comparative analysis provokes the question: How can we envisage a shift towards stronger accountability mechanisms of crowdwork platforms to ensure respect for labour rights in their digital production chain? The next section considers several avenues.

The ways forward: A multi-level response

The first policy recommendation regards the promotion of private governance mechanisms. An advantage of these soft measures is their flexible character and their applicability across various jurisdictions (Berg et al. 2018; Cherry 2019). Voluntary codes of conduct should be strengthened by other social audit instruments. Certification schemes can increase consumers' awareness about the labour conditions of workers providing their services through crowdwork platforms. Besides the advocacy effect, they could be a way of increasing transparency of the entire platform-mediated production process, thanks to which crowdworkers would become more visible to the consumers. Tracing back the various stages of human labour supporting the development of AI, from data annotation to verification, would likely be more complex than identifying workers producing physical products. This may be a particularly challenging task in the case of "multi-layered" platforms, where workforce management involves multiple partner companies or subcontractors (Tubaro 2021). Hence, it may be more problematic, although not impossible, to introduce similar mechanisms as "fair trade" labels on food products (Graham, Hjorth and Lehdonvirta 2017, 154). External monitoring by independent certification companies, auditors, civil society groups or trade unions will be needed to provide strong incentives for compliance. Otherwise, these instruments will be simply too weak to bring a meaningful, sustained change to the working conditions, as well-documented in the GSCs context. Stronger accountability mechanisms beyond private sources of regulation are needed to make platforms exert pressure on requesters to consider the ethical treatment of workers.

Another field of the required regulatory intervention relates to the transparency of platforms' operations. The first dimension of transparency refers to platforms' internal, algorithmically driven operations affecting crowdworkers. Platforms are already subject to a range of obligations under existing and emerging regulations. Important digital rights, such as the right to information about the use of automated monitoring and decision-making systems, the right to an explanation for automatically taken decisions, and the right to a human oversight are enshrined *inter alia* in the EU General Data Protection Regulation (GDPR). These rights and obligations are further specified in the proposal for a Directive on improving the working conditions in platform work, under which digital labour platforms are required to inform platform workers about automated monitoring and decision-making systems that significantly affect their working conditions (Art. 6), to provide for regular human monitoring and evaluation of the impact of automatically taken decisions on working conditions (Art. 7) and to ensure an explanation for such decisions (Art. 8). Likewise, the ILO Centenary Declaration for the Future of Work, adopted on 21 June 2019, calls on all Members to put in practice "policies and measures that ensure appropriate privacy and personal data protection, and respond to challenges and opportunities in the world of work relating to the digital transformation of work, including platform work" (Part III(C) (v)). The prime example of a domestic-level regulation is the Spanish "Rider's Law" (Royal Decree-Law 9/2021), under which the workers' representatives have the right to be informed about the parameters of algorithms affecting decision-making which may influence the worker (Art. 64 (4)(d) Worker Statute). An important weakness of this regulation is the lack of a redress mechanism (Villarroel Luque 2021).

These digital rights are pivotal for the fulfilment of fundamental human and labour rights such as the right to work, non-discrimination or access to remedy. To achieve this objective, however, other accompanying instruments are essential. It is crucial not to limit legislative efforts to algorithmic transparency and fairness, since social problems cannot be equated with technological problems that can be fixed through appropriate programming (Kocher 2022). What is needed is a comprehensive legal accountability system which entails not only that platforms ensure transparency of their internal operations, but also disclose relevant information about the work arrangements that they orchestrate and prevent any risks of violations of labour standards.

The proposed Directive on improving the working conditions in platform work provides for transparency obligations of digital platforms, although the scope of these regulations is limited. Art. 11 requires platforms which are employers to declare work performed by platform workers to the competent labour and social protection authorities. Art. 12 (1) mandates platforms to provide relevant authorities with information about the general terms and conditions that apply to platform-based contractual relationships. The scope of this obligation is narrowed down only to such terms and conditions which are *unilaterally determined* by the platform and apply to a large number of contractual relationships. This undermines the relevance of this transparency obligation with regard to some crowdwork platforms where clients establish or co-determine the payrate and other terms of how work is provided.

Policy makers should give more consideration to regulatory strategies harnessing the fact that platforms have oversight over the work performance. All abuses of labour rights (e.g., non-compliance with working time or minimum wage regulations) are fully traceable by the platforms. Crowdworkers might be "invisible" to labour inspectors and clients, but certainly not to platforms, which are the locus of all transactions and possess the exclusive data underlying the processes. Legislators could leverage this power to improve regulatory oversight and enforcement of labour standards. In the words of Rogers (2018, 315), "the move to platforms may be creating some institutional preconditions for better work, by centralizing regulatory capacity within large, sophisticated firms." In fact, the regulation and remedy of the "data-driven fissuring" may be thus more feasible than the one in the "classic" fissuring model adopted in the garment industry (Rogers 2018, 314). Drawing on the accountability concept presented by Landau and Hardy (2021), platforms could play a dual role: they would be both accountability holders requiring compliance with applicable regulation by all actors involved in their ecosystem and would themselves be held accountable to oversight authorities. In other words, they would be held liable not only for the transparency of their algorithms and for disclosing information about terms and conditions unilaterally determined by them, but also for detecting labour law violations by requestors. For example, when the clients specify the criteria of a target group of crowdworkers to whom tasks will be distributed (e.g., country and gender), it is in principle for them to comply with the anti-discrimination regulations, but we could envisage the platforms' responsibility for preventing such practices. Protection from discrimination could be, thus, conceived as a shared responsibility of platforms and clients.

Finally, to overcome the issues related to the extraterritorial reach of crowdwork platforms, a multi-level response is needed. Scholars have emphasised the importance of an international, rather than national governance framework (Novitz 2020; Berg, Cherry and Rani 2019). The need to establish an international governance system that obliges platforms and their clients to ensure certain minimum rights has also been expressed in the report of the Global Commission on the Future of Work, an independent group commissioned in 2017 by the ILO Director-General (ILO 2019). While there is still little clarity on the adequate international-level response to the issues of platform work, this topic remains on the ILO's agenda. As approved by the Governing Body in November 2021,[17] a tripartite meeting of experts on decent work in the platform economy will be held in October 2022. Time will tell whether it will come to a general discussion or a designated standard-setting initiative in this area. The Governing Body can decide to discuss it at the 112th Session (2024) of the International Labour Conference.[18] Reaching a consensus of all constituents on this politically tense issue within a standard-setting initiative will surely be challenging (De Stefano and Wouters 2021, 139), much as it has been the case with GSCs.[19]

As we await further regulatory developments at the international level, it is crucial to remember that it is, ultimately, for the states to ensure that platforms assume responsibility for work practices in their ecosystems. The turn to national, mandatory HRDD responses in some countries in the supply chain context is in this regard promising, as it signals that such a domestic regulation of transnational business operation is feasible.

Conclusions

The primary objective of this chapter was to advance normative responses to make crowdwork platforms accountable for labour standards in their ecosystems. The current focus of the debate has been predominantly on the classification of platforms as employers– an option that is valid for some scenarios, although it does not resolve all problems faced by crowdworkers. The chapter advocated for strengthening the existing regulatory framework by introducing mandatory mechanisms that would not only ensure algorithmic transparency of platforms' operations but also make platforms responsible for ensuring adherence to labour standards. Crowdwork needs to be addressed by public–private regulation whereby corporate social responsibility instruments and state-based regulations reinforce each other. Moreover, state-based regulation has to be complemented by an international and regional governance framework. Such a multi-layered, hybrid response is needed to target the structural characteristics of global crowdwork and bring its exploitative practices to an end. Only then will we be able to speak of crowdwork as a pathway for inclusive development across the globe.

Notes

1. PhD researcher, European University Institute, Florence. Contact nastazja. potocka-sionek@eui.eu. This chapter draws from my previous paper "How to regulate 'digital piecework'? Lessons from global supply chains", published in *Lavoro e Diritto*, 3–4 2021, pp. 645–77. I am very grateful to the editors of this monograph and to the participants of the seminar "A Research Agenda for the Gig Economy and Society" for invaluable feedback on the first draft of this chapter. I am also extremely thankful to Prof. Claire Kilpatrick, Prof. Antonio Aloisi, Dr. Nicola Hargreaves, Dr Sophie Duroy, Hannah Adzakpa, Aikaterini Orfanidi and Marc Steiert for their generous comments on earlier versions of this chapter. I gratefully acknowledge Prof. Simon Deakin, Prof. Colin Fenwick and Sylvie Armstrong an inspiring discussion and feedback on my earlier work on this topic. The usual disclaimer applies.
2. European Commission, Proposal for a Directive of the European Parliament and of the Council on Improving Working Conditions in Platform Work COM (2021) 762 final.
3. This shall be the case if at least two of the criteria listed in Art. 4 (2) are met, i.e., when platforms (a) effectively determine or set upper limits for the level of remuneration; (b) impose rules with regard to conduct towards the recipient of the service or performance of the work; (c) supervise the performance of work or verify the quality of the work results; (d) effectively restrict crowdworkers' freedom to organise their work; and (e) effectively restrict the possibility to build a client base or to perform work for any third party.
4. This framework is built upon three pillars: (1) states' obligations to respect, protect and fulfil internationally recognised human rights and fundamental freedoms; (2) enterprises' obligation to comply with all applicable laws and to respect human rights; and (3) the need for rights and obligations to be matched to appropriate and effective remedies when breached.
5. Recommendation CM/Rec (2018)2 of the Committee of Ministers to Member States on the roles and responsibilities of internet intermediaries (Adopted by the Committee of Ministers on 7 March 2018 at the 1309th meeting of the Ministers' Deputies), point 11.
6. UN HRC Resolution 26/9, UN Doc. A/HRC/26/L.22/Rev. 1 (26 June 2014).
7. OEIGWG Chairmanship Third Revised Draft 17.08.2021; see https://www.ohchr .org/Documents/HRBodies/HRCouncil/WGTransCorp/Session6/LBI3rdDRAFT .pdf.
8. These include freedom of association and collective bargaining, the elimination of discrimination in respect of employment and occupation, the elimination of forced or compulsory labour and the effective abolition of child labour (ILO Declaration on Fundamental Principles and Rights at Work 1998).
9. As stated at https://appen.com/crowd-wellness/.
10. As stated at http://faircrowd.work/.
11. Act no. 2017-399 of March 27, 2017 relating to the duty of vigilance of parent companies and ordering companies.
12. Act on Corporate Due Diligence Obligations in Supply Chains, BGBl I 2021, 2959.
13. Act relating to enterprises' transparency and work on fundamental human rights and decent working conditions, LOV-2021-06-18-99.

14. For example, neither of them provides for civil liability. Moreover, a substantial limitation of the German Act is that due diligence requirements apply to the operations of the company and its direct suppliers. Only when companies gain "substantiated knowledge" of potential violations in their indirect suppliers are they required to conduct a risk analysis (Krajewski, Tonstad and Wohltmann 2021).

15. European Commission, Proposal for a Directive of the European Parliament and of the Council on Corporate Sustainability Due Diligence and amending Directive (EU) 2019/1937 COM (2022) 71 final.

16. The proposed Directive only covers large European companies with more than 500 employees and a net turnover of over EUR 150 million. Two years after the entry into force of the Directive, this threshold will be lowered to 250 employees and a turnover of at least EUR 40 million if a minimum of half of this turnover was generated in at least one of the "high-impact" sectors specified in the Directive. For non-European companies, the same threshold applies, but there is no requirement concerning the number of employees.

17. GB.343/Decisions.

18. GB.341/INS/3/1(Rev.2), para. 26.

19. The 105th Session of the International Labour Conference (ILC) included a general discussion on GSCs. In its Conclusions, the ILC expressed concern that "current ILO standards may not be fit for purpose to achieve decent work in global supply chains", and called on the ILO to "consider what guidance, programmes, measures, initiatives or standards are needed to promote decent work and/or facilitate reducing decent work deficits in global supply chains" (Conclusions concerning decent work in global supply chains, ILC, 105th Session, Geneva, 2016, para. 25). Three subsequent meetings were held: the meeting of experts on promoting decent work and protecting fundamental principles and rights at work in export processing zones (2017), the meeting of experts on cross-border social dialogue (2019) and the technical meeting on achieving decent work in global supply chains (2020). The ILO Office was further tasked with a review "to clearly identify if there are any gaps in the current body of normative and non-normative measures," which will be assessed by the tripartite working group on options to ensure decent work in supply chains. (GB.341/INS/13/2/Decision). To date, it has not come to an adoption of a new international labour standard on this matter.

References

Aloisi, Antonio. 2020. "Hierarchies Without Firms? Vertical Disintegration, Personal Outsourcing and the Nature of the Platform." In *Quaderni del Premio «Giorgio Rota»* 8, 11–32. Torino: Centro Einaudi.

Amengual, Matthew, and Sarosh Kuruvilla. 2020. "Editorial Essay: Introduction to a Special Issue on Improving Private Regulation of Labor in Global Supply Chains: Theory and Evidence." *International Labour Review* 73(4): 809–16.

Anner, Mark, Jennifer Bair and Jeremy Blasi. 2013. "Toward Joint Liability Supply Chains: Addressing the Root Causes of Labor Violations in International Subcontracting Networks." *Comparative Labor Law and Policy Journal* 35(1): 1–44.

Bair, Jennifer. 2017. "Contextualising Compliance: Hybrid Governance in Global Value Chains." *New Political Economy* 22(2): 169–85.

Barrientos, Stephanie, and Sally Smith. 2007. "Do Workers Benefit from Ethical Trade? Assessing Codes of Labour Practice in Global Production Systems." Third World Quarterly 28(4): 713–29.

Bérastégui, Pierre. 2021. "Exposure to Psychosocial Risk Factors in the Gig Economy: A Systematic Review." Report 2021.01. European Trade Union Institute.

Berg, Janine, Miriam A. Cherry and Uma Rani. 2019. "Digital Labour Platforms: A Need for International Regulation?" *Revista de Economía Laboral – Spanish Journal of Labour Economics* 16(2): 104–28.

Berg, Janine, Marianne Furrer, Ellie Harmon, Uma Rani and M. Six Silberman. 2018. "Digital Labour Platforms and the Future of Work: Towards Decent Work in the Online World." Geneva: International Labour Office.

Cherry, Miriam A. 2019. "A Global System of Work, A Global System of Regulation?: Crowdwork and Conflicts of Law." *Tulane Law Review* 94(2): 1–62.

Choudary, Sangeet Paul. 2018. "The Architecture of Digital Labour Platforms: Policy Recommendations on Platform Design for Worker Well-Being." Future of Work Series, Research Paper 3. Geneva: International Labour Office.

Choudary, Sangeet Paul. 2020. "The Platform Manifesto." https://platformed.info/the -platform-manifesto/.

Cossart, Sandra, Jérôme Chaplier and Tiphaine Beau de Lomenie. 2017. "The French Law on Duty of Care: A Historic Step Towards Making Globalization Work for All." *Business and Human Rights Journal* 2(2): 317–23.

De Stefano, Valerio. 2016. "The Rise of the 'Just-in-Time Workforce': On-Demand Work, Crowdwork and Labour Protection in the 'Gig-Economy'." *Comparative Labor Law and Policy Journal* 37(3): 471–504.

De Stefano, Valerio, Ilda Durri, Charalampos Stylogiannis and Mathias Wouters. 2021. "Platform Work and the Employment Relationship." ILO Working Paper No. 27. Geneva: International Labour Office.

De Stefano, Valerio, and Mathias Wouters. 2021. "Embedding Platforms in Contemporary Labour Law." In *A Modern Guide to Labour and the Platform Economy,* edited by Jan Drahokoupil and Kurt Vandaele, 129–44. Cheltenham, UK and Northampton, MA, USA: Edward Elgar Publishing.

Degryse, Christophe. 2016. "Digitalisation of the Economy and its Impact on Labour Markets." Working Paper ETUI 2016.02.

ETUC. 2022a. "Commission Delivers 'Bare Minimum' on Corporate Sustainability Due Diligence." 23 February 2022. https://www.etuc.org/en/pressrelease/commission -delivers-bare-minimum-corporate-sustainability-due-diligence.

ETUC. 2022b. "Uber & Deliveroo Fail EU Tests on Self-Employment." 25 January 2022. https://www.etuc.org/en/pressrelease/uber-deliveroo-fail-eu-tests-self-employment.

Fairwork. 2021. *Work in the Planetary Labour Market. Fairwork Cloudwork Ratings 2021.* Oxford, United Kingdom.

Fieseler, Christian, Eliane Bucher and Christian Pieter Hoffmann. 2019. "Unfairness by Design? The Perceived Fairness of Digital Labor on Crowdworking Platforms." *Journal of Business Ethics* 156(4): 987–1005.

Fudge, Judy. 2018. "Why Labour Lawyers Should Care About the Modern Slavery Act 2015." *King's Law Journal* 29(3): 337–406.

Gereffi, Gary. 2001. "Shifting Governance Structures in Global Commodity Chains, With Special Reference to the Internet." *American Behavioral Scientist* 44(10): 1616–37.

Gol, Elham Shafiei, Mari-Klara Stein and Michel Avital. 2019. "Crowdwork Platform Governance toward Organizational Value Creation." *Journal of Strategic Information Systems* 28(2): 175–95.

Graham, Mark, and Mohammad Amir Anwar. 2019. "The Global Gig Economy: Towards a Planetary Labour Market?" *First Monday* 24(4).

Graham, Mark, Isis Hjorth and Vili Lehdonvirta. 2017. "Digital Labour and Development: Impacts of Global Digital Labour Platforms and the Gig Economy on Worker Livelihoods." *Transfer* 23(2): 135–62.

Graham, Mark, Jamie Woodcock, Richard Heeks, Paul Mungai, Jean-Paul Van Belle, Darcy du Toit, Sandra Fredman, Abigail Osiki, Anri van der Spuy and M. Six Silberman. 2020. "The Fairwork Foundation: Strategies for Improving Platform Work in a Global Context." *Geoforum* 112: 100–13.

Howson, Kelle, Fabian Ferrari, Funda Ustek-Spilda, Nancy Salem, Hannah Johnston, Srujana Katta, Richard Heeks and Mark Graham. 2021. "Driving the Digital Value Network: Economic Geographies of Global Platform Capitalism." *Global Networks*: 1–18.

Human Rights Watch. 2022. "EU: Disappointing Draft on Corporate Due Diligence." 28 February 2022. https://www.hrw.org/news/2022/02/28/eu-disappointing-draft-corporate-due-diligence.

Humphrey, John F., and Hubert Schmitz. 2008. "Inter-Firm Relationships in Global Value Chains: Trends in Chain Governance and Their Policy Implications." *International Journal of Technological Learning, Innovation and Development* 1(3): 258–82.

ILO. 2011. *Report IV: Labour Administration and Labour Inspection, International Labour Conference, 100th Session.* Geneva: International Labour Office.

ILO. 2019. *Work for a Brighter Future, Global Commission on the Future of Work.* Geneva: International Labour Office.

ILO. 2021. *World Employment and Social Outlook 2021: The Role of Digital Labour Platforms in Transforming the World of Work.* Geneva: International Labour Office.

Kocher, Eva. 2022. *Digital Work Platforms at the Interface of Labour Law. Regulating Market Organisers.* Bloomsbury Publishing.

Kolben, Kevin. 2011. "Transnational Labor Regulation and the Limits of Governance." *Theoretical Inquiries in Law* 12(2): 403–37.

Kovács, Erica. 2017. "Do We Really Wish You Were Here? Hungary and Distance Work." In *Core and Contingent Work in the European Union: A Comparative Analysis*, edited by Edoardo Ales, Olaf Deinert and Jeff Kenner, 83–110. Oxford: Hart Publishing.

Krajewski, Markus, Kristel Tonstad and Franziska Wohltmann. 2021. "Mandatory Human Rights Due Diligence in Germany and Norway: Stepping, or Striding, in the Same Direction?" *Business and Human Rights Journal* 6(3): 550–58.

Krzywdzinski, Martin, and Christine Gerber. 2021. "Between Automation and Gamification: Forms of Labour Control on Crowdwork Platforms." *Work in the Global Economy* 1(2): 161–84.

Kuruvilla, Sarosh, Ning Li and Lowell Jackson. 2021. "Private Regulation of Labour Standards in Global Supply Chains: Current Status and Future Directions." In *Decent Work in a Globalized Economy. Lessons from Public and Private Initiatives*, edited by Guillaume Delautre, Elizabeth Echeverría Manrique and Colin Fenwick, 185–209. Geneva: International Labour Office.

Landau, Ingrid, and Tess Hardy. 2021. "Transnational Labour Governance in Global Supply Chains: Asking Questions and Seeking Answers on Accountability." In

Decent Work in a Globalized Economy. Lessons from Public and Private Initiatives, edited by Guillaume Delautre, Elizabeth Echeverría Manrique and Colin Fenwick, 43–74. Geneva: International Labour Office.

LeBaron, Genevieve, Remi Edwards, Tom Hunt, Charline Sempéré and Penelope Kyritsis. 2021. "The Ineffectiveness of CSR: Understanding Garment Company Commitments to Living Wages in Global Supply Chains." *New Political Economy* 27(1): 99–115.

LeBaron, Genevieve, Jane Lister and Peter Dauvergne. 2017. "Governing Global Supply Chain Sustainability through the Ethical Audit Regime." *Globalizations* 14(6): 958–75.

LeBaron, Genevieve, and Andreas Rühmkorf. 2019. "The Domestic Politics of Corporate Accountability Legislation: Struggles over the 2015 UK Modern Slavery Act." Socio-Economic Review 17(3): 709–43.

Lehdonvirta, Vili. 2016. "Algorithms That Divide and Unite: Delocalization, Identity, and Collective Action in 'Microwork'." In *Space, Place and Global Digital Work*, edited by Jörg Flecker, 53–80. London: Palgrave Macmillan.

Locke, Richard M. 2013. *The Promise and Limits of Private Power: Promoting Labor Standards in a Global Economy*. Cambridge: Cambridge University Press.

López, Carlos. 2021. The Third Revised Draft of a Treaty on Business and Human Rights: Modest Steps Forward, But Much of the Same. *Opinio Juris* (blog), 3 September 2021. http://opiniojuris.org/2021/09/03/the-third-revised-draft-of-a-treaty-on-business-and-human-rights-modest-steps-forward-but-much-of-the-same/.

Macchi, Chiara, and Claire Bright. 2020. "Hardening Soft Law: The Implementation of Human Rights Due Diligence Requirements in Domestic Legislation." In *Legal Sources in Business and Human Rights: Evolving Dynamics in International and European Law*, edited by Martina Buscemi, Nicole Lazzerini, Laura Magi and Deborah Russo, 218–47. Leiden: Brill | Nijhoff.

Nolan, Justine, and Gregory Bott. 2018. "Global Supply Chains and Human Rights: Spotlight on Forced Labour and Modern Slavery Practices." *Australian Journal of Human Rights* 24(1): 44–69.

Novitz, Tonia. 2020. "The Potential for International Regulation of Gig Economy Issues." *King's Law Journal* 31(2): 275–86.

Pretelli, Ilaria. 2018. "Improving Social Cohesion through Connecting Factors in the Conflict of Laws of the Platform Economy." In *Conflict of Laws in the Maze of Digital Platforms*, edited by Ilaria Pretelli, 17–52. Publications of the Swiss Institute of Comparative Law n. 86. Schulthess: Éditions Romandes.

Rani, Uma, and Marianne Furrer. 2021. "Digital Labour Platforms and New Forms of Flexible Work in Developing Countries: Algorithmic Management of Work and Workers." *Competition & Change* 25 (2): 212–236.

Rogers, Brishen. 2018. "Fissuring, Data-Driven Governance, and Platform Economy Labor Standards." In *The Cambridge Handbook of Law of the Sharing Economy*, edited by Nestor M. Davidson, Michèle Finck and John J. Infranca, 304–15. Cambridge: Cambridge University Press.

Rühmkorf, Andreas. 2018. "Global Supply Chain Governance: The Search for What Works." *Deakin Law Review* 23, Special Issue: 63–82.

Schmidt, Florian Alexander. 2019. "Crowdsourced Production of AI Training Data: How Human Workers Teach Self-Driving Card How to See." Working Paper Forschungsförderung, No. 155. Düsseldorf: Hans-Böckler-Stiftung.

Sjåfjell, Beate, and Jukka Mähönen. 2022. Corporate Purpose and the EU Corporate Sustainability Due Diligence Proposal. *Oxford Business Law Blog*, 25 February 2022.

https://www.law.ox.ac.uk/business-law-blog/blog/2022/02/corporate-purpose-and-eu-corporate-sustainability-due-diligence.

Trebilcock, Anne. 2015. "Due Diligence on Labour Issues. Opportunities and Limits of the U.N. Guiding Principles on Business and Human Rights." In *Research Handbook on Transnational Labour Law*, edited by Adelle Blackett and Anne Trebilcock, 93–108. Cheltenham, UK and Northampton, USA: Edward Elgar Publishing.

Tubaro, Paola. 2021. "Disembedded or Deeply Embedded? A Multi-Level Network Analysis of Online Labour Platforms." *Sociology* 55(5): 927–44.

Tubaro, Paola, and Antonio A. Casilli. 2019. "Micro-Work, Artificial Intelligence and the Automotive Industry." *Journal of Industrial and Business Economics* 46(3): 333–45.

Vallas, Steven, and Juliet B. Schor. 2020. "What Do Platforms Do? Understanding the Gig Economy." *Annual Review of Sociology* 46(1): 279–94.

Villarroel Luque, Carmen. 2021. Workers vs Algorithms. What Can the New Spanish Provision on Artificial Intelligence and Employment Achieve? *Verfassungsblog*, 27 May 2021. https://verfassungsblog.de/workers-vs-ai/.

Woodcock, Jamie, and Mark Graham. 2020. *The Gig Economy: A Critical Introduction*. London: Wiley.

Index